KATE SAPIN

ESSENTIAL SKILLS FOR YOUTH WORK PRACTICE

2ND EDITION

Los Angeles | London | New Delhi
Singapore | Washington DC

Los Angeles | London | New Delhi
Singapore | Washington DC

SAGE Publications Ltd
1 Oliver's Yard
55 City Road
London EC1Y 1SP

SAGE Publications Inc.
2455 Teller Road
Thousand Oaks, California 91320

SAGE Publications India Pvt Ltd
B 1/I 1 Mohan Cooperative Industrial Area
Mathura Road
New Delhi 110 044

SAGE Publications Asia-Pacific Pte Ltd
3 Church Street
#10-04 Samsung Hub
Singapore 049483

Editor: Alice Oven
Assistant editor: Emma Milman
Production editor: Katie Forsythe
Copyeditor: Sharon Cawood
Proofreader: Audra O'Brien
Marketing manager: Tamara Navaratnam
Cover design: Wendy Scott
Typeset by: C&M Digitals (P) Ltd, Chennai, India
Printed and bound by CPI Group (UK) Ltd,
Croydon, CR0 4YY

Library of Congress Control Number: 2012939780

British Library Cataloguing in Publication data

A catalogue record for this book is available from
the British Library

MIX
Paper from
responsible sources
FSC® C013604
www.fsc.org

ISBN 978-0-85702-832-7
ISBN 978-0-85702-833-4 (pbk)

ESSENTIAL SKILLS FOR YOUTH WORK PRACTICE

SAGE has been part of the global academic community since 1965, supporting high quality research and learning that transforms society and our understanding of individuals, groups and cultures. SAGE is the independent, innovative, natural home for authors, editors and societies who share our commitment and passion for the social sciences.

Find out more at: **www.sagepublications.com**

CONTENTS

LIST OF BOXES

LIST OF PRACTICE EXAMPLES

ABOUT THE AUTHOR

Kate Sapin is Programme Director of Community and Youth Work Studies in the School of Education at The University of Manchester, England, where she has worked with others to develop participative programmes of learning about community and youth work since 1985. Her community and youth work experience includes work with young parents, economic migrants and homeless people as well as area and centre-based work, education outreach (IT skills, English language) and campaigns.

AUTHOR'S NOTES ON THE SECOND EDITION

This second edition of *Essential Skills for Youth Work Practice* has been hugely supported by positive feedback from youth work practitioners, students and colleagues involved in the professional education of community and youth workers on the first edition. Thank you for your encouragement and ideas, which I have attempted to incorporate into this new version. Since the first edition was published, I have also had the advantage of more experience of work with full-time students who are new to the field. Their perspectives and questions have helped to structure a new chapter that specifically addresses the issues involved in setting up and undertaking fieldwork practice placements (Organising student placements, Chapter 12). So, thank you! I hope that experienced practitioners will continue to find the book relevant to their thinking, particularly when taking up a new post, as I have also slightly reoriented the early chapters to reflect the first stages of starting work in a new community.

Thank you to the young people and colleagues I have met through youth work practice. Thanks also to past and present course participants, tutors, assessors and supervisors, employers and other colleagues I have worked with on the University of Manchester's community and youth work learning programmes. Your experiences and insights have formed this book. Thanks also to those who contributed to the first edition: Tania de St Croix, Leigh Cook and Amelia Lee.

My love and thanks to family and friends for their encouragement and support, especially Leah Sapin for her helpful comments on the text and Sam Sapin for his assistance with diagrams. Special thanks, too, to Anita Baishnab, Joanna Connor, Alison Healicon, Mary Kenny, Kathy Lawson and Marcella Walsh for keeping me on track.

INTRODUCTION

Youth work, as defined and outlined in *Essential Skills for Youth Work Practice*, is a form of professional practice with young people that can be carried out by individuals and organisations in a wide range of settings. The distinguishing characteristics are associated with practice, that is, in the ways in which youth workers interact with young people and their communities. Youth workers exercise their power judiciously, approach young people positively and informally, and engage them in enjoyable activities; most importantly, youth work is based on voluntary relationships with young people who choose to participate. Youth work practice involves a commitment to developing relationships based on respect for young people, listening to them and valuing mutual learning. The aim is to involve young people in decisions about issues that affect them, rather than simply to provide information, advice or services. Young people have fun, learn from each other and participate in the design and implementation of activities, projects and services. The intention is not to prescribe methods and outcomes. Although often serving a positive, therapeutic and preventative function for young people and society, youth work attempts to focus on developing opportunities for young people to explore their options and develop their understanding of choices and consequences.

Youth workers might work with young people aged anywhere between six and eighteen years old although many organisations or projects would focus on a more specific age group within that range. Abilities, rates of maturation and circumstances vary widely amongst individuals, but, in general, children below the lower end of the spectrum usually require more supervision of activities and adult intervention than is typically provided by youth workers. Younger children are often less ready to undertake responsibility for social interactions outside of their family or structured environment such as school. Individuals above the upper age range are usually more interested in and ready for adult responsibilities, activities and services. Statutory services in the UK have suggested that youth workers work primarily with young people aged 13–19 (National Youth Agency, 2004) although this is by no means universal. The young people who participate are those who enjoy the independent social opportunities provided by youth work. Most youth workers also work with others in the community through volunteer programmes and cross-generational work.

Young people's transition to maturity is a process of development involving a series of changes affected by nature, circumstances and choices. Most individuals undergo major physical, mental, social, emotional, sexual, domestic and psychological changes and development during the period that youth work might be available to them. Youth work is one of the ways in which adults can work with young people to provide positive, creative and challenging experiences to support these transitions. Opportunities are developed for young people to build and act upon to further their understanding of the personal, moral, spiritual, social, economic and political aspects of their lives. Through participation in youth work, young people develop confidence. The skills, knowledge and awareness acquired can assist them to make informed choices for themselves and for anyone for whom they are or become responsible. The process is at their pace, on their terms and based in their realities.

The approach to youth work outlined in *Essential Skills for Youth Work Practice* is based on youth work experience and analysis of practice. The structure, content and approach comes from discussions, evaluations and other collaborative projects with experienced youth workers, community workers, activists and informal educators for nearly 30 years at the University of Manchester. This *praxis*, that is bringing together learners and practitioners to reflect on ideas and experience, has established some values and principles for youth work and provided a rich variety of examples and suggestions about ways to build relationships and work together with young people in different settings. The book has been written to present the findings of this research in a structured format to support further youth work practice and learning.

Essential Skills for Youth Work Practice attempts to reflect the wide range of experience that has contributed to this book. Experienced practitioners and individuals embarking on their careers have participated. Their paid and unpaid work has included focused work with young people, as well as with children, young adults and mixed generational groups. While the majority of contributors have been based in England, individuals involved in similar work in other countries and on exchange programmes have also played their part. The youth workers, as well as the young people and the communities they work with, include individuals who have self-defined or come together as white or black British, Bangladeshi, African, African-Caribbean, Jewish, Indian, Pakistani, Chinese, Vietnamese, Travellers, refugees, young parents, disabled people, lesbian, gay, bi-sexual, transgender, women, tenants and residents, and more. Many have been based in local government departments and other services relevant to young people, whilst others have worked in 'third sector' organisations, such as non-government organisations and charitable trusts. The projects, groups, organisations, networks, multi-agency structures and communities in which they work have been defined by geographic area, housing development, community of interest or specific need, issue or activity. Both similarities and differences have been explored to inform the analysis and examples presented here.

The book follows a staged approach to undertaking youth work from getting to know the context for practice to developing projects with young people and sustaining development. The sequence of chapters was inspired not only by evidence from youth workers talking about what they do, but by Henderson and Thomas' 'nine stage process of neighbourhood work' (2002: 30) that starts with finding out about local people and ensuring their collective involvement in community work. *Essential Skills for Youth Work Practice* takes the reader through the process of youth work practice, from initial contacts with young people to their participation in the management of projects. Part A provides a definition of youth work, an explanation of the practice-based approach of the profession and the underlying values and principles for practice. Part B looks at the skills of forming groups, bringing young people together to have fun, learn and deal with the ups and downs of working together. Part C looks at how youth work can make an impact through enabling young people to participate in developing and managing research and other projects.

Part A – Building Relationships starts the book with some of the ways in which youth workers begin practice in a new setting by gaining an understanding of the context for practice and having a proactive approach to establishing professional contacts and relationships with young people. Chapter 1, 'Understanding youth work', provides a framework for youth work practice that is underpinned by values and principles. The chapter includes a checklist based on Davies' (2005) 'manifesto' for youth work that enables youth workers to identify practice that is in keeping with professional roles and responsibilities (see Box 1.5). Chapter 2, 'Locating youth work in different settings', suggests that youth workers need to be clear about the type of work that the organisation undertakes and includes a checklist for induction to ensure that this information is discussed with new workers or students on placement (see Box 2.7). A sample 'SWOT' analysis of the strengths and limitations of an organisation's policies and practice is included, which may be useful for students undertaking such an exercise (see Box 2.9). Chapter 3, 'Reaching out', suggests a number of ways to make initial contacts with young people and the issues that may need to be taken into consideration when presenting oneself in different settings. Chapter 4, 'Establishing voluntary relationships', is intended to assist a youth worker to consider professional boundaries when getting to know young people and provides some examples of ways to do this (see Box 4.5). The chapters in this first section could be used to structure a response to the inevitable interview question for a youth worker post: 'what will you do in the first few months after taking up this job?'

Part B – Working Together provides examples of work developed and carried out with young people, and starts with Chapter 5, 'Bringing young people together', which provides a planned approach to developing group work based on young people's interests. Chapter 6, 'Having fun', looks at some of the decisions that need to be made when involving young people in a range of enjoyable activities. Chapter 7, 'Working on issues', looks at anti-oppressive practice in more detail, with examples of how to raise issues related to inequity, such as exclusion and negative discrimination, and how to address situations as they arise. Chapter 8, 'Sustaining growth in groups', concerns ways to handle clashes between individuals and arguments in groups so that groups and the individuals continue to grow and develop. Chapter 9, 'Enhancing young people's participation', focuses on strategies to involve young people in decision making. The chapters in Part B provide guidance for planning and carrying out group work with young people that could be used to answer a range of job interview questions about handling diverse situations in youth work.

Part C – Sustaining Development looks at practice to nurture youth work practice and the profession. Chapter 10, 'Developing a project proposal', looks at the research required to plan a piece of work and put together a proposal for new work, whether addressed to a manager from within the organisation or to an external funder. Chapter 11, 'Managing a project', attempts to provide an overview of some of the skills required to manage projects, whether as a student on placement or a manager of a large organisation. Relevant skills include defining the purpose of the project, managing resources and working with staff in ways that are transparent and practicable. Chapter 12, 'Organising student placements', identifies the issues for students, host organisations and course providers when planning and facilitating work-based learning. Chapter 13, 'Using supervision', examines how youth workers maintain a professional focus to their practice by using and providing supervision. Issues to consider when establishing professional boundaries and a suggested agenda for sessions are suggested with some practice examples of using supervision to work on issues in practice. The chapters in this section could be used to structure a presentation for an interview as a youth work manager about the responsibilities of the post.

Each chapter begins with a summary of its content. The headings highlight some relevant essential skills, which are discussed and then listed at the end of the chapter with a selection of recommendations for further related reading. Bibliographic details for all text references and recommended reading are listed at the end of the book.

Tables and diagrams based on key theories as well as analysis of youth work experience appear in numbered boxes referenced throughout the text. Illustrative scenarios drawn from practitioners' practice are presented to provide issues for consideration rather than to prescribe specific approaches. These practice examples are numbered and referenced within the text. Except where indicated otherwise, the practice examples are presented from the perspective of an individual youth worker.

The boxes and practice examples are listed and page referenced after the Contents page. Definitions of youth work terms and phrases are listed in an appendix as suggested interpretations of some of the terms commonly used in practice.

PART A

BUILDING RELATIONSHIPS

The first part of *Essential Skills for Youth Work Practice* focuses on the skills required for building appropriate youth work relationships with young people and their communities. The foundations for professional youth work relationships are respect and mutual learning. According to Gandhi, youth workers may have more to gain:

> And believe me, from my experience of hundreds, I was going to say thousands, of children, I know that they have perhaps a finer sense of honour than you and I have. The greatest lessons in life, if we would but stop and humble ourselves, we would learn not from grown-up learned men, but from the so-called ignorant children. (1931: 361)

Chapter 1 explores how understanding the purpose of youth work based on professional values and principles can lead to positive, participative and anti-oppressive practice. Consideration is also given to varying roles and responsibilities, constraints on practice and issues related to safeguarding. Chapter 2 looks at the varied organisational settings for youth work and different types of work that take place. Chapter 3 outlines the initial stages of making contact and getting to know young people. The nature of the autonomous and voluntary relationships that are the foundation for youth work practice is examined in Chapter 4. Together, the four chapters establish a professional framework for practice that links values and principles with guidance on building professional relationships in a new community or role. Part A should also provide a student with the tools to start building relationships in a placement and carry out an organisational analysis.

1

UNDERSTANDING YOUTH WORK

This chapter introduces the links between the purpose of youth work, the core values and principles for youth work practice and an understanding of the roles and responsibilities of a youth worker, which underpin the first steps in building professional relationships with young people and their communities.

IDENTIFYING YOUTH WORK VALUES AND PRACTICE

Youth work is professional practice with young people based on certain core values and principles requiring the establishment of voluntary relationships with young people, links with communities and other relevant organisations, and professional supervision from experienced practitioners. Respect for young people is at the heart of youth work values in a profession that works 'where young people are' with a positive, participative and anti-oppressive approach. Through engaging in open and honest dialogue with young people, youth workers aim to value different perspectives and address expressed needs and interests. Attempts are made to recognise young people's rights to be treated with dignity as individuals, reject negative labelling and challenge negative stereotypes, whether based on ageism or other oppressive attitudes, by promoting positive images and examples of young people's lives. The process involves careful listening to young people about their understanding of themselves and their situations.

The values provide an ethical foundation that informs professional principles and practice. The principles apply the general values more directly to youth work practice and define the essential activities of enabling young people's voluntary participation and actively seeking accountability to them and their communities. The significance of this close relationship between values and practice is that youth workers need to be involved in continuous professional reflection and development to ensure that personal experiences and perspectives are used appropriately and that any boundaries and barriers to their role are clarified and addressed. The relationship between youth work practice and professional values and principles is illustrated in Box 1.1, which suggests a framework for youth work that can transform young people's lives and communities.

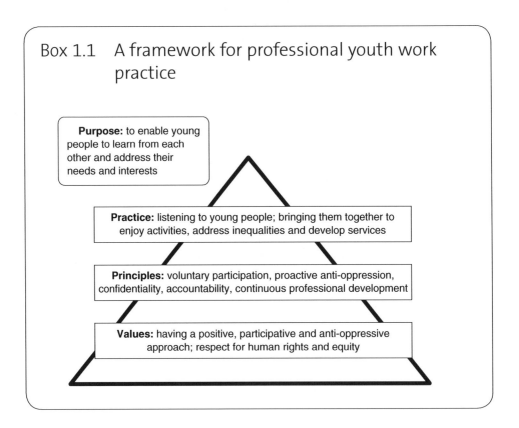

Box 1.1   A framework for professional youth work practice

Purpose: to enable young people to learn from each other and address their needs and interests

Practice: listening to young people; bringing them together to enjoy activities, address inequalities and develop services

Principles: voluntary participation, proactive anti-oppression, confidentiality, accountability, continuous professional development

Values: having a positive, participative and anti-oppressive approach; respect for human rights and equity

Clarity about the purpose of youth work and the relationship of values and principles can help youth workers to develop and carry out professional youth work practice. A starting point could be to 'locate' the congruence between youth work values and principles and personal standpoints. The concept of 'location' is commonly used in youth work to refer to the identification of a position in relation to different perspectives, such as a political ideology or social class, and recognising how this may influence any interpretations of new situations. 'Locating oneself' requires an analysis of experiences and understanding of how things work, perhaps in relation to others' perspectives. A match between personal and professional values will mean that learning how to apply these values to youth work practice will be strongly underpinned. The Free Child Project acknowledge this personal link in their definition of 'community youth development work' as:

> a strategy, philosophy, and personal approach to acknowledging the ability, authority, and knowledge of young people as powerful, purposeful catalysts for personal, social, cultural, and institutional growth and transformation. (Fletcher, 2008)

APPLYING VALUES AND PRINCIPLES TO PRACTICE

The application of positive, participative and anti-oppressive values has a range of implications for youth work practice, the activities developed and youth workers themselves. A *positive approach*, for example, could include encouraging young people's educational development and promoting equitable social change; an appreciation of young people's needs for fun, warmth and nurture, as well as youth workers' enjoyment of their work. Enjoyable activities not only encourage young people to participate voluntarily, but may also counter some of the effects of individuals' negative experiences or societal oppression. Rather than seeing young people as problems, victims or individuals in need of help, youth workers recognise their strengths and encourage them to undertake activities that make a positive difference. (See also Chapter 6 for examples of how enjoyable activities, such as socialising, arts and games, can enable young people to make changes in their lives.)

The *participative nature* of youth work recognises young people's rights to choose whether to be involved and to make decisions about issues that affect them. Recognising, valuing and building on participants' contributions and experiences means that young people are 'at the centre' of youth work practice. Participative practice brings young people together in groups to gain support and learn from each other, and encourages them to 'keep it real' by exploring genuine and realistic options. Young people develop greater control over their lives whilst learning new skills, taking responsibility and finding out about new opportunities. Rather than simply providing a service, youth work encourages young people to find their own solutions to problems and develop their own plans and projects. (See also Chapter 9 for ideas about opportunities for young people to become involved in decision making.)

Respect for young people and their human rights informs an *anti-oppressive approach*, which is clearly related to equity, whether for individuals, groups of young people or for young people as a whole in society. Youth work acknowledges and addresses young people's all too frequent exclusion from decision making, as well as the neglect, rejection and denial of opportunities experienced by some young people more than others. Some individuals, due to circumstances related to birth or upbringing, may be denied safety, security, love or a healthy environment. Societal attitudes and practices, such as racism, sexism, heterosexism, classism, ageism and ableism, benefit a privileged, often minority group and can exclude others from equal access to rights and opportunities as varied as education, employment, housing, health services, legal protection and leisure activities. Youth work can offer alternative opportunities as well as assist young people to make sense of their circumstances and broaden their understanding of their options. (Practice Example 1.1 provides an example of the power of practice underpinned by the professional values that means young people are welcomed with a positive, participative and anti-oppressive approach.) The pervasiveness of oppressive influences on attitudes and behaviour requires youth workers to have an active and positive approach to individuals and groups that are oppressed and an understanding of how societal attitudes may affect their own perceptions. (See also Chapter 7 for some ideas on developing proactive anti-oppressive youth work.)

PRACTICE EXAMPLE 1.1

The power of value-based practice

The best thing about going to the youth centre was that I didn't feel like a stranger. Since I started high school, I haven't been able to get on with the people in my class and it never seemed to be the right time to talk with anyone about it. But when I came to the youth centre, we got stuck in straight away to talking about how to decorate the 'quiet room'. No one seemed to care that I didn't have nice clothes or that I didn't know anyone before I got there. (A young member of a youth organisation)

Linking the values to professional practice are ethical principles: voluntary participation, anti-oppressive practice, confidentiality, accountability and continuous professional development, which together help to define professional boundaries. Power, control and autonomy become key issues for reflection on practice. Through debriefs and supervision, youth workers identify how information was shared with young people to 'tip the balance of power' (Davies, 2005) in their favour and how their capacity to make autonomous decisions was achieved. Youth workers should not just provide services to a passive clientele or assert social control. For example, rather than simply providing young people with solutions to problems, a youth worker will involve young people in identifying their own method or plan to address their issues. Levels of participation by traditionally excluded groups and evidence of oppressive attitudes or practices are identified. Considering how accountability is maintained, such as openness about resource allocations, and how to ensure young people are made aware of any constraints on confidentiality, are also important questions for establishing professional practice. Some examples of applying the principles to practice are listed in the table in Box 1.2.

Box 1.2 Youth work principles and ethical practice

Principle	Examples of ethical practice
Voluntary participation	Allowing young people to choose whether or not to participate
	Creating welcoming and accessible environments, resources and services
	Keeping young people informed about opportunities and resources
	Providing opportunities for young people to have a voice
Anti-oppressive	Recognising that youth work is for the benefit of all young people, particularly those whose human rights are at risk
	Seeing youth work as an agency for change: taking positive steps to address oppressive language, attitudes, practices and structures, and challenging negative discrimination
	Respecting differences and building bridges between different groups and individuals
	Identifying and promoting positive role models, images and participation by individuals and groups often excluded from participation or facing societal oppression
	Educating self and others about the causes and effects of oppression and the implications and application of anti-oppressive perspectives, such as feminism, a black perspective, a social model of disability, global youth work
	Continuously reassessing practice through consultation and evaluation by others directly affected by oppression
Confidentiality	Being aware that information about individuals should not be recorded or passed on to others without their knowledge except in very exceptional circumstances

(Continued)

(Continued)	
Principle	**Examples of ethical practice**
Confidentiality (Continued)	Recognising that young people may disclose information to youth workers that they are not ready to tell others
	Preferably prior to disclosure, informing individuals about any boundaries to confidentiality, especially information that might require further action or intervention, such as illegal activities or circumstances that endanger individuals, particularly children or young people
Accountability	Involving young people and other members of the community in developing youth work activities, opportunities and decisions
	Ensuring that resources are allocated according to clear criteria
	Seeking out feedback and ideas from diverse groups and individuals
	Recognising that a youth worker's perspective on appropriate practice may be in conflict with that of other individuals or professions
	Prioritising work that benefits young people over work that addresses others' interests or concerns
Continuous professional development	Seeking out information and training about other perspectives on practice
	Developing clarity about the role of a youth worker, use of self and professional boundaries through supervision
	Monitoring and evaluating practice, responding to feedback and accepting responsibility for own actions, shortcomings and education

RECOGNISING YOUTH WORK ROLES

While the focus of the chapter so far has been on face-to-face work with young people, youth workers' roles vary considerably and can include different types of work with a range of target groups and issues, tasks and duties, sometimes reflected in a job title. Some youth work concentrates more on a developmental, educative or protective role, such as providing support or guidance for young people to become responsible adults, particularly when more standard provision seems to be ineffective. A 'youth development worker' may focus on young people's positive transitions to adulthood, whilst a 'participation worker' may promote young people's involvement in social and political change. The terms 'enabler'[11], 'facilitator' or 'emancipator' focus on the process of developing young people's understanding of their own and others' power and control. 'Animators' or 'informal educators' work with young people to develop their self-expression through art, drama, poetry or music and may also be known as 'arts development workers'. A focus on particular activities used 'as a vehicle' for informal education may also be highlighted, such as a 'sports development worker' or 'health development worker'. However, these various terms are often interchangeable and may be defined differently by others.

Youth workers who are restricted to work only with young people through organisational targets or duties may find that their perspective and activities are rather limited. Youth workers who are able to allocate time to outreach work and participation in local committees and forums will be able to find out about relevant issues, communicate the value of youth work and involve other members of the community as volunteers and activists. Communities are the context and environment for young people's lives and therefore for youth work. Knowing about the communities that young people come from and live in assists mutual understanding and can provide support for practice. Networking and interaction with parents, neighbours, local shopkeepers and other relevant agencies and societal structures develops links with stakeholders, i.e. others who are interested in or affected by young people. The title 'youth and community worker' may be used in recognition of the value of involving members of the community or of working with young people within the context of their communities. Youth and community workers may also observe and intervene in community and institutional processes and tasks to promote young people's participation, whereas a 'community development worker' would also work with communities to develop their capacity for managing and improving the quality of their lives.

Youth workers undertake a range of tasks and duties, including face-to-face work, linking with other organisations, taking responsibility for managing other staff or volunteers and looking after venues, budgets and resources. Responsibilities may be related to the setting in which the youth work takes place, such as the geographical area, organisation or facility, as much as job title. Access and responsibilities for resources can vary considerably. For example, a centre-based youth worker may be responsible for the workers and activities within and around the centre as well as maintenance and upkeep. A youth warden may have responsibilities for the environment within a garden, playground or sports facility. An area youth worker would probably cover a wider geographical area and may have managerial responsibilities for youth work activities and workers in more than one project or centre. A street-based or detached youth worker may only be responsible for resources that could be easily carried. Some examples of the tasks and duties that a youth worker may be called upon to carry out are listed in Box 1.3.

---

[1]Please note that the term 'enabler' is also sometimes applied to an individual who intentionally or unintentionally supports another to continue a destructive habit, such as drug or alcohol abuse.

Box 1.3   Youth work tasks and duties

Face-to-face work

- Establish contact with young people in different settings defined by area and/or target group through outreach work and detached work.
- Build relationships with young people individually and in groups.
- Bring young people together in groups and shared activities.
- Involve young people in assessment of interests, planning, monitoring and developing, as well as participating themselves in relevant activities, projects or services.
- Facilitate discussions, arts-based activities, community/environmental projects, open days, residentials (overnight stays), outdoor education and sports.
- Raise topics related to personal and social education (for example, health, fitness, smoking, drugs, the environment, relationships, bullying, globalism).
- Address issues related to anti-oppressive practice, such as racism, sexism, heterosexism, disabilism, classism, ageism, sex trafficking, child labour and domestic abuse.
- Act as an advocate for young people's interests, for example, representation in decision making, improvements in resources and services for young people.

Links, networks and partnerships

- Find out about community stakeholders, resources and potential partnerships.
- Carry out research to identify local, regional, national and global community interests, issues and links.
- Develop cross-generational activities and projects.
- Work with other agencies to develop services and facilities across communities.
- Work with parents and other community groups to address issues and improve services and facilities.
- Work with others as a member or leader of a staff team.

Management and organisation

- Design and produce information, publicity and recruitment material, such as leaflets, posters and presentations.
- Recruit, induct, supervise and train paid and unpaid staff and volunteers.
- Involve young people and other members of the community in the management of projects and the organisation.
- Develop and implement policies, codes of practice and ways of working.
- Manage and coordinate activities, projects and resources, such as buildings and equipment.
- Deal with administrative and office tasks; maintain records of finance and budget control.
- Identify and procure resources and funding for projects.
- Draw up business plans, write reports and make formal presentations to funding bodies.

> **Service-oriented work**
>
> - Advise and guide young people, their parents and other professionals and service providers.
> - Provide personal and social education, mentoring, support and careers guidance.
> - Provide instruction in skills and knowledge related to sports, outdoor activities, keeping fit, martial arts, drama, art, funding applications and committee management.

BEING CLEAR ABOUT WHO YOUTH WORK IS FOR

The primary focus of youth work is young people. Youth work is more than a community or societal provider of services to unwilling or passive recipients and is not just a 'helping profession' that defines the problems and controls the solutions. The differences between youth work and other professions lie in how help is defined and offered. In particular, a youth worker allows young people to have a genuine say in whether to accept any help. When youth workers offer specific assistance to an individual who is experiencing difficulties or blocks to progress, and that assistance is accepted as a genuinely useful resource, mutual respect is retained. Services that call into question an individual's independence or ability to make his or her own choices can be humiliating and disempowering (Best, 2000). The practice avoids patronising, irrelevant or over-directive support through young people's participation in identifying interests and defining activities.

Youth workers are often called upon to become involved in providing services to young people, their parents or other professionals, or in addressing issues of concern to social institutions, such as the government or a housing association. Youth workers are well placed to offer advice and support for work with young people deemed by others to be 'hard to reach' or 'detached' and can become quite knowledgeable about young people's interests, issues and needs. Their understanding of how to provide appropriate services and existing networks of support and information can be very useful in the design, provision and management of a range of services related to young people, such as education, health and leisure. Other 'stakeholders' in young people's lives may also be able to offer different types of support and contribute their perspectives to youth work. Care needs to be taken that tackling specific issues related to young people's lives according to others' agendas does not take over from a youth work role.

Although youth workers are interested in developing more than 'quick-fix' solutions, a range of services for young people are often offered in response to the expressed interests of young people themselves. Some examples of relevant services for young people that youth workers may offer, sometimes in partnership with others, can be found in the table in Box 1.4. Youth workers' involvement here is generally to ensure that services are responsive to young people's concerns and are flexible, attractive and accessible. Identifying young people's levels of interest and control over service provision and access may indicate whether or not a youth worker should become involved. Most youth workers would not engage in services where the main purpose is to control or curtail young people's activities against their will.

Box 1.4 Services and facilities for young people

Type of service	Possible relevant activities
Educational	Alternative education, mentoring, training in outdoor pursuits, sports and social facilities, homework clubs
Advice and guidance	Sexual health, information about drug use, mental health counselling, careers advice, housing assistance, signposting to relevant services and support
Caring	Holiday play schemes, camps and after school clubs, crèches, playgroups, breakfast clubs
Support	Young mothers'/parents'/fathers' groups, young carers' groups, mental health groups, identity-specific groups
Housing	Refuges, sheltered accommodation, emergency housing, half-way housing
Environmental	Gardening and clean-up projects, park and playground design, mural creation, recycling, sustainability efforts
Media	Internet cafés, radio stations, DJ facilities, local newsletters, drama, music and art studios, social networks
Leisure	Cafés, youth centres, sports activities, indoor games, social networks
Health	Counselling services, multi-agency health clinics, health promotion, condom distribution, needle exchange, keep fit classes, healthy eating groups
Social control?	Diversionary or preventative activities, surveillance and supervision.

Youth work carries a more profound purpose than simply providing leisure and recreation-based activities, care or diversionary services. The facilitation of diversionary and preventative activities related to young people's experimentation with risky activities or anti-social behaviour can only be described as youth work if the activities build on young people's interests and stated needs and they have a say in how the programme is designed and carried out. The presentation of interesting activities for young people, such as sports, crafts and music can form part of youth work in many settings within schools, youth centres, churches, enterprises, and so forth – but the service needs to be designed, evaluated and developed through dialogue with young people. The goals should be to involve young people in facilitating or managing the activities and to promote their ownership and control of any plans or strategies (see Practice Example 1.2). Otherwise, the 'service' can become an exercise in social control.

A service becomes participative

An after-school club run by youth workers provided a service for local parents and carers by looking after children and young people whilst their carers were at work, busy elsewhere or simply needing respite. The youth workers' aims were to develop self-esteem and confidence amongst the members accessing the club. The members were asked how the club could be improved, and they started by stating which activities they preferred. Soon they were designing the programme and publicity. Before long, they became involved in the management of the club. The members realised that young disabled people had few opportunities to socialise with others in the neighbourhood and arranged for a partial merger with a local disabled young people's project. The members successfully challenged the notion that the club was just a service for parents and carers. They changed the aims of the after-school club to make it a service for all young people in the community and tackled issues such as access, integration and independence by listening to other young people's ideas on what kind of service they wanted.

PRACTICE EXAMPLE 1.2

RECOGNISING ROLE CONFLICT

Conflicts in role can arise when activities or services are designed to control young people rather than enable their self-expression and autonomy. Youth workers need to recognise the difference so that they can decide when to 'take a stand' and to define and defend their professional boundaries, and when flexibility and cooperation can work for the benefit of young people. Compatibility or conflict in roles may not always be straightforward or consistent, as Practice Example 1.3 demonstrates. A project that was funded to divert young people from crime was developed into a youth work project through participative practice.

Diversion or participation?

A football project was funded as a 'diversion from crime' initiative. The youth workers involved the team members in managing the project. The young people developed the funding application, recruited and inducted new members, handled the finance, trained volunteers and organised the travel arrangements, tournament participation and sponsorship deals. They also set up a support group for volunteers amongst previous members, parents/carers and local members of the community who became coaches and referees. Using youth work methods, the football project developed from being a 'take care of our badly behaved young people' service for the community into a community-based initiative where the young people took a leading role.

Increased bureaucratisation or efforts to control individuals or groups can lead to excessive monitoring and oppressive surveillance of young people's activities. Through partnership work with other agencies or funding that becomes available for particular projects, some workers have been drawn into a surveillance role without questioning or necessarily recognising the changes and their implications for youth work practice. Records of contacts, hard outcomes and working to a pre-planned programme are procedures often expected and required by funders, but detailed record keeping, particularly when information can be accessed by others, does not usually comply with youth work principles of accountability and confidentiality. For example, assessed alternative education, prevention training and probation services can require information sharing with far-reaching effects, such as failure, withdrawal from a programme or imprisonment. When recording and maintaining detailed records turns into judging young people's behaviour or becomes a punitive intervention, most youth workers would no longer describe the practice as youth work. Youth workers aim to identify and address discrimination and injustice rather than contribute to further oppression. Attempting to encourage socially acceptable behaviour or respect for others with young people who are being treated unacceptably and disrespectfully could be seen as collusion with oppression.

Youth workers may be asked to work on a one-to-one basis with young people and to target 'interventions' with named individuals or a caseload of 'clients'. Individuals may be identified as in need of intervention to promote their involvement in education, training or employment, with 'youth workers' acting as learning mentors or personal advisors. Action programmes may be devised and implemented to address these aims with little involvement of the young people. Programmes are then assessed on whether these named individuals return to learning or enter employment rather than on any contribution made to the quality of community life, personal flourishing or social relationships that may arise out of the process.

Such intervention work is an example of one of the many ways in which adults retain and demonstrate care, protection and control of young people as they move from childhood needs for protection to undertaking adult responsibilities. A youth work approach would be to provide young people with the opportunity to make considered and informed decisions based on a better understanding of situations and consequences. While most young people progress towards adulthood taking on new or different responsibilities for financial, economic, social, career and domestic matters, some experience more difficulties in making these transitions than others, sometimes due to their particular circumstances or make-up. Youth workers need to be aware that undertaking a protective rather than an interactive relationship can lead to role conflict.

Bernard Davies' (2005) manifesto for youth work sets out some criteria to identify whether practice clearly relates to the principles of youth work. Applying this checklist (in Box 1.5) can assist in the identification of role conflict and compatibility, particularly when working within an organisation that may have a very different approach to working with young people.

Box 1.5   Davies' (2005) checklist for youth work practice

- Is this really youth work?
- Do the young people choose to become involved? Is their engagement voluntary?
- Is the practice seeking to tip the balance of power to young people? Are the young people viewed and welcomed as young people?
- Are young people's contributions respected and valued?
- Is the practice starting where young people are? Is the expectation that young people will be able to relax, meet friends and have fun?
- Is the practice focused on young people as individuals?
- Is the practice respectful of young people's peer networks and actively responsive to them?
- Is the practice respectful of young people's wider community and cultural identities and actively responsive to them?
- Where young people choose, is the practice seeking to help them strengthen their community and cultural identities?
- Is the practice seeking to go beyond where young people start? Is it encouraging them to be outward looking, critical and creative in their responses to their experience and the world around them?
- Is the practice concerned with how young people feel, as well as with what they know and can do? (Davies, 2005: 7)

BEING CLEAR ABOUT ONE'S OWN MOTIVATION

Youth workers often have a specific motivation for work with young people that can form part of a desire to improve the world and/or the people living in it.

Motivations can vary, ranging from a desire to right wrongs and resolve social and political problems to ensuring that others do not have to suffer through similar personal difficulties. Belton, for example, defines 'radical youth work' practice as 'being informed by political and moral values: opposition to capitalism and authoritarianism, belief in equality and respect for the environment' (2010: 69). The Development Education Association also provides a relevant example with a definition of 'global youth work' as:

> informal education with young people [that] encourages a critical understanding of the links between personal, local and global issues. It seeks their active participation in bringing about change towards greater equity and justice. (Williams and Edelston, 2010: 10)

An organisation may have a focus on non-violence or community spirit, concerns which are clearly compatible with young people's well-being and interests. Box 1.6 provides some further examples of youth work as a 'mission'.

Box 1.6   Youth work as a 'mission'

Some youth workers and organisations may have specific motivations for involvement in youth work, for example:

- a religious community that provides opportunities for young people to form relationships with others, sharing their beliefs to preserve a culture or faith
- a philanthropic organisation that feeds homeless young people or offers shelter or mentoring
- a political party that has a youth wing to support the development of future leaders
- a campaigning organisation that recruits young people to projects aiming to improve society or the environment, including involvement in clean-up tasks, volunteering opportunities and befriending schemes
- a uniformed organisation with value-based aims, such as the Scouts and Guides who aim to create a better world or the Air and Sea Cadets who aim to foster good citizenship.

Clarity about whether individual motivation is compatible with the values and principles of youth work can assist youth workers to address young people's interests rather than impose a particular agenda. Youth work motivated by strong ideological beliefs can provide interesting options for young people; whereas beliefs in the superiority of particular groups or life choices and the imposition of belief systems onto young people are inappropriate. A youth work organisation should not be involved in indoctrination, coercion or exploitation of young people, or involve them in destructive or exclusive groups (except perhaps some targeted provision). An awareness of organisational or individual motivations can increase young people's control over participation or opt out.

IDENTIFYING UNACCEPTABLE YOUTH WORKER BEHAVIOUR

As youth workers hold privileged positions in the lives of young people, clarity about professional boundaries and respecting young people's rights are important factors in youth work relationships. Youth workers have a high level of responsibility for the care and safety of young people, particularly when working with younger age groups or in residential settings. Reliability and trustworthiness are important traits to evidence and promote. Young people could be vulnerable or at risk from violent, exploitative or otherwise inappropriate relationships or behaviour, and should not encounter this in their relationships with youth workers. The values and principles of youth work that define good practice are intended to protect young people from physical or verbal abuse, being unfairly blamed or 'scape-goated' and from receiving inaccurate or inappropriate information and advice.

Specific definitions or expectations of acceptable professional behaviour can vary in different situations and organisations. Recognition of an individual's suitability for youth work usually depends on standpoints that could include legal, moral or political standards as well as professional ethics. Legislation may determine whether individuals with particular histories, such as sexual exploitation or violence, are allowed to be in the company of young people, much less work with them. Evidence of certain illegal or risky behaviour, specific judicial sentences or particular mental health diagnoses will preclude involvement in some youth work organisations or in some countries, for example some organisations will not use volunteers or employ individuals with a history of drug use or violence. (See Box 1.7 for some further examples of unacceptable youth worker behaviour.)

While youth work organisations and youth workers need to take serious and sensible precautions when recruiting staff to ensure the safety of young people in their care, youth workers who have relevant negative experiences may have a lot to offer young people facing similar difficulties and choices in their lives. Youth workers often draw on past experiences to inform their youth work practice, particularly in relation to some of the more challenging issues such as addiction or anger management and abusive or violent relationships. Individuals who have been involved in 'anti-social' activities or crime and have been able to turn around their lives can provide valuable insights for young people. For these reasons, a criminal record does not necessarily preclude involvement in youth work. First-hand experience of the criminal justice system can also provide a deep awareness of some of the implications and consequences of certain life choices and circumstances, which can inform youth work practice.

Box 1.7   Unacceptable youth worker behaviour

Most organisations would find the following activities to be unacceptable during working hours:

- wilful, knowing or negligent failure to comply with relevant legislation or organisational policy
- exercising undue influence on young people or other members of the community for personal or financial gain
- carrying out youth work activities whilst under the influence of drugs or alcohol
- flirtatious behaviour, sexually provocative dress or sexual intimacy
- preferential treatment or attention for individual young people.

Many organisations would also find evidence of 'moral unfitness' outside of working hours unacceptable, for example:

- involvement in illegal activities, particularly any sexual activity with a legally defined 'minor'
- drunkenness or other risky behaviour carried out in public, particularly if posted on a social networking site accessible to young people.

(See also Chapter 12 for examples of staff misconduct.)

Individuals applying to work with young people on a paid or unpaid basis can expect potential employers to check criminal records. While record systems vary in relation to accuracy, relevance and ease of access, many employers will be required by organisational policy and/or law to check the criminal records of anyone applying to work with children and young people, whether on a paid or voluntary basis. Others will insist on doing so. Applicants need to be prepared to discuss their past experiences with potential employers. Appropriate policies about employing ex-offenders generally take into account factors such as the severity and circumstances of the offence, how long ago it was committed and evidence of learning from the experience.

KEEPING UP TO DATE WITH LEGAL CONSTRAINTS

Youth workers need to be aware of relevant legislation and legal boundaries to inform their own choices about action to take, as well as any advice given to young people. While most individuals are clear about what constitutes theft, assault, road traffic violations and use of illegal substances, additional knowledge of their application and relevance to youth work is useful. Many youth work organisations require youth workers to have specific training in issues and legal responsibilities related to safeguarding, health and safety, physical restraint and sexual harassment prior to any physical contact with young people. Other relevant information could include laws related to human rights, crime and disorder and any specific rights and protection afforded to different groups. Mental health, immigration, trafficking and forced marriage: awareness may also be relevant areas of study, and knowledge of legislation related to employment would be essential for posts with responsibility for selecting or managing staff. As legislation is subject to change, maintaining currency and relevance about legal constraints, rights and responsibilities through relevant training is a requirement of professional youth work practice.

The values and principles of youth work are not always compatible with changing legal requirements or organisational policies and practice. Like other 'people-oriented' occupations and professions, youth work requires individual and flexible responses to situations that depend on individuals rather than stock answers. To maintain clarity of purpose and awareness of possible conflicts in role, youth workers need to be involved in continuous professional development to keep up to date with legal, political and moral issues that may affect the information and views that they hold and sometimes pass on to young people. The identification of appropriate responses requires discussion with young people and colleagues in relation to ethical and professional values and evaluation and planning through supervision.

RECOGNISING AND USING SUPPORT AND SUPERVISION

Appropriate support can help a youth worker to plan and engage in best practice, define professional boundaries and handle role conflicts that may arise. Such support may be provided within the organisation from a manager or colleagues, and may also be available from experienced individuals and groups external to the organisation who can provide advice or guidance from diverse perspectives. The availability and need for external support will vary greatly depending on individuals, their employment arrangements and their organisational setting. Young people and colleagues within the organisation may provide sufficient direction, challenge and encouragement, and the culture and approach of the organisation may comply with professional youth work practice. However, some youth workers work to restrictive job descriptions, policies, procedures and codes of practice that would mean external support would be necessary to find ways to function professionally. Attempting to change attitudes and practices within an organisation requires support, a strategy and a will to engage in challenging activities. Many youth workers need to seek additional support with external supervision (see also Chapter 12) and networking with other agencies to ensure that professional values and principles are upheld in practice.

ESSENTIAL SKILLS FOR UNDERSTANDING YOUTH WORK ROLES AND RESPONSIBILITIES

- Identifying youth work values and practice
- Applying values and principles to practice
- Recognising youth work roles
- Being clear about who youth work is for
- Recognising role conflict
- Being clear about one's own motivation(s)
- Identifying unacceptable youth worker behaviour
- Keeping up to date with legal constraints
- Recognising and using support and supervision

 FURTHER READING

For further reading about ethical youth work practice, Banks (2010) discusses ethics and youth work as well as some of the dilemmas faced in professional practice. Davies (2005) also provides some examples of how the checklist in Box 1.5 might apply to an analysis of ethical youth work practice.

For further reading about safeguarding, see Cleaver et al. (2009) which explores the principles and process of having 'children at the heart of safeguarding practice'. Munro (2008) suggests ways to assess risk. The Charity Commission (2009) provides some useful guidance on the web for developing relevant polices with legal compliance for the UK. Alderson (2008) provides a context for practice with Young Children's Rights. The NSPCC's (2011) Safe Network website collects together some very useful guides for safe practice, including information about recommended numbers of staff, online safety checks and sample forms for attendance, excursions and photographs.

2

LOCATING YOUTH WORK IN DIFFERENT SETTINGS

This chapter suggests ways to get to know about the organisation and practice settings in which youth work takes place and the factors that may affect activities, methods and young people's participation, such as the organisational context and the type of youth work undertaken.

FINDING OUT ABOUT THE ORGANISATION

Information about the organisational setting in which youth work takes place, enables a youth worker to understand the organisation's expectations around duties and responsibilities, as well as any opportunities or constraints that may affect practice. A number of factors can be relevant, such as decision-making structures, organisational priorities and purpose, as well as current activities and wherewithal for new developments. Key areas of information are who makes the decisions, who funds the activities, who is being targeted and what type of work is being carried out. Finding out about actual practice as well as the relevant policies and procedures on paper is important as organisational documents and job descriptions may not always tally with the reality of day-to-day work. The information-seeking and analytical process outlined in this chapter can be described as 'locating' the organisation in relation to other youth work (see Box 2.1). The process would be carried out during and following induction so that the strengths of the organisation and any limitations on practice are clearly understood. A checklist at the end of this chapter provides suggestions for topics to be covered in the induction of new members of staff, volunteers or students on placement, from an introduction to the working environment to exit arrangements (see Box 2.7).

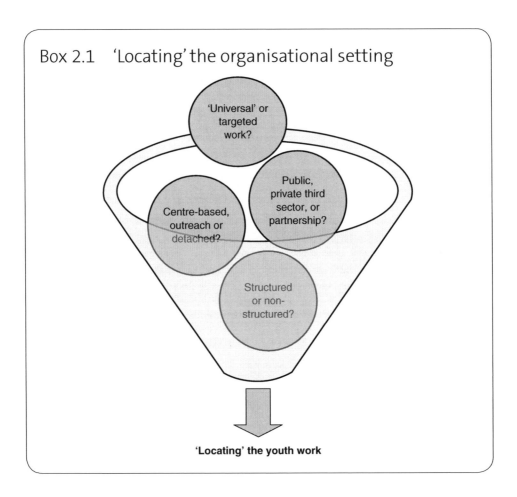

Box 2.1   'Locating' the organisational setting

'Universal' or targeted work?

Public, private third sector, or partnership?

Centre-based, outreach or detached?

Structured or non-structured?

'Locating' the youth work

Finding out whether an organisation is public, private or 'third' sector or a cross-sector partnership means finding out about sources of funding and their requirements in relation to direction and accountability. Public sector youth work may be funded and/or provided by national, regional (such as county/state) or local (city/town) government services or departments. Private sector youth work is carried out on a 'for-profit' basis, for example by self-employed or freelance individuals or companies generating an income for themselves and/or shareholders. The third sector is meant to be independent of government or the need to generate a profit and includes international, national or local charitable bodies, non-government organisations (NGOs) and other 'not-for-personal-profit' groups, such as social enterprises (businesses that have an environmental or other social purpose). Examples of possible attributes of the different sectors and their funders are provided in Box 2.2. However, individual organisations vary considerably and may not conform to general attributes of a sector in relation to decision making, where the power lies or how changes are implemented.

Box 2.2   Youth work in different sectors

Public sector youth work:

- could involve statutory and standardised services backed up by legislation
- could benefit from costs being fully covered
- may focus on significant groups or issues
- is accountable to tax payers or citizens/voters via elected members
- may rely on being able to demonstrate success in relation to specific targets or outcomes
- may be dependent on the relevance to current political issues and agendas.

Private sector youth work:

- could be a profitable social enterprise providing a sustainable balance between social and/or environmental mission and financial goals
- could be an ethical business able to minimise the negative impact on society or the environment
- is accountable to owners or shareholders
- may mean salary and job insecurity as covering costs depends on income generation
- may need to charge fees, which would restrict access to those with the wherewithal.

Third-sector youth work:

- may be able to focus on minority interests, e.g. local community and 'grass roots' associations
- may be willing to focus on emerging needs or interests with greater flexibility and responsiveness
- can use any surplus revenue to further the organisational aims, rather than to pay shareholders
- could be a charity dependent on short-term grants and donations and restricted in relation to trading activities
- is generally accountable to the public via a board or committee that does not benefit financially.

(Continued)

(Continued)

Cross-sector partnerships for specific activities, projects or organisations:

- could build on the strengths of all parties to provide efficient and sustainable options, e.g. the accessibility of a third-sector organisation with the systems of a private sector business
- need to be carefully constructed to ensure clarity of roles and mutual benefit
- could involve increased bureaucratisation and dependence.

The focus on organisations in this section does not mean to imply that all youth work takes place within formally constituted organisations. A group of parents, local volunteers or activists may get together on an ad hoc basis to facilitate enjoyable leisure activities for young people. Neighbours joining up for an annual street party or trip to the seaside may find themselves considering questions such as who is involved or the type of activities that would define the type of youth work in which they are engaged. Young people facilitating their own activities, such as a weekly basketball tournament, may wish to apply for funding to access other resources. Ad hoc groups can be very flexible and responsive to local needs. Individual adults may simply offer their time and resources, which can mean building on enthusiasms. (Practice Example 2.1 provides an example of such a group.) However, excluding unsuitable participants may be difficult and dependence on goodwill may make planning problematic. Participants in these less structured third-sector settings may come to a point where identifying the strengths and limitations of the arrangement can inform decisions about whether becoming a constituted group would be beneficial or detrimental to their work with young people.

PRACTICE EXAMPLE 2.1

Working without rules

I started a football session with a mate of mine on Tuesday nights because we liked football and we knew that the kids around here had nothing to do except get into trouble. I managed to get permission to use some grounds attached to a religious centre nearby. We can't use their toilets and we don't have anywhere to get changed or shower, but they said that we can use their field. So anyway, about a dozen kids show up – not always the same ones, but pretty much. They just found out by word of mouth. Everybody around here knows us anyway. We don't have any club rules; we just have football regulations. Except we don't have teams – they change every week. And we usually don't bother keeping score. Actually, that's not true. We did have one rule. No hitting – or else you can't come back the following week. Then one week one kid hit another kid. We all stood around in the rain shouting about it. Then everyone said, 'See you next week', so we got rid of that rule.

Interagency work, multi-agency partnerships or other cooperative cross-sector arrangements may involve pooled resources or shared responsibilities, which can blur the distinctions between different sectors. In these situations, both positive and negative attributes of the participating sectors may apply. Long-term government financial support for a third-sector organisation, for example, can lead to a local self-help group having to address the current political climate and becoming dependent on elected members' support. Further investigation into external bodies may be necessary to identify the direction and focus of youth work that is funded or managed by decisions made elsewhere.

Identifying existing and potential links with other relevant organisations, networks and services may reveal additional available support or resources for youth work. Youth workers may share resources and expertise or develop work with a range of other agencies working with young people from different sectors. Examples include health services, the police, housing associations, schools, social services and a range of third-sector organisations. Issues as diverse as school exclusions, healthy eating, community safety or concerns about an individual young person can lead to joint work or funding being allocated. For example, another organisation's expertise in specific areas such as drugs, crime or sexual health may evolve into interagency work for a targeted group of young people. A partnership could involve joint agencies working at any level of service provision, from face-to-face work to management. Individual links may be developed as being able to signpost young people to individuals working in specialist services is very useful. Alternatively, another agency may reach out to youth workers. Public services and other agencies are often keen to utilise the contacts and relationships that youth workers have to support their need to engage or reach young people. Developing partnerships can enhance current resources and/or provide opportunities for future cooperation. Box 2.3 has some examples of partnerships that could be relevant.

Box 2.3　Cross-sector partnerships

- A subgroup of a youth forum agrees to put together materials for the police about young people's perspectives, which become part of the initial training for new workers joining the police service.
- A multi-agency group coordinates public sector services for children and young people within a politically defined area and involves representative staff from education, probation, health and social services, as well as youth workers who support young people's representation and feedback.
- Youth workers work alongside healthcare professionals in a sexual health clinic to offer more informal and accessible support to young people using the services.
- A group of young people agree to participate in selecting a new member of paid staff. Training is provided to ensure understanding of legal and ethical practice in equal opportunities selection procedures.

(Continued)

(Continued)

- A partnership between government-funded education services and a local charitable trust utilises teachers and youth workers to provide educational activities within a community-based setting for young people 'excluded' from school.
- A local church provides a venue for youth workers funded by local government to provide informal social education for young people in the area.
- A national network, which establishes charitable status, gathers individuals and representatives from a range of organisations facilitating youth work to establish good practice guidelines in relation to a particular issue that are then adopted by the participants.
- A cooperative relationship between a private enterprise holiday camp and a charitable youth work organisation means that outdoor pursuit facilities and training is provided for young people unable to afford a holiday.

WORKING WITHIN NON-YOUTH WORK ORGANISATIONS

In the interests of young people and their rights, youth workers often work within organisations that are not involved in youth work and alongside other professionals. Such work may be undertaken in order to access certain groups of young people or to enhance opportunities for young people. For example, youth workers may work within schools or colleges, prisons, or housing offices. When youth work roles are valued, working within non-youth work organisations can be a useful way to access different groups of young people and to influence how other professionals interact with them.

Youth workers attempting to practise within an organisation, activity or venue that is set up for reasons other than youth work may find that different working practices are expected. Activities may be oriented towards societal needs rather than young people's interests. Projects in housing offices may relate to 'diversionary activities' for young people involved in 'anti-social' or 'risky' behaviour which is annoying the neighbours, rather than addressing the young people's concerns. Other professionals may expect youth workers to wear a suit, insist on being addressed as 'miss' or 'sir', or, perhaps most problematically, require attendance. If asked to report on young people's lack of attendance with the knowledge that any breaches may lead to disciplinary action or incarceration, many youth workers would draw a line on the grounds that non-voluntary relationships go beyond youth work principles. However, the offer of resources and opportunities to facilitate access to young people may take precedence over professional misgivings. A decision to remain working in a situation that requires young people's participation may depend on whether the work is perceived to be positive and otherwise participative.

Finding ways to negotiate a compromise rather than withdrawing from a shared piece of work or project may be possible.

Establishing a base within a school or college building can be a very efficient method of contacting large numbers of young people and can provide them with easy access to youth work during breaks in the school timetable. Young people can raise confidential issues, such as the prospect of a forced marriage, whether or not to 'come out' about their sexuality or domestic abuse disclosure, without the knowledge of family or community. Youth workers based in educational settings may also find themselves providing informal or more formal education to young people and staff. Youth workers may facilitate sessions in personal, health or social education classes on drugs awareness, sexual health and identity or self-harm. Staff may call upon their expertise in 'race' relations or handling conflict to provide training or to resolve issues arising in the school. Other roles could include mentoring, linking schools and communities, supporting students or pupils who are excluded temporarily from classes, or providing alternative education for longer-term exclusions. In some situations, youth workers may have close working relationships with a school nurse, a psychologist, the local police assigned to the school, welfare officers and home–school liaison workers, as well as teachers and staff. The ability to communicate with other professionals about youth work values and principles can assist the development of cooperative working.

Youth workers sometimes work in prisons, young offenders' institutions or detention centres to enhance the availability of educational, social and leisure activities to young people who are involuntarily detained having been found guilty of committing a crime. As the organisation could be involved in isolation or punishment to redeem or rehabilitate a young person, youth workers may find little leeway within the controlled and controlling environment to develop voluntary relationships or create opportunities for young people to be involved in decision making. To retain professional identity in this setting, the effective use of resources and clarity about the role can help find ways to offer opportunities and choices which alleviate the constraints of the organisation (as can be seen in Practice Example 2.2).

Youth workers may find that their work becomes more about surveillance or social control than leisure activities, education or liberating and self-defined projects. Professional judgement may be limited by organisational procedures getting in the way of approaching young people as individuals. A key area is an expectation that information about young people will be passed on to others working in the organisation, which a youth worker would be reluctant to do without good reason. Youth workers need to use their communication skills and understanding of their role to assert their values and principles and develop working relationships with other professionals that do not compromise their practice with young people. Information about these matters may only be revealed by experience. Continuous organisation-wide reflection on the strengths or weaknesses of different projects and potential opportunities/threats from organisational changes, as well as development through supervision and evaluative discussions with young people, can assist youth workers to learn more about their organisations. The use of Davies' (2005) checklist in Chapter 1 (Box 1.5) may be useful to identify whether the work is compatible with the role of a youth worker. A 'SWOT' analysis, looking at strengths, weaknesses, opportunities and threats, is illustrated in Box 2.9, later in this chapter.

Youth work or surveillance?

I'm involved in an intensive supervision project with young men who have come out of prison. As a youth worker, I am ideally placed to work with these young men. I know them. I've been there. I know what they are going through. There are only three guys that I meet regularly for about three months to keep track of them. It's like I'm their big brother. They come out of prison and there's nothing else for them. They've lost their families and homes. There's no one there. Next time they're arrested, it will be for serious crimes and adult prison. They need someone to set them on the right path. This is their last chance. I know it's not the same as youth work, but I've got all of the right skills to work with these guys. They can't pull the wool over my eyes. So when we talk about options and what happens after they do something, they know that meeting me is part of what they have to do. So it's their choice. They come and see me or they go back to prison. In that way, I try and keep it as much like youth work as possible. When they come to see me, they choose what they talk about and whether to join in. Unfortunately, I have no control over what happens to the paperwork. But that sometimes is helpful. I tell the guys, look, if you don't come to the sessions, it goes down in this paper and you'll be going back to prison. It gives them some structure and they know what's going on and that I will be fair with them.

IDENTIFYING SOURCES OF DIRECTION AND SUPPORT

Discussions about the organisation in order to understand its practice in relation to youth work requires an understanding of responsibilities within that organisation. A manager and co-workers may be key contacts for providing daily direction and support for practice, although in time this may be provided or augmented by someone other than the designated individual. Identifying members of a committee or board directing operations and finding out their perspectives on youth work may also be relevant. Talking with colleagues and reading organisational documents should reveal where the power lies: who makes decisions and what informs those decisions. Channels of communication and sources of power can usually be identified by asking who is responsible for different types of decisions, such as the overall direction of the organisation versus planning activities or buying a multi-purpose bus versus stationery. Identifying the chain of command can reveal the role of young people in making decisions. For example, in the 'chain of command' diagram illustrated in Box 2.4, the Executive Board is in touch with the funders and the manager, but does not appear to be in contact with the young people. In this arrangement, any decisions the Board makes about the young people's interests may be based only on information passed through the youth worker and the manager. See Chapter 9 for ideas about developing young people's participation in organisations.

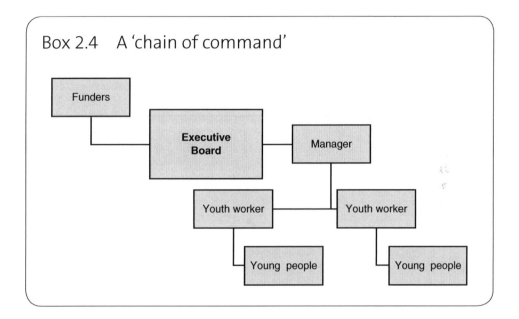

Box 2.4   A 'chain of command'

IDENTIFYING TYPES OF YOUTH WORK

Finding out whether the youth work offered by an organisation is structured or non-structured, 'universal' or targeted can assist a youth worker in understanding organisational priorities and plans. Some youth work, such as fixed or short-term projects, may need to be more tightly planned and organised with clearly identified outcomes and procedures, whilst other opportunities are more flexible and open, without a fixed 'agenda' or predetermined expectations. Ideally, the type of youth work is identified and organised in relation to the interests of the young people, as well as the remit and resources of the organisation. Tensions can arise if the approach does not fit the type of work that has been funded, or if the values or principles of youth work are compromised to such a degree that the benefits of youth work cannot be realised. The diagram in Box 2.5 provides some examples of attributes associated with structured and non-structured youth work, although some activities may contain aspects of both types.

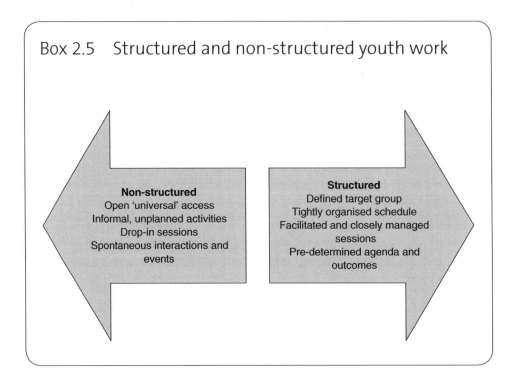

Box 2.5   Structured and non-structured youth work

Non-structured
Open 'universal' access
Informal, unplanned activities
Drop-in sessions
Spontaneous interactions and
events

Structured
Defined target group
Tightly organised schedule
Facilitated and closely managed
sessions
Pre-determined agenda and
outcomes

Curriculum-based programmes are an example of structured work that can demand more scheduled commitment and specific outcomes than other forms of youth work. Outdoor education, for example, may be planned to develop skills, widen experiences and raise self-esteem and confidence. Assessment of risk for challenging opportunities, such as gorge walking or high-rope activities, may require participants to follow fairly rigid instructions. A residential involving training in outdoor activities can provide young people with a great sense of achievement leading to increased confidence and self-esteem especially when fears are overcome. In addition to personal challenges, there is a strong emphasis on caring, sharing and working as a team. Throughout the course, students experience the countryside which can also develop their understanding of the natural environment. Other structured youth work could include competitive activities or creative projects leading to a performance or display, which may target young people with specific interests and require consistent attendance. Such structured work has a place in youth work practice when young people express interest.

An example of non-structured youth work is a youth centre or mobile unit that offers a drop-in service to young people who access available resources at their own pace with minimal supervision. Youth workers are often in the background or chatting casually with young people, intervening when directly approached or to join a debate. Typically, such provision would provide games equipment, such as a pool table or computer suite, and lounging area. This type of activity could be offered to any young people within a defined geographical 'catchment' area or could target specific groups by restricting entrance or opening times. For example, the schedule for a mobile unit's locations may prioritise areas designated as lacking in other services for young people, or a centre may allocate certain slots in the timetable to 'girls-only work' or sessions for specific sports or educational opportunities.

Some organisations or programmes will target work with particular defined groups of young people to address specific issues identified by the funders. Rather than attempting to offer 'universal' provision for all young people in the area, a specific activity or project may be designed to address individuals in particular circumstances, usually because of an assessment or perception of particular groups of young people as being in need of focused attention. Projects may target particular types of behaviour, particularly that which is, or is perceived to be, dangerous, illegal, 'anti-social' or 'risky', or certain groups of young people, such as those not in school or not in paid employment. Care needs to be taken to ensure that targets are not based on a deficit model, which perceives certain young people as 'disadvantaged' or nuisances.

Targeted projects are often designed to offer opportunities to young people who are experiencing difficulties in life, to deter them from getting involved in additional difficulties or to prevent current problems from escalating and may be required to demonstrate that specific outcomes have been met. Examples could include alternative education projects for individuals who are excluded or have self-excluded from school, are 'under-performing' in school or have learning difficulties. Such projects may need to evidence improvements in attendance and academic achievement as well as behaviour, such as a reduction in substance misuse, illegal activities or teenage pregnancy. The indicators used to identify the group perceived to be most 'at risk' and 'in need' of youth work may be labels imposed by others rather than self-defined.

LOCATING KEY POLICIES AND PROCEDURES

An organisation's policies and procedures for safe and professional practice may be backed up by written documents or simply passed on through example and discussion. Training and induction may be obligatory in order to pass on information about rules and procedures designed to address an organisation's concerns about the safety of young people and equipment, accidents on excursions and potential allegations of sexual or racial harassment. Records of personal information and interaction may be expected; statistical data may be compiled; parent and carer provider permissions may be sought. Detailed procedures may attempt to cover every eventuality although, clearly, guaranteeing protection is impossible. Knowledge of any constraints to confidentiality or liability is necessary so that accurate information can be given to young people on these key matters.

The anticipation of potential hazards that could arise from an activity is clearly a commonsense procedure for anyone taking responsibility for others. More formal written records of risk assessments are also often required by organisations during planning and review of programmes and projects. Consideration needs to be given to safeguarding young people's and staff members' well-being and the potential for accident and injury. Identifying risks and those who could be at risk from a particular activity has the purpose of identifying ways to reduce or remove the potential for harm. This attention to health and safety should mean that contingency preparations can be identified. However, in some instances, concerns about risk management mean that activities are severely curtailed. Youth workers also need to be aware of situations that may give rise to accusations about their misconduct or blame to be accorded by an organisation, whether or not these claims are justified. Written records may be used as evidence in insurance claims or court investigations so are generally expected to be regularly reviewed and updated.

Policies that are designed to protect the organisation against litigation and disciplinary action can have a detrimental effect on practice. Contact with young people may be curtailed by extensive risk management or requirements for data entry. Key aspects of youth work such as flexibility, spontaneity or informality may be undermined by exaggerated emphasis on procedures and could devalue the contribution of professionals who often make decisions based on their understanding of a particular situation. Informal work with young people often thrives on being able to make exceptions to rules, rather than imposing regulations based on general rather than individual circumstances. However, an individual needs to be aware of the organisation's policies and their implications in order to know when support for actions may be withdrawn. Breaching protocols and regulations means taking personal responsibility for one's actions, which can be risky in terms of making mistakes and potentially experiencing disciplinary action and job dismissal.

IDENTIFYING THE VENUES

Information about venues, programmes and resources for current activities provides a foundation upon which to build and ensures that new ideas and initiatives do not simply duplicate previously established work. A new worker will want to find out whether the organisation's programme of work involves centre-based, outreach, detached or online settings since practice and resource requirements will vary accordingly. While the interests and needs of young people may be accommodated in locations ranging from purpose-built facilities to natural open spaces, appropriate and efficient use of resources depends on knowing about the locations and any potential for development of new activities. Issues such as planning, risk and accessibility also need to be considered.

Centre-based activities can take place in small rooms that fit only a tiny number of targeted young people, or in large, publicly accessible venues where anyone can drop in, which clearly makes a difference in relation to staff ratios and identifying risks. Some settings may be more accessible for specific groups or individual young people, more suitable for certain activities or suit a particular youth worker's own skills and interests. Whereas a room without much more to offer than shelter from the weather may be appropriate for individuals seeking a supportive and relaxed environment, young unemployed people wanting support in developing their skills in music, sports or car mechanics, for example, may need a space with more equipment and resources. Some settings have been designed for specific use and activities whilst others, such as unused shops or churches, may require creativity to adapt the space or funding to improve the building.

Youth workers often use other organisations' locations for outreach work with young people. Specific interests, such as wall climbing or roller-skating, may be requested by young people particularly interested in those activities, or might be accessed to expand the interests and experiences of young people who have not had the opportunity to try out these activities previously. Youth work can involve travel to new places or environments through excursions, camping, exchanges or other overnight residentials. Identifying an ideal setting for youth work is not always easy to predict. Going on a residential to a new setting may not be appropriate until a disruptive or boisterous group has bonded; alternatively, using the opportunity to bring young people together through shared new experiences may be very appropriate. These activities clearly have implications for risk assessment and carers' consent. Considering the make-up and history of a group can assist a youth worker in predicting and preparing for certain eventualities, whilst discussions with the young people themselves will inform planning.

Detached youth work involves making contact with young people in their own settings by going out to meet them where they naturally congregate, usually in outdoor settings. Through detached work, a youth worker can learn from direct experience about the context of young people's lives and any geographical, cultural or other territorial boundaries that they may use to organise themselves. Youth workers can also develop their knowledge of the communities they work with and the issues arising for young people and their neighbours. Detached youth work provides the opportunity to reach out to young people who cannot or choose not to become involved in other youth work settings, and often engages groups that may not feel welcome in other settings. Sometimes the young people themselves may be referred to as 'detached' or 'hard to reach', as they may not engage with other social structures or agencies. A detached group could include individuals whose experience of problematic relationships with school, family, carers, the criminal justice system or other professionals may have taught them to be wary of social systems or authorities.

A detached youth worker works outside of any youth work venues and becomes a 'visitor' in the young people's environment (see Box 2.6 for some examples of areas in which detached work might take place). An important part of a youth worker's approach is to recognise and acknowledge that the balance of power is clearly distinct from most other situations where adults tend to have more control over interactions with young people. Unlike discussions with parents, carers or adult professionals, young people in detached settings establish their own rules over conversations and activities and can also decide whether or not to allow a youth worker to become involved. In a detached setting, young people's participation is clearly voluntary in that they can simply move away if they do not wish to engage.

> ## Box 2.6   Areas for detached work
>
> - a bench or bus shelter where young people congregate to socialise
> - a natural shelter, such as a cluster of trees or rocks, that provides some protection from the weather
> - a section of a multi-storey car park or abandoned waste ground where homeless young people come together for mutual support or survival
> - a street corner where a group meets to gossip and have a laugh or conduct business, such as drugs or crime
> - a section of a park which provides a group of friends with a bit more privacy and distance from complaining neighbours
> - areas where young people are waiting for other provision or services, such as outside schools, courtrooms or health clinics
> - a publicly accessible bike or skateboard ramp, football field or basketball court where young people join in or participate as spectators, supporters or commentators.

Virtual youth work has developed alongside the internet and social networking. Youth work organisations use web pages to disseminate information about relevant issues, communicate with young people in a variety of ways and to celebrate young people's achievements. The medium has particular strengths for isolated young people. For example, virtual youth work is a useful way to work with young people in rural areas where travelling to youth centres is particularly problematic. Individuals who may be worried about asking certain questions or disclosing information about themselves can also benefit from the anonymity that may be possible with virtual contacts. As youth work thrives on social contacts, social networking can be very advantageous for young people's exchange of ideas and information. Posting films and photos about youth work activities can also publicise non-virtual events.

An awareness of good and safe practice in relation to virtual youth work is emerging amongst practitioners. Some of the risks associated with social networking are similar to those in other settings, such as bullying or exclusion, but will require different types of responses to face-to-face youth work. Newer issues, including lack of awareness of privacy and internet safety, such as spending too much time on-screen, disclosing personal information and engaging unknowingly with sexual predators, need to be taken into consideration when planning virtual youth work. Youth workers could also benefit from reflection on their own web presence to ensure that the images and information they disseminate are positive and professional.

CHECKING INDUCTION

The organisational context, type of youth work and settings for activities will determine a number of issues related to practice that need to be discussed during induction. For example, some organisations or youth workers have certain expectations about acceptable and unacceptable behaviour, particularly when a youth work activity takes place in another organisation's venue or whilst on a supervised excursion. Some facilities or organisations ban or eject young people who are clearly under the influence of mind-altering substances, attempt to bring such substances into premises where youth work is taking place, are physically violent or verbally abusive towards others, engage in risky behaviour or behave in ways that are unsafe, dangerous or in an attempt to bully or intimidate others. Other organisations have very few rules, but manage to convey their expectations of considerate behaviour through example and discussion. Rules should, whenever possible, relate to attempts to ensure young people's safety rather than simply to control or for no genuine purpose. (See also Chapter 8 which discusses ways to make group agreements.)

Some organisations provide planned inductions as well as relevant documentation for new staff or volunteers involving young people, staff and members of communities. In other situations, a youth worker may need to facilitate their own orientation or augment the induction by asking questions and observing. The sample induction checklist in Box 2.7 might be used to check that key topics are addressed, either by an organisation designing induction procedures or by an individual starting work in a new organisation.

Box 2.7   An induction checklist

Tour of premises/venue

- ❑ Desk or a base, telephone, computer: shared or individual
- ❑ Own contact telephone number, email address
- ❑ Equipment access, e.g. log-in for computer or photocopier, mobile/cell phone, voicemail, storage for games, apparatus, stationery supplies
- ❑ Facilities and use, e.g. house-keeping arrangements, refreshments, local amenities
- ❑ Available transport, car parking, bike storage
- ❑ Access to building: time restrictions, security requirements, identity card, codes/keys

Meeting the staff

- ❑ Identifying the manager: the individual who will ensure understanding of tasks and duties, monitor quality of work; answer questions about expectations; provide day-to-day support and direction
- ❑ How and when this management will take place: daily/weekly/before each session
- ❑ Key individuals: their roles and contact details
- ❑ Who/how to contact if unable to attend work or a meeting
- ❑ Staff/team meetings and training
- ❑ Professional supervision: whether an internal staff member will provide regular sessions to discuss professional practice or whether this may be accessed externally

(Continued)

(Continued)

Information about the organisation

- ❑ Organisational aims and targets, funding and accountability issues
- ❑ Key areas of activity, annual reports, publicity
- ❑ Key policies, codes of practice, procedures, particularly child protection, health & safety, confidentiality, social networking protocols, what to do if a fight breaks out
- ❑ Complaints: who to go to when things go wrong
- ❑ Organisation's timetable and activities
- ❑ Information about target groups, interests, local communities
- ❑ Planned or expected outcomes
- ❑ Record-keeping, monitoring, evaluation and report requirements
- ❑ Exit interviews: particularly for temporary or short-term work, projects or placements
- ❑ Time in lieu arrangements, holidays
- ❑ Pay, claiming procedures and timetable
- ❑ Expenses: what (if any) expenses may be incurred; claiming procedures
- ❑ External training and conferences: procedures for booking and budget availability

Programme of work

- ❑ Individual timetable with venues/other personnel
- ❑ Individual's role, specific duties, responsibilities, priorities, start date
- ❑ Recommendations for establishing appropriate relationships with young people
- ❑ Specific instructions regarding confidentiality, child protection or lone working

ANALYSING THE ORGANISATION

Starting out in a new organisation often requires some focused attention over a period of time beyond the induction period for development of the youth worker's understanding of the organisation and the context for practice. Over a period of months, new youth workers engage in finding out not only how the organisation works, but analysing and evaluating effectiveness and professionalism. The process generally continues throughout a youth worker's involvement with an organisation, but is more focused when starting out in a new organisation or project. A useful set of questions to guide the analysis is McKinsey's 'Seven S model' of organisational relationships (Waterman et al., 1980), illustrated in Box 2.8. The seven interrelated and co-dependent areas for investigation, include the structure, systems, style, staff, skills, strategy and shared values of the organisation. Finding out about these areas and the levels of harmony or congruence between them can provide a profound basis for understanding how the organisation works, as well as its capacity for change.

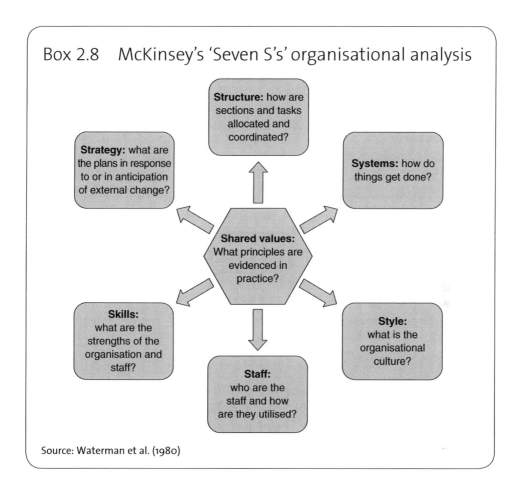

Box 2.8   McKinsey's 'Seven S's' organisational analysis

Structure: how are sections and tasks allocated and coordinated?

Strategy: what are the plans in response to or in anticipation of external change?

Systems: how do things get done?

Shared values: What principles are evidenced in practice?

Skills: what are the strengths of the organisation and staff?

Style: what is the organisational culture?

Staff: who are the staff and how are they utilised?

Source: Waterman et al. (1980)

An analysis of current strengths and weaknesses as well as potential opportunities and threats through a 'SWOT' analysis (attributed by Leigh in Pershing, 2006, to various influences and sources) can provide a useful framework for getting to know an organisation and where change may be necessary. Finding out about existing strengths on which to build can help to identify where appropriate support and direction may be found. Any weaknesses that need to be addressed may provide avenues for developing useful initiatives. Clearly, any immediate threats will indicate actions requiring high priorities, and opportunities may well provide ideas for how to implement these actions. (See Box 2.9 for a sample 'SWOT' analysis.) Internal as well as external factors are useful to consider through observation, discussion and reading of evaluation reports, publicity and previous funding applications that usually contain valuable statistics about the organisation. Internal issues may come to light relating to the experience and qualifications of staff; the availability and sustainability of resources; activities and take-up by young people (the numbers of young people attending); or the involvement of volunteers and communities.

Box 2.9   A sample 'SWOT' analysis

	Positive	Negative
Current	**STRENGTHS**	**WEAKNESSES**
	Experience of reaching out and engaging detached young people	Insufficient range of activities to keep young people interested
	Diverse staff reflecting the catchment communities	Slightly chaotic filing 'system' for records of completed projects
	Good networks with range of sector organisations	Insufficient recycling or up-cycling to make best use of resources
	New, very motivated volunteers recently recruited	Timetable confusions and conflicting demands on resources
Future	**OPPORTUNITIES**	**THREATS**
	New youth worker just appointed	Temporary funding for projects about to run out
	Potential partner offering free use of venue for outreach work	
	Drama performance by young people coming up that could promote activities and attract funders	Inadequate training for volunteers may lead to unprofessional practice
		Current government cuts affecting core funding

Some youth workers have the privilege of working within an organisation that has a coherent set of aims and policies based on youth work values and principles, or one that recognises and values the youth work contribution to their provision of compatible services. In these situations, identifying appropriate support and direction for practice can be straightforward. Others may find themselves in the position of having to promote or defend their approach with colleagues who have alternative or conflicting principles, perhaps working in multi-agency partnerships with diverse professionals or where youth work is not managed by youth workers. Youth workers may have to explain the voluntary, participative and enjoyable nature of youth work practice to others whose job it is to require attendance, provide pre-planned programmes or facilitate highly formal meetings. Challenging one's own organisation in order to adhere to youth work principles may not be advisable as a first step when starting work in a new job, but can be part of the role of a youth worker. Support from outside the organisation may be necessary to develop an effective strategy for maintaining a youth work approach to practice.

Analysing and evaluating an organisation's strengths also requires knowledge of the young people whose interests the practice is meant to address. The next chapter, Chapter 3, considers the skills involved in going out to meet young people in their communities alongside the youth worker's ongoing developing understanding of the organisational setting. Analysing the organisation may be carried out as a mental exercise, made a regular agenda item for discussion in supervision or put together as a detailed written piece. The 'Seven S' and 'SWOT' analyses can be very useful when compiling a portfolio of evidence of work-based learning for a youth work training course or professional development programme. Chapter 10 in this book provides further guidance for those involved in placements or projects for learning programmes. The material in that chapter may also be useful for new workers and their supervisors, particularly the information about reflection and evidencing learning.

ESSENTIAL SKILLS FOR LOCATING ORGANISATIONS

- Finding out about the organisation
- Working in non-youth work organisations
- Identifying sources of direction and support
- Identifying type of youth work
- Locating key policies and procedures
- Identifying the venues
- Checking induction
- Analysing the organisation

 ## FURTHER READING

See Rogers' (1981) excellent outline of various stages for setting out in detached work. See also Tiffany's (2007) *Reconnecting Detached Youth Work: Standards and guidelines for excellence* that provides what the title says and the Federation for Detached Youth Work's website: www.detachedyouthwork.info/, which includes some useful definitions of aims and roles, with various free downloads containing methods and tools for use. For further reading about detached work, Davies and Cranston's (2008) report on youth work and social networking provides some useful ideas for safe practice. Chapters on policy and practice in part 2 of Wood and Hine's (2009) *Work with Young People* explore the impact of varied settings on roles.

3

REACHING OUT

A youth worker establishes contact with young people by reaching out to a wide range of groups and individuals, listening to what they say and engaging in conversation. Starting with gaining an overview, making contacts and networking, this chapter looks at different methods of outreach and self-presentation with young people, their families and communities, colleagues and other professionals. Reaching out is most effective when the youth worker is ready to learn from the young people. As Planck said:

> The reason why the adult no longer wonders is not because he has solved the riddle of life, but because he has grown accustomed to the laws governing his world picture. But the problem of why these particular laws and no others hold, remains for him just as amazing and inexplicable as for the child. (1949:92)

GOING OUT TO WHERE YOUNG PEOPLE ARE

Youth work is an active process where youth workers take the initiative to locate and meet young people often on their terms or on their 'territory'. This process requires communication skills, flexibility and a willingness to learn. Developing confidence in negotiating the area and interacting with young people are key resources for safe practice. Venturing out to streets, parks, schools, prisons or homes to find certain individuals or groups of young people may take youth workers to unfamiliar areas. Starting work in a new community may lead to new ways of seeing things and communicating, as well as using a wide range of creative methods to reach different young people.

The process of reaching out starts with going out into the area to get a feel for it. Some workers prefer to walk or cycle around a neighbourhood in order to be able to see more, have closer contact with the community and feel less like a detached observer. Others find that an initial drive around allows them to develop an overview of the area. Such outings will indicate where young people 'hang out' in unsupervised or detached groups and the location of the shopping areas, cafés or streets where young people socialise or find entertainment. Close observation can identify how major roads, housing projects or school boundaries define or split particular communities, which can be a major cause of territorial behaviour and a key factor in planning youth work activities. Housing can also reveal a lot about an area and its population. For example, household sizes, patterns of housing and state of upkeep and repair can indicate potential interests in spaces for socialising or opportunities to enhance career prospects. In youth work, this knowledge is used to support an appreciative approach to young people's lives rather than to develop a deficit model. (Box 3.1 has some examples of ways to gain an overview of an area through observation, literature searches and networking.)

Box 3.1   Gaining an overview of an area

Observation

- Look around: walk or cycle around the area.
- Look at maps of the area.
- Identify any public or open spaces.
- Go into shops and markets to get a feel for the area.
- Drive around at different times of the day/evening/night.
- Notice where young people congregate.

Literature search

- Check out plans for development and regeneration.
- Browse information about local organisations in public posters and leaflets.
- Look at listings in telephone books and libraries.
- Read local papers and carry out internet searches for information about local politics and events.
- Look at reports, newsletters and bulletins from one's own and others' organisations.

Networking

- Ask young people what they think about their area and its amenities.
- Listen to young people's stories.
- Ask other residents about the neighbourhood and community relations.
- Visit relevant organisations to identify potential resources and contacts.
- Attend local meetings to find out about local issues.

Over a period of time, a youth worker uses different methods to locate and contact young people and their communities. Going out at varying times of the day to explore diverse areas will help a youth worker to identify different groups of young people. Although some young people establish their 'territory' in a location that can be easily accessed and meet regularly in a specific area or shelter, others may seek out more private locations, particularly if they are hiding or running away from families, carers or other authorities. A youth worker who leaves the area at 8:00 p.m. may miss the group of homeless young people who occupy the park at night or the young sex workers on the streets. Youth workers who take time to observe what is going on in an area will also meet parents, caretakers and others related to young people, including friends and enemies, partners and employers. These contacts can inform the development of appropriate 'intervention strategies' and provide ideas for future interactions with young people.

The process of outreach work should be two-way so that when contact is made with individuals and groups, ideas about events or opportunities are also discussed. Publicity distributed through various media should include offers of opportunities to meet. Initial forays into communities with publicity and information about youth work may develop into 'off-site' projects targeted to reach particular groups, such as detached work and outdoor activities. Although the focus of the outreach work is on making contact with young people, networking with other professionals and stakeholders can lead to a 'snowball' effect, where ever-increasing types of information is gathered to gain a wider perspective on what is going on in a community. For example, participation in community meetings and events provides opportunities to audit and discuss residents' concerns, which could lead to a better understanding of community issues and could lead to volunteers coming forward to help out. (Box 3.2 has some examples of ways to make contact with a range of young people and other stakeholders.)

Box 3.2   Making contacts

- promote understanding of youth work through door knocking, leaflet drops, poster campaigns and publicity about youth work opportunities
- discuss interests and options with pupils in school, detached groups and users of particular services such as libraries, health centres and sports facilities
- talk with young people about what is on offer, find out why some do not access current activities or what may prevent participation
- network with other professionals to identify opportunities for new developments, partnerships, overlaps and gaps in provision
- attend residents' committees and local community groups to identify community concerns or changes in the area that may affect young people.

Particular attention may be required to reach some individuals. While young people can often be found in familiar settings or existing groups, others may be more isolated, detached and previously 'un-reached' by youth work or other services. Some young people face barriers to participation created by established societal oppression whether overtly or unwittingly. Others may be in circumstances where their needs are not addressed due to neglect or ignorance. A youth worker needs to make a positive effort to reach such individuals. Rather than labelling young people as 'non-attenders', 'hard-to-reach' or 'not interested', youth workers attempt to locate such individuals through adopting a range of different ways to undertake outreach work (see Practice Example 3.1).

Targeted outreach to encourage attendance at youth work activities may be necessary to ensure that underrepresented groups know they will be welcomed. Paying attention to the identities of the young people who are being contacted, which groups are not represented, and identifying specific ways to reach them could also be part of an anti-oppressive approach to outreach work. Monitoring whether contacts have been made with young women as well as young men, various ethnic groups, disabled and non-disabled young people, with lesbian, gay, transgender and questioning (LGBTQ) young people as well as individuals who are not 'out', individuals from different housing complexes and schools, from various areas, etc, can help to establish a more targeted outreach programme to reach a more representative range. Using materials designed with particular groups or communities in mind, such as positive images, relevant 'life stories' or languages or mention of specific issues, can help to reach a particular group. Such focused practice can be useful to ensure that the interests of particular groups are addressed and also communicate that all are welcome.

Different forms of outreach

Outreach in homes

Parental support is really important in this community because the young people depend on their parents for transport to sessions. Also, most of them need parental permission to attend. My role as an outreach worker often takes me to their homes – so I see them in an environment that they are familiar with. Usually, everyone is more relaxed if I meet them at home, rather than if they have to come into the centre before they know anyone. I also find that if I can create a bond with other members of the family, the young people tend to attend the youth sessions more regularly.

Street-based work

Most of the young people I work with would not come to the youth centre so I generally contact them outside in the parks or on the streets. Some of them have attended the youth centre before and have been excluded because of alcohol or drug abuse or violent behaviour. Some of them just don't like the youth club environment. I was given some funding to work with targeted groups of young people to reduce 'juvenile nuisance' in the area. After making initial contact, we developed a good relationship which allowed the young people to tell me what they thought of the park, which lead to them being involved in its re-development.

(Continued)

PRACTICE EXAMPLE 3.1

(Continued)

Multi-agency or cooperative work

We find that a large number of young people come to the health centre for advice and services about drugs, sexual health and sexual activity, concerns about weight and mental health. We developed a support group on site that is very well used. I don't think that they would have come to a 'mainstream' youth work group and they certainly wouldn't have felt comfortable raising these issues in a youth centre; they come to this group because it is accessible and related to their needs.

Networking

I collect suggestions from other professionals about organisations to visit and specific contacts who might be useful. I always ring up first to see if I can get an invitation to observe or to talk at school assemblies, residents' association meetings, in prisons and organised care environments. I always make it clear that I am from an external organisation, but generally join in any activities going on and exchange small talk with all of the people I meet, such as secretaries, building caretakers and other professionals.

Online networks

I've found that use of online social networks attracts a lot of young people to our web-based publicity and information. It's a great way to make contacts. I'm not sure that we recruit to our centre-based work this way. But, we can reach out to young people who may be shy, isolated in rural areas, not wanting to 'come out' publicly as LGBTQ, or have questions they are too embarrassed to ask face to face – and keep in touch with them.

Youth workers may be directed to contact certain individuals or groups of young people by their employing organisation, other agencies or partnership work. For example, a residents group may complain about young people 'hanging around' a particular street corner; the police may highlight an area with high youth crime rates. A school may designate certain individuals for home visits. Youth workers need to be cautious when directed to work with particular contacts as the nature of the relationship may no longer be voluntary or meaningful to the young person. Clarity about the purpose of such contacts is essential so that youth work principles are not compromised.

HAVING A NON-JUDGEMENTAL APPROACH

For youth workers who are venturing into new cultures or communities, particularly when going into other people's homes, a non-judgemental approach to different ways of living will enable learning about what is going on and positive relationships to develop. Some youth workers find this difficult, particularly if young people are living in circumstances very different to their own experience. Young people may live in poverty or apparently without the benefit of care and attention, which a youth worker may not have previously encountered. Responding to such unexpected situations with shock or asking intrusive questions is ill advised. Such responses can communicate a negative evaluation of others' circumstances without sufficient knowledge of cause or context. 'Putting oneself in others' shoes' by imagining oneself having to 'cope' in certain environments is generally unrealistic due to a lack of understanding of the availability of options and opportunities. In general, youth workers would avoid making comparisons between their own living arrangements and a young person's circumstances, or assuming that other people's choices or coping strategies are wrong. Practice Example 3.2 (below) provides an example of how easy it is to make inappropriate judgements and how supervision can be used to develop a non-judgemental approach.

Learning to be non-judgemental

During a supervision session, a youth worker described his reactions to a visit to a young person's home carried out with another worker. 'I was sitting in the living room when the young person's mother offered to make me a cup of tea. I had to refuse because there were dog hairs all over the furniture, piles of old clothes and papers all over the room and dirty plates on every surface. I hate to think what the kitchen was like.' The supervisor asked the worker whether he knew how many people lived in the house. When the worker identified that there were seven people, including three adults working full-time, two adolescents and a toddler as well as the dog, the supervisor asked the worker how practicable it would be to maintain a tidy environment. Given that the house only had two bedrooms, it was likely that the other downstairs room was being used as a bedroom and the living room was additionally functioning as a laundry room, storage space and dining room. It was quite possible that the plates were from a recent meal and that the clothes had just been washed and were waiting only to be ironed. When comparing the situation with his own living arrangements, the worker was able to identify his lack of understanding of what he had seen and of the potential stresses and strains impacting on this household. He agreed that his impressions could have been an over-reaction and that even if the room had been unhygienic, it was really none of his business.

PRACTICE EXAMPLE 3.2

Many youth workers go through a range of emotional, cultural and spiritual 'journeys' before learning how to accept or understand others' situation without jumping to conclusions or assuming that they could do better. Some individuals struggle to curb their emotional response or accept that different cultures have different ways of living. A non-judgemental approach can develop through getting to know individuals in varied circumstances and having two-way communication. Awareness and understanding of the range of lifestyles that people inhabit are built up through experience, so that, in time, most youth workers are rarely shocked by what they see or hear, which gives time to consider a calmer response. Many youth workers find that this learning leads to a deeper understanding of their own circumstances and experiences, which can also benefit their understanding of how others perceive them.

Bearing in mind the potential for domestic relations to affect a young person's access to youth work, tact and diplomacy are a requirement in young people's homes. In most situations, youth workers would greet others living with the young people in a friendly manner and pass on information about their role and work. Youth workers rarely intervene to 'fix' young people's lives as the consequence is that power is taken away from the young person. Having information available about refuges, food banks or charities giving away clothing and furniture can be useful for signposting when asked. However, should a young person appear to be in genuine danger, most youth workers would raise this with the individual concerned in order to identify whether the fears are justified. Alerting other authorities, such as the police or social services, ideally would only be done with the knowledge of the young person.

GETTING TO KNOW EXISTING GROUPS

For a youth worker new to an area, existing youth work activities can provide instant access to contacts. New workers will need to establish their own relationships with the young people. Whether quietly and slowly or 'with a splash' will depend on the youth worker's own individual style and on the type of facilities or activities going on. In a youth centre with a laid-back approach to provision of various leisure activities, a new youth worker can often simply observe what is going on and mingle without the need for formal introductions. By gradually joining in conversations or activities, a youth worker can be integrated quite naturally into the setting; whereas in some youth centres, young people are encouraged to take 'ownership' of the management and facilitation of activities, as well as take part in the selection and induction of new workers.

Contacting young people already accessing facilities needs to be recognised as a limited exercise. Over-reliance on existing members for 'word-of-mouth' recruitment can lead to rather homogenous groups who are unwelcoming to individuals perceived as 'different'. Apparently superficial or even indiscernible distinctions can sometimes lead to bullying or clique-ish behaviour. Most groups benefit from regular new membership to avoid becoming static so outreach work is generally ongoing.

MEETING YOUNG PEOPLE AT SCHOOL

An awareness of issues affecting youth work within an educational establishment, such as attendance and protocols, can assist a youth worker in identifying appropriate methods for establishing contact. Protocols about how to meet with young people may require some formal introduction and negotiation. Access to young people may be arranged through school assemblies, lunchtime drop-ins or visits to class. Youth workers based in a school may have regular contact with young people, with an office base, access to a common room or scheduled time for work with certain groups. Making contact through school could affect young people's perceptions of youth work. Attendance at school is generally obligatory, often a legal requirement and sometimes a costly privilege that young people are not able to question. Teachers and parents usually demand or expect some level of compliance with norms. Explanations about the contrasting voluntary nature of youth work and the emphasis on self-directed activities can help to highlight any misconceptions about youth work practice.

Relying on school as a means of meeting young people could miss those who might be most interested in youth work activities. Youth workers need to remember that whilst most young people attend school regularly, others only attend intermittently or not at all, due to responsibilities at home, fears of various kinds or exclusion orders imposed by the school. Some young people have valid reasons for finding school an inappropriate use of their time. A job description which designates specific priority groups may be difficult to carry out if school is the only contact with young people. Considering additional ways to contact and involve young people will improve outreach work.

Outreach work with a particular school may result in contacts with individuals from similar economic or social backgrounds. Reliance on friendship groups can then lead to the development of a monoculture where others feel excluded. Finding ways to locate and involve individuals in different backgrounds and circumstances could lead to more integration within and outside of youth work activities.

PRESENTING SELF

The initial contacts that a youth worker makes with young people can set the tone for future work and relationships. During initial connections with young people, a youth worker finds out about them by listening to them talk about their interests and concerns. At the same time, a youth worker passes on information about the organisation and what is on offer for the young people and their communities. Introductions with key individuals, groups, organisations and services are part of the process. Good listening skills and clarity about the role of the youth work and the organisation are therefore essential in this first stage of getting to know the young people.

In reaching out and listening to young people, the youth worker communicates to them the importance of their views. Having an interest in learning from young people and enjoying their company are essential to youth work practice. Those youth workers who enjoy being with young people and finding out what they have to say are rewarded with new learning and positive relationships with a wide range of individuals. Often, young people have had poor experiences in their previous relationships with adults. A youth worker who meets young people on their own terms may be very different from what they have been led to expect from adults. Whatever time is necessary to establish the relationship between a youth worker and young people is generally worthwhile.

Contact with young people assists youth workers in planning, facilitating and evaluating youth work activities, services and projects. Identifying where young people live, what music they listen to, their religion or ethnic group, their peers, their school, what clothing or sports they like and so forth is not simply a way of getting to know the young people. It is also a way of identifying which young people may be on the fringe of communities or feel excluded. By finding out about young people and being open to what they have to say, youth workers begin to identify some of the barriers faced by young people and their needs.

HAVING CONVERSATIONS

Conversations that take place in and around other enjoyable activities are the mainstay of youth work. Youth workers and young people get to know each other, identify interests and pass on information through casual conversation, whilst more serious discussions provide opportunities to challenge each others' assumptions and raise awareness of issues. Although a youth worker provides space for conversation and brings in issues for discussion, the power is with the young person to 'disengage' and the youth worker accepts that relationships may take time to develop. Box 3.3 has some suggestions about ways to engage in conversation.

A calm and confident approach to conversation with young people is conducive to two-way communication and is generally easier than when a worker presents a false persona in a mistaken attempt to curry favour or be accepted. When a youth worker feels positive about the young people and interested in what they have to say, initiating and responding can be an enjoyable part of the process of getting to know each other; whereas worrying unduly about one's own 'performance' or finding the young people unresponsive, inattentive or aggressive can make this stage quite difficult.

Box 3.3   Starting conversations

- Identify what is going on: observe the young people and listen to any ongoing conversations. Take notice of details and identify key ingredients such as the setting, the current topics, who is involved, any emotions being displayed, body language, new jargon or slang. You don't need to use their language; you just need to understand it!
- Listen to young people's stories; hear what they have to say.

- Think about what you are going to say: identify a topic that has been raised and which you find interesting. Respond to their conversations rather than changing the direction of them.
- Join the conversation as an equal rather than asserting your right to speak, being confrontational or offering advice. Try not to interrupt anyone. A question may be perceived as intrusive. Acknowledging agreement with something that has been said can be an effective way of communicating that you are listening respectfully, are interested and have understood.
- Don't be put off if you get no response. Hang on and try again after a few minutes.
- Allow the young people space and time to respond. Listen.
- As the conversation progresses (if it does), stay within the topics that the young people are discussing. Don't raise questions about issues or facts that are outside the immediate subjects or arena of discussion.
- Don't collude with anything that you're not comfortable with, such as laughing at sexist jokes or condoning illegal behaviour. You don't have to express your views on every issue, but don't agree if you disagree. Be yourself and express your opinions without expecting everyone to be in agreement.
- After the conversation, reflect on what happened. 'Replay' the conversation to identify any issues and points at which the conversation could have developed differently, particularly your own interventions. Think about whether there were any issues raised to cause concern and your feelings about the topics and dynamics of the conversation.
- Discuss any issues and feelings in supervision and consider topics raised that could be returned to if the opportunity arises or handled differently next time around.

A youth worker needs to recognise that young people grouping in outdoor spaces, whether open to the public or just available for access, usually consider themselves to be on their own territory. Many young people do not have alternative access to space where they can invite friends, socialise with others or express their opinions freely. An appropriate and effective way to communicate with young people does not convey collusion with illegal or risky behaviour and recognises young people's rights to their own space. Unless good relationships are already established, conversation with a group of young people on a street corner should not imply that the youth worker has power over their behaviour. For example, 'Do you think you should be smoking that joint?' or 'Aren't you a bit young to be out at this time?' would rarely be effective intervention strategies in this setting. A youth worker who 'joins' such a group will soon find that the young people can and will walk away unless 'their space' is clearly recognised and respected. A better intervention would be responding to an issue raised by a young person or to something that one of the young people had said. Discussions about behaviour may need to wait for an opportunity related to the young people's discussion. For example, a young person saying that he had a bad cough or was feeling tired could provide an opening for a discussion about smoking or sleep; worries about not having any money may lead to conversations about jobs and careers. Finding the right moment can mean responding to topics arising, sometimes rather creatively, rather than having a set agenda.

Detached work usually starts with initial observations and low contact visits to identify the best approach with a group. Establishing group routines, such as when and where they meet, protocols within the group and any activities that might require risk assessment can help youth workers to make best use of their contacts. Interactions build up gradually through greetings and non-intrusive 'small talk'. Different 'intervention strategies', such as offering information, opportunities or events, would follow.

While a prescriptive approach to any youth work will always find exceptions that work perfectly well, most youth workers wait until they have developed a positive relationship with individuals before passing comments on minor or common misbehaviour carried out in their presence, particularly in an outdoor, detached setting. Some workers ignore language, attitudes or behaviour that they would more readily challenge in a centre-based setting. Moving on to another location or group would be preferable to colluding with or seeming to approve of any misdemeanours. Inside a youth centre, rules about dangerous or 'risky' behaviour, such as drinking, smoking, fighting, and carrying out sexual or criminal activity are generally established practice. Youth workers in a youth centre would strive to limit or curtail such activities through discussions of the issues and consequences of 'bad behaviour'.

IDENTIFYING RISK

Youth workers need to balance an optimistic approach to work with young people and communities with an awareness of potential pitfalls or dangers. This balance can be achieved through ongoing assessments of risk and the development of associated protective measures. In general, a commonsense approach develops through discussion with others, as well as through consideration of organisational policies. Any youth worker who goes out into unknown communities may be considered to be 'at risk'. Not much youth work would be carried out if concerns about workers' safety were allowed to take over and create an atmosphere of fear.

Lack of experience, negative experiences or the reputation of certain individuals or groups can contribute to insecurities taking over in certain situations. An assessment of the risks associated with going out into a community could begin with an understanding of the youth worker's own feelings, experience and knowledge. A starting point can provide direction for necessary preparations to alleviate or address worry, which will vary with individuals. If a youth worker is worried about personal safety, further precautions could be taken. Just as any individual would think twice about venturing into an isolated and unknown territory in the dark, so should youth workers consider reasonable precautions. Some sensible safety measures, such as the identification of support and emergency routines, may assist an anxious worker to overcome unreasonable fears.

An essential skill of youth work practice is to find a way to work with young people without being afraid. A youth worker who is scared of young people or frightened of a particular area is unlikely to be able to carry out useful youth work. Feelings of fear can be analysed to identify causes and come to an understanding of whether they are realistic or prejudicial. Negative stereotypes can be created by certain negative media images, distorted history and lack of experience. For example, a youth worker may have concerns about a group's response to their different identity, whether it be about race, class, age or sexuality. The worker may have heard about the group's racism, homophobia or other negative behaviour. Confidence can be developed through gradual exposure to the new group, discussion of fears with other experienced youth workers who have knowledge of the group, and reading to challenge attitudes and stereotypes. Practice Example 3.3 describes how a youth worker's confident approach to door-to-door outreach work benefitted on-going centre-based youth work.

Door-to-door outreach work

Noticing that a large number of young people were 'hanging around' outside a block of flats, a youth worker approached the group to talk about activities at the youth centre. Although the centre was only a few streets away, the young people said that their parents had instructed them not to venture beyond the immediate vicinity. The youth worker decided to go door-to-door around the flats to distribute information about the youth centre.

The majority of residents were fairly friendly and almost all had something to say about the young people, usually 'somebody needs to do something about those young people always getting into trouble'. The youth worker responded lightly with 'I've really enjoyed meeting the young people downstairs', or 'They seem quite lively and interesting', or 'It's hard, isn't it, for young people these days – because everything is so expensive'. Although she felt a bit uncomfortable about declining invitations to come inside, her refusals were accepted politely.

Reflecting on the exercise in supervision, the youth worker was reprimanded for not following the lone working policy and not taking another worker with her to provide back-up should she have an accident or be physically attacked. While the youth worker explained that she didn't feel she had been in any danger and that working solo had enabled her to have more natural conversations than would have been possible with accompanying colleagues, her supervisor was adamant that a partner was essential and would not negatively affect her work. The youth worker agreed that any future outreach would be undertaken with greater attention to safety.

The supervisor and youth worker agreed that the outreach work had been useful. A number of new contacts had been made and information about the youth work activities had been distributed. Quite a few individuals had identified themselves as parents of the target age group. Providing telephone contact numbers, sample programmes and photos

PRACTICE EXAMPLE 3.3

of the facilities seemed to go down well. Negative attitudes towards young people had been discussed and a couple of residents had expressed interest in volunteering at the centre.

In the short term, attendance at the youth centre was unaffected. However, about a month later, the youth worker (with a partner) went around the flats to invite the residents to an event at the centre. About a dozen people who had been personally contacted through the visits attended. Over the following weeks, attendance increased dramatically as young people came and brought their friends.

MAKING ARRANGEMENTS FOR SAFE PRACTICE

Safe practice often means assessing the probability of risk and the level of impact of any consequences of risks as well as identifying ways to mitigate or reduce risk with alternative actions or contingency planning. The potential conflict between responsible protection and safety with potentially risky activities is not always easily resolved. Employing organisations may require extensive 'risk assessments' and a lone working policy to protect their staff and avoid high insurance costs and litigation if a youth worker is hurt or injured whilst working. Managers are aware that whilst any setting carries an element of risk, the financial, legal and organisational impact or consequences of injury or harm are more far-reaching when an individual is at work. Overprotection can have its downsides. A requirement for the use of brightly coloured all-weather gear, for example, may well protect against wind, rain and traffic accidents, but may also give an inappropriate impression of being part of a uniformed security or police service.

Some health and safety procedures can reinforce negative views of certain groups of young people and limit opportunities for positive work. For example, youth services often have policies prohibiting work with young people without others present. The policy is seen to protect the young person from abuse from the youth worker. The youth worker is also protected from false accusations because a colleague is present as a potential witness. Making home visits or giving young people lifts in their cars on their own is often discouraged or prohibited due to concerns about accidents or attacks. The policy protects the organisation, but may also limit the scope of work through preventing or inhibiting one-to-one conversations.

Youth workers with greater levels of confidence and experience can be encouraged to work alongside those with less. Recognising the difference between young people who are expressing strong opinions, anger or other negative emotions and individuals or circumstances that could be personally dangerous may only come through experience. Youth workers develop antennae to pick up indicators that someone may be about to switch from expressing themselves through words to violent behaviour. This ability means that youth workers can be more confident in their interactions with young people, a skill that will develop through praxis, co-working and supervision.

ORGANISING SAFE DETACHED WORK

As detached work aims to provide opportunities for positive interactions with young people and communities, safety precautions that serve to create an atmosphere of fear or perceive young people or members of their community as dangerous are generally ill advised. Youth work organisations may require detached youth workers to undertake additional precautions to ensure their well-being, as well as comply with risk assessment, health and safety procedures or the demands of insurance. (See Practice Example 3.4 of the precaution that one organisation takes to attempt to ensure safe detached work.) A balance between intrusive or excessive measures to ensure safety and sensible arrangements needs to be found so that youth workers can approach young people with confidence and a relaxed manner. Although some youth workers prefer a more flexible approach and perceive certain precautions as interfering with practice, they need to be aware that not adhering to an organisation's requirements can result in the withdrawal of support or dismissal should an accident or dangerous incident occur.

Preparations for detached work

Our manager requires us to carry emergency phone numbers like organisational contacts and legal advisors, a personal attack alarm and change or petty cash for public transport. We have a phone card for emergency telephone calls and a choice about whether we carry a mobile (cell) phone. We have to wear identifiable clothing with the organisation's logo on and carry an identity card. We always work in pairs or small groups with an established meeting point with other team members. We have a pre-planned escape route and leave details about where we are going with a colleague who isn't out with us, who we report to at the end of the shift. We all have to be trained in handling needles, first aid and self-defence. Once I got into a routine of doing all this, none of it seemed intrusive except for the 'corporate' rain gear, which I think makes us look like officials.

I always leave any valuables, money, expensive clothing and my car at home. I'm not sure what messages certain labels give out and I don't want to worry about damage or loss. It's not because I think the young people are thieves – it's just one less thing to think about.

As a team, we make sure to be aware of isolated or risky hiding places. Basically it's street sense. We don't split up and we make sure that we can see a co-worker at all times. We always have someone delegated to be particularly observant, to watch what's going on around us. We're always more cautious if a situation or group is new to us and let the others know if anything is worrying us. We try to define the area of work prior to going out and stick to this, and agree specific start and finish times and stick to them too. We also keep our eyes open for accessible venues in the area for respite, both for ourselves and for the young people. Sometimes a local key member of the community will offer an emergency contact point or access to a toilet. We are also on the lookout for alternative accommodation in case a group wants to get involved in activities like discussions or games.

PRACTICE EXAMPLE 3.4

Having said all that, I do detached work because I really enjoy talking with young people in a relaxed setting! We have a real laugh and they seem to enjoy the fact that we don't come across with authority or try to control their conversations and behaviour. We get to know more about them through talking with them in the park than we could ever have in the centre. I know that I will always remember some of the conversations that we have had.

ASSESSING RISK FOR THE YOUNG PERSON

Managers of youth workers and volunteers need to be aware of the potential risks or consequences for young people in relation to engaging with youth work or youth workers. New experiences can bring physical, emotional and other stresses or danger for which some young people are not fully prepared. Taking reasonable precautions whilst enabling young people to experience new situations can be a difficult balance to keep. Certain situations demand particular attention, such as lone working and one-to-one work. When others are not around, young people may be at risk from inappropriate behaviour from a member of staff or volunteer; a youth worker could also be at risk from allegations of the same. Whether or not the allegations are warranted, without witnesses both parties can be in difficulties. Involving young people, their communities and youth work colleagues in risk assessments can provide a more secure foundation for understanding certain procedures and decisions that may need to be made when planning. (See Box 3.4 for some examples of planning methods that can assist in addressing risks.)

Box 3.4   Planning to address risks

- Involve young people as well as staff in risk assessment and planning.
- Provide induction, training and supervision for youth workers and volunteers.
- Use experienced members of staff to supervise less experienced individuals.
- Monitor the behaviour, attitudes and practice of staff and young people.
- Have adequate insurance for staff and young people.
- Plan carefully, particularly for any new or different activities.
- Be clear about any limitations in relation to capacity, skills and safety.
- Be available to listen and talk about issues arising.
- Discuss the implications of lone working and one-to-one work.
- Involve young people in the evaluation and review of activities.

Although some young people are supported by family and friends when they attend youth work activities, some are not. Some may attend against parents' or carers' wishes. Young people may encounter individuals and groups who have different perspectives, experiences, beliefs or value systems from their families or communities. Being exposed to challenges and changes to their ideas, language, knowledge and experience can be difficult for some young people. The physical or emotional challenges of trying out new activities are usually exciting, but can be overwhelming. They may find out about risky or illegal behaviour that is new to them. Providing opportunities for young people to talk about these issues and feelings and make sense of them is an important aspect of youth work.

NOT LETTING THE FIRST CONTACT BE THE END OF THE STORY

Youth workers need to be cautious about targets that assume youth work is easily predictable, defined or quantifiable. Youth work can be constrained by reliance on measurable and tangible outputs. Evaluation that only looks at the number of groups or individuals contacted can provide a false picture of the success or failure of youth work. Young people's learning and development through involvement in youth work will vary according to the individual and the group. More qualitative research methods may be required to recognise and value these changes.

Youth work depends on establishing relationships, which take time to develop. Unfortunately, funding for youth work is often limited to short-term programmes, which may mean that making contact with young people is the beginning and end of the story. Pressures to demonstrate statistical success can lead to a meaningless collection of superficial contacts. Rather than providing time to establish relationships and develop group work, some projects are terminated after the initial contact and distribution of information. Some youth workers are frustrated by being pulled out to work with another group that has been identified as 'a problem' when they have only just begun to establish links with a community. Others can carry out this limited role in creative ways that involve young people and other community members so that the whole community benefits. For example, peer education projects can involve young people in passing on information so that the work has longer-term impact.

ESSENTIAL SKILLS FOR MAKING CONTACT

- Going out to where young people are
- Having a non-judgemental approach
- Getting to know existing groups
- Meeting young people at school
- Presenting self
- Having conversations
- Identifying risk

- Making arrangements for safe practice
- Organising safe detached work
- Assessing risks for the young person
- Not letting the first contact be the end of the story

FURTHER READING

Driskell's (2002) manual for 'creating better cities' includes relevant material for identifying stakeholders. Hawtin and Percy-Smith's (2007) practical guide for compiling a community profile contains some useful information about research on communities and making contacts in an area. See also Chapter 11 of this book, which outlines a method for involving young people and others in relevant research.

4

ESTABLISHING VOLUNTARY RELATIONSHIPS

This chapter explores how youth workers establish and maintain appropriate relationships with young people by providing a welcoming environment and responding positively to individuals, engaging in dialogue that respects the reality of their lives and being clear about professional boundaries. Taking time to establish relationships is key to effective practice.

As youth work relationships are generally more informal than those that young people have with other adults, care needs to be taken to find an appropriate balance between approachability and professionalism. Young people need to be clear that although youth workers tend to have a sense of humour, enjoy themselves at work and have interesting opinions about rules and authority, they will not collude in unacceptable behaviour. Establishing professional boundaries, therefore, requires youth workers to identify what they find unacceptable and to communicate this clearly and honestly to young people. Unlike in many other relationships young people encounter, youth workers provide opportunities for them to exercise a high level of power and control. Youth workers discuss decisions made about the allocation of resources and planning activities and attempt to be clear about the reasons for their choices. This accountability and openness about relevant decision making enables young people to understand 'where the youth worker is coming from' and to trust them to be honest and reliable. Establishing this relationship involves the youth worker in maintaining the values and principles outlined in Chapter 1, and enables young people to choose whether to accept or reject any offered activities, suggestions or advice.

WELCOMING YOUNG PEOPLE

A welcome that respects and accepts young people as individuals is an important first step in establishing a voluntary relationship. Recognising that young people may feel uncomfortable in new situations, youth workers notice when new members arrive and monitor their responses to activities and other members, in order to identify an appropriate welcome. Providing a warm welcome to all young people usually requires that a youth worker enjoys the company of young people and embraces participative and anti-oppressive values. The method of welcoming young people to their first encounter with youth work and to any subsequent meetings should suit the individuals and circumstances and need not involve an elaborate greeting or induction procedure. A young person may feel welcomed simply by being accepted by a group when joining an ongoing activity. Another may prefer to be introduced to an individual who provides an orientation to available activities and resources. Recognising that barriers, such as shyness or feeling different, can prevent young people from accessing activities, youth workers attempt to provide posters, procedures and arrangements that simultaneously communicate a welcome to diverse young people in varied circumstances and include the information that a wide range of issues and questions can be raised and discussed. (Practice Example 4.1 gives an insight into a first visit to a youth work session from a young person's perspective.)

PRACTICE EXAMPLE 4.1

A young person's first impression

When I first came to the youth group, I didn't know what to expect. At first I couldn't even see any adults. It looked like the whole place was just kids. At first it made me nervous. I kept looking around for somebody to tell me off, keep quiet or stop putting my feet on the furniture and I wasn't sure what would happen if some of the scarier-looking kids started giving me a hard time. After a while I noticed a couple of youth workers playing pool with some kids and another one was sitting with some others playing some kind of game with a board and cards. I felt better when I saw one of the adults break up an almost fight without any shouting or big deal. I also saw some interesting posters – particularly ones about different types of families – including ones with just grandparents and small children. And in the toilets there was a list of emergency phone numbers that included numbers to ring if you were worried about suicide, rape, pregnancy and all sorts. There was some great music going on and next door, kids were playing basketball. It was all very exciting.

The flexibility of youth work means that different styles of welcoming can be provided to suit a diversity of young people, whether first-timers or ongoing participants. The level of extroversion, openness and humour that a youth worker employs may determine whether young people are overtly rallied to join in or more gently informed about options. Box 4.1 provides some examples of different styles of youth work practice. Young people will have similarly varying styles and may respond better to a youth worker with a very different style. While one young person may view a particular youth worker as detached, aloof or even aggressive with young people, others may value that worker's even-handedness, clarity and humour. As relationships are voluntary rather than assigned, a young person may approach different youth workers at different times to suit specific circumstances or current needs. Further on in this chapter, increasing one's self-awareness is recommended so that youth workers can identify their style, which may be affected by gender, cultural background and/or individual preferences. Some youth workers may seek to change styles or develop greater flexibility if their approach feels inappropriate in a particular setting or with a specific individual or group.

Box 4.1   Different styles of practice

Extroverted?

- Some youth workers find it easy to contribute to a large group; others prefer a quiet chat in a corner with one or two people.

Open?

- Some youth workers do not reveal information about themselves; others are keen to share their personal experiences and opinions.

Humorous?

- Some youth workers smile, laugh, tell jokes and funny stories; others have a more moderate demeanour.

Active?

- Some youth workers enjoy joining in games and activities; others prefer to encourage from the sidelines.

Quiet?

- Some youth workers would rather speak with individuals to communicate information; others can easily raise their voice to get everyone's attention.

Warm?

- Some youth workers come across as serious and focused; others exude a warm and carefree exterior.

Structured?

- Some youth workers have a laidback approach; others are more organised and structured.

Welcoming young people will continue after the first encounter whether attendance is a regular occurrence, follows an unexplained gap or comes after an enforced absence. The welcome can continue to communicate the youth worker's beliefs in the right of young people to attend and the expectation of positive participation, which will contribute to the establishment of a voluntary relationship. If a young person was aggressive or disruptive in a prior meeting, that individual needs to be offered the opportunity for a fresh start in a new session. A youth worker should not harbour, or at least, not communicate, ill feelings or negative attitudes towards a young person. The welcome would not usually depend on an explanation or apology for any gaps in attendance and would generally indicate that whatever may have taken place previously, the opportunity to move on is being provided. Equally important is the need to avoid demanding or expecting a response from the welcome. The story in Practice Example 4.2 demonstrates the importance of extending a welcome to young people despite an apparent lack of response.

PRACTICE EXAMPLE 4.2

'Matching the mood'

A young person had been attending a youth centre for some months without becoming involved in any of the activities. He tended to sit in a quiet corner rather than interact with others or use any of the games or equipment available. The youth worker made a point of welcoming him to the sessions, but after a few attempts to make conversation, it seemed clear that the young person did not want to talk. The young person continued to attend the sessions and the youth worker made sure to spend some time in the young person's company, usually just sitting next to him. While the young person did not seem interested in conversing, he did not appear to object to sharing the sofa and seemed content to observe the youth worker's interactions with the others. Without pressuring the young person to talk or join in the activities, invitations were always extended to him and his decision not to participate was respected. One evening almost without warning, the young person began to talk with the youth worker about some of the seriously unhappy feelings he was experiencing.

Following the young person's disclosures, the youth worker explored the approach that he had used with his supervisor. They agreed that the reason the young person was eventually able to talk was because he had come to trust that the youth worker would not push him further than he wanted to go. The youth worker was not sure whether more direct questioning at an earlier stage would have enabled the young person to 'open up' more quickly. The process seemed to have taken rather a long time. Subsequent chats with the young person confirmed, however, that he would not have attended the sessions if he had been 'forced' or expected to talk and that he had been unable to discuss his feelings with anyone else up until that point.

RESPONDING TO YOUNG PEOPLE AS INDIVIDUALS

The voluntary relationship is further developed from the initial and continuous welcome through positive responses to the young people as individuals and conscious efforts to avoid labelling and making judgements. While a 'deficit model' perceives young people as needy and often inferior receivers of services, youth workers encourage young people to take responsibility for their own actions and to identify their own options for change and development in relation to the choices they make in their lives. This approach requires a youth worker to abstain from identifying solutions to young people's problems (see Practice Example 4.3).

Responding to an individual

A young mother of a baby came into an Information and Advice service facilitated by youth workers. She said that she was having difficulties finding enough money for baby clothes, nappies, a cot and a stroller. The youth worker suggested that he refer her to Social Services who might be able to help. The young woman strenuously rejected the idea, saying that they had been to her house before and that they weren't able to help. The youth worker gave her some leaflets about baby clinics in the area, referred her to a local church that he knew had recycled baby clothes and furniture, said that he would try and find out some more information and asked her to come back in a couple of days. He felt pretty good about what he had been able to do for her.

After the meeting, the youth worker asked a colleague from another agency whether she knew anything about the young woman. The colleague said that she had heard a lot about the local Travellers community. There was massive overcrowding and unemployment, very low attendance rates in school and low educational attainment, continuous problems with the police being called out to settle domestic abuse situations and high rates of crime and recidivism. She also stated that 'most of them are here illegally anyway and wouldn't be entitled to any state benefits'.

Following this conversation, the youth worker reflected on his first session with the young woman and worried that he had given her a leaflet that she may not be able to read, sent her to a church that she might not believe in and had not recognised that the social workers' involvement with the family raised questions about the baby's safety. Plus, he had not dealt with issues related to housing and food. In a panic, he discussed his concerns with his supervisor.

His supervisor suggested that he find a way to build a relationship with the young woman that was based on what she asked for, rather than labelling her with the prejudices that Travellers tend to encounter. The supervisor advised him to find out sources of income and money advice as this was what the young woman had requested. Some research about Travellers' communities was also recommended, although, as the supervisor pointed out, it hadn't been clearly established that the young woman was from that community.

The next time the youth worker met with the young mother, he struggled to rid his mind of the picture of her circumstances painted by his colleague and welcomed her back as the supervisor had recommended. Although he had managed to learn a lot about Travellers that contradicted what his colleague had said, he decided to postpone checking whether she was from that community as it did not seem to be relevant. Instead, he asked how she was doing and admired the baby. He felt that he had learned to listen to what she had to say rather than identifying the issues for her.

A relationship is built with young people through attempts to hear and understand what they wish to communicate about their lives. The approach 'starts where the young person is' and generally requires a great deal of flexibility. Youth workers listen to what young people are saying, discuss their ideas and work on issues related to their expressed needs and interests without proselytising. Some of the skills and approaches used by counsellors can be useful in youth work. For example, the 'core conditions' that enable a counsellor to work effectively with a client, outlined by Rogers (1957), include the counsellor's demonstration of empathy, 'unconditional positive regard' (non-judgemental acceptance) and congruence (genuine presentation of self). The approach is intended to create a safe space for clients to develop self-awareness and fulfilment. While young people experiencing serious mental health difficulties will generally be 'signposted' to appropriate services should they be available, 'non-judgemental acceptance' and 'genuine presentation of self' are very relevant concepts for youth work practice. (See Practice Example 4.4 for a youth worker's explanation of the importance of listening.)

PRACTICE EXAMPLE 4.4

The importance of listening

I think that listening is definitely the most important thing that a youth worker can do – listening and making sure that young people have a good time. Young people have so many things going on: adolescence and transitions to adult lives, emotional and hormonal swings and changes. They have to adjust to changes in family relationships, things going on in school and friends – all kinds of issues related to sexuality and health, including drugs, HIV/ AIDS, having babies. They think about leaving home, housing, employment, discrimination, inequality and exclusion. Often they don't have anyone to listen to them. The thing about coming to the youth centre is that they can talk about these things and their views and ideas are taken seriously and sometimes even acted upon – but only when they want them to be.

ENGAGING IN DIALOGUE

Many youth workers engage in light banter with young people rather than thinking that social education or problems need to be the starting point. Taking time to listen and learn more about the young people before engaging in more serious conversation can provide a context for hearing and understanding what a young person is saying. In general, as dialogue can be initiated by either party, youth workers do not need to feel responsible for starting the conversation. Instead, their responsibility is more related to ensuring that the lines of communication are open and that young people are clear that conversations and questions are welcomed.

Thought-provoking questions rather than accusations, and honest expressions of opinion rather than directives, are other useful ways to become involved in dialogue, particularly when young people express opinions about more difficult topics. Some youth workers prefer to wait to get to know a young person or group before voicing their opinions. However, expressing disagreement can start a lively debate, which many young people and youth workers enjoy. Rapport can be established with young people despite expressing opposing views. Such discussions often provide opportunities to raise points about why certain views or language might be offensive to others in the group. Providing space for young people to express alternative views not only demonstrates respect for the individuals, but leaves avenues open for further engagement. Box 4.2 provides some suggestions for ways to maintain dialogue.

To establish equality within the dialogue, youth workers can check their understanding of what the young people are saying. Eventually, and perhaps not simply in one conversation, the aim is to explore issues fully so that each party comes to recognise more about the other's perspective. In community development and conflict resolution circles, the technique is described as 'democratic dialogue' which is required for inter-cultural, inter-community or cross-generational understanding. As Pruitt and Thomas said:

> The more conceptual frameworks differ, the more the interpretations are likely to be at odds and the greater the challenge of achieving understanding. What is needed in these situations is not necessarily more communication but more understanding (2007: 16).

Establishing this form of dialogue means that youth workers minimise the focus on themselves. The focus of the conversation is on identifying the young person's understanding rather than winning an argument or ensuring that the young people see the youth worker's perspective. Judging when to interject and help to steer a discussion or offer an opinion is a skill that is learned through experience. Reflecting on conversations in recordings or supervision, youth workers may find that their interventions could have been timed or worded differently. Considering whether and when to interject with an alternative perspective at particular points in the conversation can provide guidance for future practice.

Box 4.2   Maintaining dialogue

- Focus on the young person.
- Provide opportunities to ask questions or find out information rather than always providing the answer.
- Approach young people positively rather than prejudging or labelling.
- Take time to listen rather than worrying about your own situation, work and schedule.
- Attempt to understand the meaning of what someone is saying rather than listening without hearing.
- Allow young people to find their own examples and demonstrate their knowledge rather than showing off and scoring points.
- Expect to learn from the young people rather than telling them 'like it is'…
- Check understanding of the situation rather than interpreting possible meanings.

(Continued)

(Continued)

- Acknowledge what the young person says rather than disagree.
- Ask about opinions rather than provide them; ask for suggestions rather than giving them.
- Check young people's own feelings or responses rather than demonstrating or expressing your own.
- Allow young people to think 'out of the box'; don't resist new ideas or perspectives.
- Design activities with high levels of participation and creativity; don't just control or divert attention and energy.
- Invite feedback; don't resist criticism.
- Encourage young people to express themselves; don't talk too much.
- Allow young people time to explore their ideas; don't move into decisions or actions too soon.
- Encourage young people to share their experiences and feelings; don't problem solve.

Youth workers encounter young people who are experiencing unjust treatment and are avoiding, challenging or simply putting up with their unpleasant or oppressive situations. The youth worker's response to such information will vary according to the method of learning about the young person's experiences, as well as details about the environment and individuals involved. For example, if bullying is observed, an immediate response may be called for, whereas if young people talk about being bullied at school, simply listening to their experiences may help them find ways to deal or cope with their situations. Alternatively, youth work responses can include more proactive educational, emotional or supportive functions. A youth worker may respond by providing a social context. The information may serve to reassure individuals that they are not alone and that the cause of the problem is not personal. A more emotional response, showing warmth and compassion, may be appropriate in some instances. Some young people may prefer to pursue diversionary interests and may benefit from not dwelling on life's inequities. Encouraging a young person to consider options and consequences may have to wait for a suitable time and place. Providing the appropriate level of support and presenting opportunities for young people to develop their confidence and readiness to talk will assist them in identifying and making their own choices in relation to any action, reaction or coping mechanism they decide to implement (see Practice Example 4.5).

A youth worker's relationship with young people is not simply responsive. Youth work has a positive and proactive role in promoting social justice, recognising discrimination and addressing barriers to equality of opportunity. A youth worker raises and discusses issues such as racism, sexism, ableism, heterosexism, class oppression, ageism and unfair treatment of individuals. The attitudes and practices of young people, colleagues and other agencies working with young people may provide barriers to participation that need to be addressed. Through positive images, supporting individuals experiencing discrimination and challenging oppressive attitudes and practices, a youth worker encourages young people and colleagues to have an active approach to addressing inequality (see also Chapter 7 on anti-oppressive practice).

Providing appropriate support

PRACTICE EXAMPLE 4.5

A young man told a youth worker about the 'bullying' he received from a teacher at school. The young person said that no matter how hard he tried, he could not understand the course work. He was constantly in trouble for not completing his assignments and the teacher was always 'going on' at him. The youth worker, who was experienced in working with excluded young people, wondered whether the young man had undiagnosed learning difficulties. Although the youth worker thought that the young man might well have been unfairly treated, he did not reveal any anger about the situation. He provided the young man with the opportunity to express his feelings, describe his learning experiences and explore his options. The focus of the discussion was on what the young man could do to change the situation that he was in and what the consequences of different choices might be. Possible options included making a complaint, asking for help or ignoring his teacher. During this discussion, the teacher's apparent unfair treatment became less of a concern than the possibility of being able to find a way to complete his school work. The youth worker provided the young man with information about dyslexia. They talked about the possibility of being screened and discussed his feelings about this – as well as the advantages and disadvantages of this process. Decisions about his first steps, such as talking with his parents, asking the head of year for an appointment and talking with his teacher, were also discussed. Through this process, the youth worker provided support for the young person to make his own decisions so that he could take more control of his situation.

RESPECTING YOUNG PEOPLE

Respect plays an important role in youth work and relates to the young people, the youth worker and their relationships. The process of building a relationship based on respect starts with 'respect for the person' rather than the person's status, beliefs, opinions or history. To do this, youth workers separate the young people from their reputation and previous actions to provide them with opportunities to express themselves. In general, youth workers do not expect instant respect from young people as this respect may need to be earned. Most youth workers recognise the value of having respect for themselves, and their professional value base and boundaries rather than demanding this from others.

Youth work respects others' potential for change and development and recognises their achievements. Demonstrating a respect for others' basic human rights to dignity, privacy and equality of opportunity is the first step. Youth workers are often involved in encouraging young people to recognise the rights of individuals to free speech and assisting them to see a distinction between respect for the person and respect for what they have to say. A youth worker does this by supporting young people's rights to say something even when others strongly disagree. Through a range of responses and activities, youth workers foster young people's abilities to respect themselves, each other and other people in their lives, including the youth workers.

The level and degree of respect demonstrated and demanded between a youth worker and young people should be mutual and even-handed. Most youth workers do not expect or demand respect for their own achievements, knowledge or strengths; the emphasis is to pass these on to young people if they are interested or want them. Attempts to provide a positive role model, for example, can be based on a perception of a young person's current role models as immoral or operating on an inferior value base, which is not a respectful approach. Demanding respect from young people as an older, wiser, more mature or successful individual can be counter-productive to establishing a youth work relationship, which is generally on a more equal level (see Practice Example 4.6 for ideas on different approaches to practice).

PRACTICE EXAMPLE 4.6

Different styles of work on respect issues

Challenging disrespect: If I overhear a young person disrespecting another or if someone disrespects me, I point this out. I might ask them how they would feel if someone treated them like that or tell them that the particular behaviour is offensive or explain how it makes someone feel. I don't think you can ignore it when someone is rude or uses offensive language or puts someone else down. We have to pass on an understanding of basic human rights and the need to treat others fairly and humanely. I show respect to them so they show respect to me.

Showing respect: I know that many of the young people's experiences are about not being respected – so I don't expect them to show me respect. I try to demonstrate respect to them. I hope that over time this will 'rub off'. I think that young people have so many authority figures telling them how to behave all the time and I'd rather try something different. It may take time, but I respect where they are coming from and take it from there. Eventually, they respect themselves. Eventually, they come to respect me.

Analysing respect: Sometimes young people don't realise how their own behaviour contributes to situations. So we talk about rights and responsibilities – choices and consequences – and try to link these themes into how respect can be earned. We talk about what goes on in their interactions with teachers, parents and the police, and talk about their reactions, unfair treatment and being ignored and how they can handle it.

Respect for young people as individuals is generally linked to an understanding that they are capable of making choices and taking some control over the decisions that they make. Some interventions or interactions may be more useful with specific groups or situations – and most youth workers will use a variety of 'standing by' approaches as well as 'getting involved'. Young people often ignore frequent challenges, which can communicate a negative stance. Appropriate encouragement and praise can help to counterbalance interventions that point out mistakes. Deciding when, how, why and where to intervene may require a number of factors to be analysed. An individual's confidence and responsiveness, the potential effect on the individual and others, and whether alternative actions may prove more effective, may all determine what might be said or whether to say anything at all.

Youth work practice is contextual, based on the realities of the particular young people with whom the youth worker comes in contact. While different youth workers may use their own individual strengths in varying ways to engage with young people, build credibility and/or provide alternative perspectives, a relationship starts with the specific young people and their experience, preferences and realities.

LOCATING AND 'USING' SELF

As individual personal histories, identities, abilities, skills, knowledge and values can shape and affect perspectives on and reactions to young people, issues and colleagues, a clear awareness of self can support the development of professional practice and relationships. Particularly significant influences include experiences of privilege or oppression in relation to the social constructs of class and race, sexism, ableism and heterosexism. Supervisors, colleagues, family members, reading and reflection can be used in this process of 'location of self'. This knowledge can assist youth workers to recognise how they may be perceived by others who come from different backgrounds and to avoid having judgemental responses to situations that are outside their experience. Taking time to reflect on how their identity affects their practice can help youth workers to analyse their assumptions and the context of their beliefs (see Box 4.3 for some examples of ways to 'locate self').

Box 4.3   'Locating self'

Youth workers can 'locate self' by identifying and evaluating:

- Their experiences, by asking themselves questions such as: Was I brought up in a secure or chaotic environment? With strict religious or political ideologies or unstructured values? Within the safety and security of a loving family or with domestic abuse? Did I experience economic comfort or poverty? Did I live in a peaceful community or with war, gangs and riots?
- their strengths as well as any weaknesses or gaps
- their identity in relation to age, gender, race, class, ability, religion and politics
- how they might be perceived by others
- any differences between their own experiences and perceptions and those of the young people they work with

(Continued)

(Continued)

- their role as a youth worker and how thisrelates to young people, the organisation, the community, society
- self-disclosure and how much information about themselves is necessary to pass on or reveal
- the core values of youth work and their anti-oppressive perspectives, including feminism, a black perspective, a social model of disability
- how the core values of youth work and their personal values or paradigm relate to each other
- how they would define appropriate relationships with individuals and groups of young people
- how they perceive professional behaviour with other workers
- their own power – whether personal (due to their experience), locational (due to their identity) or positional (due to their job status)
- how they can continue to learn and grow.

Although youth workers share information about decisions relevant to youth work, sharing information about their own lives is an individual matter. Being honest and open does not require disclosure about personal histories or circumstances. Most youth workers tend to be cautious when utilising their own experience, opinions and personalities in their interactions with young people. Quite often the information is irrelevant. Young people's circumstances may appear to be similar or comparable, but individual levels of confidence and assertiveness will affect options and opportunities. In some circumstances, a thought-provoking example from experience can be useful as an encouragement to think differently about a person or issue. Rather than prescribing a specific course of action, youth workers may use incidents or aspects of their lives to provide a new perspective, for example how lives can turn around or change. Other youth workers are very open about their experience and use their interpretations of their lives as a regular method of practice. Practice Example 4.7 illustrates youth workers' very different approaches to using their experience.

PRACTICE EXAMPLE 4.7

Using experience in practice

- I feel that my own experience of living with domestic abuse has informed my practice in that I recognise similarities in individuals' circumstances, attitudes and actions. I know that everyone is different and I don't try to impose my interpretations on others, but I also know that I am very well aware of the impact of domestic abuse on self-esteem, confidence, abilities to take up offered opportunities and forming trusting relationships. It means that I can recognise and look out for signs and offer an understanding listening ear. I very rarely choose to tell my story.
- My experience of transgendered identity means that I can share my experiences with others who are questioning or seeking support in relation to their thoughts and feelings. I always say that everyone's an individual and I emphasise that I don't

expect others to make the same decisions I did. But because I know very well how hard it is to talk about transgendered identity and to find support, I find that I often tell my story as an invitation to young people to discuss their different circumstances or experiences.

The 'Johari Window' (Luft, 1982; see the figure in Box 4.4) can be used in self-reflection or supervision to identify issues that may be appropriately disclosed in youth work. The 'open window' contains information and issues that could be appropriate for discussion with young people. The 'hidden window' contains experiences that are not relevant to a youth work relationship and therefore would not be disclosed. These windows might be quite different from the open and closed windows youth workers use at home or out with friends; self-disclosure is often different in personal or work relationships. Young people can be very open about providing feedback and help to reduce the 'blind window' and their perspective on how youth workers present themselves may be quite educative. Exposure and exploration of ideas through youth work can increase a youth worker's self-knowledge. Use of the 'unknown window' may also be enhanced. Shared enjoyable activities with young people could serve to reach as yet untapped creativity normally unknown and in the subconscious.

Box 4.4   The 'Johari Window'

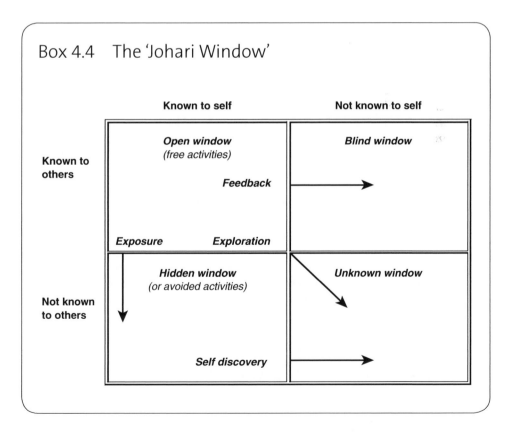

MAINTAINING PROFESSIONAL BOUNDARIES

Boundaries for appropriate youth work practice are established by youth work principles and defined by youth workers through reflection on practice with experienced supervisors. Professional boundaries ensure that youth workers can be trusted to work for the benefit of young people in ways that foster their independence. To maintain these boundaries, attention needs to be paid to power and autonomy so that an attentive and sometimes supportive or caring relationship does not slide into close personal involvement. This requires youth workers to remain aware of their role as workers, establishing their boundaries at 'the edge of the playing field' and not becoming embroiled in young people's lives as another 'player'. In order to maintain appropriate boundaries, youth workers need to reflect on their practice in the light of youth work principles and make use of supervision sessions to discuss any situations where dependency, sexual desires or friendship are impacting on youth work relationships. (Box 4.5 lists several examples of ways to maintain professional boundaries.)

Box 4.5   Maintaining boundaries

To ensure that professional relationships are developed and maintained, youth workers:

- spend time with various young people rather than allowing an exclusive clique to develop: encourage and support young people to engage with other young people and activities and with other youth workers
- steer away from preferential treatment for individuals: if one young person is informed about a job or educational opportunity, find ways to share this information more widely
- make sure that their own well-being is not dependent on a young person: if a youth worker's mood is strongly affected by a young person's actions or progress, they should focus on work with other young people
- retain a level of detachment from close or personal relationships with the young people, particularly any sexual interactions however minor: avoid being alone with any young person addressing suggestive behaviour towards oneself and alert other workers about the need for access to be limited
- take care to maintain some limits on the time that individuals discuss personal and private matters: identify alternative support structures together and inform young people about any limitations to confidentiality, such as legal or safeguarding information that may need to be passed on to others
- take reasonable measures to avoid extensive individual private time with a young person, particularly when out of sight of others
- understand and communicate the difference between an inappropriate gift (e.g. one that is expensive or used in anticipation of preferential treatment) and an allowable token acknowledgement (e.g. a card or small, inexpensive item)

- take care that behaviour (inside and outside of work) does not undermine young people's confidence in the profession: consider what they would learn from a youth worker's actions and the potential impact of that behaviour on others
- use personal social media with caution: in general, young people attending youth work should not have access to a youth worker's personal information; set up an organisation or group facility instead
- discuss responses to individuals with a supervisor, particularly any concerns or questions about the appropriateness of relationships
- reflect on their position of power and responsibility in young people's lives, being careful not to abuse or exploit this through unreasonable or personal expectations or demands.

Inappropriate relationships with young people abuse the trust that they, other youth workers and society as a whole should be able to place in an individual youth worker. Particular care and attention needs to be paid to ensuring a strict boundary is maintained within youth work regarding any actions intended to gratify sexual desires. A sexual relationship, even if the young person becomes the age of a consenting adult, will interfere with the youth worker's relationship with the individual, as well as with other members of the group. Developing a close relationship with a former member of a youth group or a close relative of a current or former member is also ill advised. If a young person seeks an inappropriate relationship with a youth worker, the youth worker must tell the young person that such a relationship is not possible. In addition, the youth worker will need to consider ways to distance themselves from the situation without making the young person feel rejected or worse about themselves. In these situations, clarity of role as a youth worker is important to explain why continuing with such a relationship would be unethical.

LETTING GO

Youth work relationships are generally temporary; young people may disengage gradually as new interests take over; others disappear more abruptly. Participation may be a completed phase that ends through gaining employment, undertaking further education, starting a family or moving away. While some young people may stay on as trainee youth workers or volunteers and others may become interested in alternative youth work activities catering for different target groups, the majority will eventually discontinue their involvement. Enabling a young person to move on into new experiences and life choices is an essential part of the process of youth work and helps to define appropriate relationships.

If a relationship has not been co-dependent or overly emotional, letting go will usually be a natural and easy progression. Having the capacity and preparedness for the inevitability of young people's moving on is not only important for avoiding 'burn out', but to ensuring that relationships do not become too close. Some youth workers have strong emotional or motivational ties to their practice, which can make this stage more significant, particularly if the reasons for a young person's leaving are less positive. Young people's departures through jail sentences, illnesses, accidents or death can be upsetting and, in these situations, a youth worker's level of detachment or attachment may be difficult to determine or control.

Offering support to young people touched by their own or others' departures may help to focus attention on a more professional approach to letting go. Constructive endings can often be planned to assist recognition of positive outcomes, whether relationships finish through choice, design or external factors. Limited term activities generally programme in a celebration or evaluation to identify the skills gained and plans for the future, and the use of social networking by organisations has meant that some form of contact can be maintained with young people who no longer attend. More unexpected events, such as the shutting down of services due to cuts in funding or a worker moving on to a new post, still usually allow sufficient notice to hold discussions of options and their implications. As a youth worker experiences multiple positive and negative events, whether planned or unplanned, a calm and confident response to letting go becomes easier to maintain and less stressful for all concerned.

ESSENTIAL SKILLS FOR DEVELOPING APPROPRIATE RELATIONSHIPS WITH YOUNG PEOPLE

- Welcoming young people
- Responding to young people as individuals
- Engaging in dialogue
- Respecting young people
- Locating and 'using' self
- Maintaining professional boundaries
- Letting go

 FURTHER READING

Banks' (2010) book about ethics in youth work provides a wealth of material about professional relationships.

For further guidance on listening and counselling, try Luxmore's (2000) *Listening to Young People in School, Youth Work and Counselling*, whose experience as a teacher, youth worker and counsellor means that the stories of young people and ideas about working with them are very relevant, or McLeod and McLeod's (2011) *Counselling Skills: A Practical Guide for Counsellors and Helping Professionals*, which identifies and explains some applicable skills and provides some useful guidance about identifying when a counsellor might be required.

Tuckman's (1965) definition of the last stage of groups as a time to celebrate and/or mourn may be a useful tool for recognising the end of a relationship and moving on. (See also Chapter 5 for more detail about the different stages.)

PART B

WORKING TOGETHER

Working Together has four chapters examining working with groups of young people. Chapter 5 looks at forming groups that address basic needs and stated interests and enable young people to learn from each other. Chapter 6 examines examples of enjoyable group activities and the importance of developing positive experiences in young people's lives. Chapter 7 focuses on work with young people in relation to some of the issues that they face through individual circumstances, development needs and societal discrimination. Chapter 8 explores ways to establish good relationships within groups and to address issues arising. Chapter 9 examines how youth work provides opportunities for young people to participate in decision making.

5

BRINGING YOUNG PEOPLE TOGETHER

This chapter examines the benefits of group work and some of the stages required to develop groups based on genuine need, such as identifying resource requirements, considering barriers to participation and prioritising conflicting demands.

Shared activities enable young people with similar circumstances, identities or experiences to develop positive relationships, learn from each other and have a voice in issues that affect them. Collectively, young people identify and articulate their own experiences in discussions with others who have a genuine understanding of their perspectives and can provide the support and/or direction to develop realistic plans for change. A youth worker brings young people together through organising contacts, creating warm environments for meetings and working with groups to acquire resources. Young people gain confidence through collective decisions and develop an appreciation of the consequences of various actions to inform future social action.

RECOGNISING YOUNG PEOPLE'S INTERESTS

Understanding what may motivate young people to join a group or make changes in their lives can provide direction for the development of viable youth work. Developing one-off activities and programmes of work, whether fixed term projects or ongoing groups, requires youth workers and young people to work with each other so that genuine motivations and interests are addressed. Some of the reasons that young people join groups are obvious: the activities on offer, such as socialising, drama or sports, are attractive to the individuals. Typical reasons for joining could include having an interest in activities that are either more exciting and creative or more safe and secure than other available options at home or on the streets. Others may join to access specific resources, such as specialised information and advice. However, other, more hidden reasons may prompt young people's attendance and stated interests may not encompass the full story. The table in Box 5.1 lists some examples of young people's motivation for attendance or participation in youth work activities that may or may not be revealed to others, or themselves. Applying the 'Johari Window' (see Box 4.4 in the previous chapter) may assist the development of an understanding of these motivations.

Identifying genuine and compatible interests is not always a straightforward procedure. Some young people may not identify or articulate their needs clearly. While in some situations, several young people may have compatible reasons for coming together or joining a group, others may have conflicting interests. Evaluating levels of enthusiasm for activities is often based on expressed interests as these are the most obvious reasons for a young person choosing to participate. Other motivations may also play a part and can affect participation. Some young people have or express more rigid preferences and will only attend youth work for a specific activity. Such specific and overt reasons may be easily identified yet subject to change. For example, a young person's aspirations to be an actor may provide an impetus for joining a drama project, but not sustain sufficient interest if only a small role is offered. Another young person may attend the same sessions with a more hidden, unarticulated need for refuge from an oppressive or abusive domestic situation. This motive may provide rich sustenance for hard work. Young people who have a general desire to become part of a group and have a good time may be inspired by a group to perform. On the other hand, this group may prefer less demanding activities. Reflection on these possible influences on group development is essential to good group work practice.

Box 5.1   Motivations for participation

For enjoyment	• To relax, have fun, play, be with others, share enthusiasms or interests, be happy, express themselves
	• To meet other people, get to know them, make friends, talk about selves, find out about others, gossip, fall in love
	• For adventure, excitement, new experiences
For specific activities	• To carry out outdoor pursuits, rock-climb, play sports or chess
	• To listen to music, become involved in arts, dance or drama, keep fit, learn something, computer access, pray, try something new

To fill gaps and/or address needs	• For praise, recognition, love, security, self-esteem
	• To feel needed, belong, be listened to, respected, treated fairly, keep busy, get involved, be responsible, achieve, gain status
	• To influence, change or assert control over social, economic and political issues that affect them
	• To gain confidence, boss others about, express themselves, feel powerful
	• To talk about issues arising in their lives, e.g. worries, concerns, fears, about the many emotional, physical, mental, domestic, sexual, behavioural and social changes and transitions going on in their lives
	• To adjust to changes in their dependence on others for boundaries, value-base, opportunities, responsibilities, finance
For a cause	• To work together, campaign, effect change, improve the environment, build community links or spirit, combat drugs/crime, have a say about current affairs and politics, access and participate in the provision or improvement of services, opportunities and resources
For services, advice or support	• For education or training, answers to questions, to gain specific skills, knowledge or awareness
	• For condoms, childcare, counselling, mediation
	• For advice and information about health, debt, drugs, alcohol, housing, employment, educational opportunities, family problems, domestic violence, peer pressure, bullying
For escape or refuge	• To get out of the house, combat isolation or boredom, feel safe or relaxed
	• For shelter, warmth, food, security, safety, protection
	• Because of desperation, there's nowhere else to go, fear, upset, conflict
Coercion	• Because of a court order or rehabilitation programme, a professional referral, it's part of the school curriculum, the teacher sent them
	• Because of peer pressure, their parents/carers sent or brought them, punishment

Pringle (1986) suggests that the significant needs during young people's development are love, security and new experiences, as well as praise, recognition and responsibility. Youth workers often prioritise work with young people who have 'fallen through the net' often provided by other social structures, such as the family or education services, and whose development needs are not being met. Maslow's (1943) hierarchy of human motivation (see the figure in Box 5.2), often depicted as a triangle rather than the rather dynamic situation he defines, recognises that most people are only partially satisfied in relation to their needs. This dissatisfaction can provide a motivation, or 'driver', for change through attempts to address unmet needs or to compensate for them. Youth work can be significant in relation to young people addressing their needs to survive, as well as for personal growth and development, by balancing provision that supports such activities with opportunities that enable young people to 'do it for themselves'. Working in groups can provide individual young people with the support to address their needs and the opportunity to work with others to create changes in their lives.

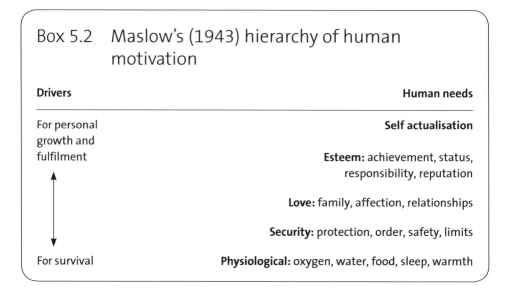

Box 5.2   Maslow's (1943) hierarchy of human motivation

Drivers	Human needs
For personal growth and fulfilment	**Self actualisation**
	Esteem: achievement, status, responsibility, reputation
	Love: family, affection, relationships
	Security: protection, order, safety, limits
For survival	**Physiological:** oxygen, water, food, sleep, warmth

According to Maslow (1943), the survival needs at the bottom of the hierarchy generally take priority over the other more intellectual desires for achievement. Different perspectives, however, due to interest, age or circumstance can affect how an individual prioritises. For example, someone interested in power may value their reputation over their need for love, sacrificing friendship for other benefits, such as finance or access to other more dominant allies. Individuals whose needs are not met in one area may find satisfaction through addressing another. For example, musical expression may compensate somewhat for a lack of love and security. (For an alternative look at human needs, see Max-Neef [1991], discussed in Chapter 9.)

Youth workers' knowledge of young people's development needs often informs their understanding of what might be relevant activities for groups. An awareness of the degree to which young people's needs are being met can also inform practice. For example, a youth worker who is aware that young people are hungry and unwelcome at home will provide a comfortable and accessible environment with refreshments in recognition of these basic physiological needs. The need for love can be addressed by bringing young people together for shared activities where they can develop friendships and other loving relationships. Recognising their need for security, youth workers address issues in relationships between group members so the young people can feel some safety in the group. Bringing young people together to broaden their understanding of possible life choices by going to new places and trying out new skills offers new experiences. Adventurous excursions to new environments enable young people to build confidence and further extend their assertiveness and survival skills. Involving young people in planning and organising such activities and sharing in decision making enables them to experience taking on responsibilities and leadership roles and addresses a need for esteem. Throughout, feedback and recognition of achievements support young people in personal growth.

General knowledge about human needs, and young people in particular, assists the development of relevant youth work, but young people's motivations are the 'drivers' for making any changes in their lives. By offering choices, voluntary participation and group involvement in deciding how needs will be addressed, young people retain their motivation and control. Youth workers facilitate opportunities for young people to explore their options with others, so that they can identify any changes that they wish to make.

As a general rule, youth workers respond positively to young people's expressed needs rather than diagnose deficiencies in their plans. For example, a young person expressing an interest in music would be signposted to relevant opportunities rather than judged in relation to their musical abilities or potential for success. Discussion could include what could be involved in pursuing a musical interest, particularly if the individual has no role models or other access to such information. Drawing upon available resources and networks and involving the young person in research to identify ways to find out more, a youth worker would assist the individual in pursuing the expressed interest. If the young person appears to lack the self-esteem necessary to pursue available options, activities that could widen opportunities for social relationships and feelings of self-worth would also be discussed. The table in Box 5.3 lists some examples of issues that may impede a young person in pursuing their options and which youth work would attempt to address.

Box 5.3   Issues related to young people's development

Areas of development	Possible issues arising
Identity Location of self	• Self-esteem, self-image, groundedness (being secure and in touch with reality), self-knowledge and confidence • Political, cultural, ethnic, class, sexual and gender identity • Racism, xenophobia, sexism, heterosexism, disablism, classism, ageism • Morality, beliefs, religion, spirituality
Health Physical, mental and emotional well-being	• Changes in appearance, abilities, puberty, growth • Pregnancy, sexual health • Boredom, self-control or other emotions including anger, disappointment, shame, loneliness • Exercise, sports, healthy eating, caring for self • Accessing health services and advisers • Addictions, substance abuse (own and others)

(Continued)

(Continued)

Areas of development	Possible issues arising
	• Eating disorders, self-harm, anxiety, depression, bereavement • Ableism, disabilism, impairments, illness • Access to green spaces, online networking, violent or pornographic online materials
Relationships With family members With friends, peers, lovers, partners With the community and the public With colleagues at work and school With professionals and figures of authority	• Communication, negotiation and social presentation, confidence and assertiveness • Conflict, arguments, disagreements • Giving and receiving love, affection, care, attention • Bullying or being bullied, hate crime, cyber bullying • Divorce, family break-up, running away, parenting • Expressing political views and opinions • Crime, domestic violence, forced marriages, sexual abuse, rape, violence, gangs (as perpetrators or victims)
Domestic arrangements	• Housing, finding a home or refuge, homelessness • Moving house, eviction, conflicts with neighbours • Being in and leaving home, care, prison, the armed forces • Seeking refugee status, asylum seeking • 'Financial literacy': handling finance, credit, planning, poverty, debt, repossession • Lack of skills in cooking, household management, repairs and maintenance, gardening • War, torture, environmental disasters
Education and work Information about options, access and pathways	• Motivation and aspirations, creativity, satisfaction • Time-management, focus and planning • Participation, progress and achievement in learning, education and employment • School exclusion, under-achievement and failure • Literacy, numeracy and computer proficiency • Dyslexia, learning difficulties • Finding and keeping a job • Access to transport, work clothes

HAVING A PLANNED APPROACH FOR BRINGING YOUNG PEOPLE TOGETHER

Bringing young people together may take place during a single session or over many months. Having established communication with an existing group, large assembly or various isolated individuals, a youth worker may be able to identify some genuine needs and interests for a group. With reflection on basic human and development needs, but mostly on young people's expressed interests in comparison with available resources, ideas for activities can begin to be formed. Possible options can be discussed with potential members so that they are involved in planning and developing viable activities and sustainable services. Depending on the evidence and level of interest, initial meetings of members may take place to discuss the aims before a more extensive resource allocation is made.

Youth work activities need to be of interest and accessible to the target group. If young people need employment, improved park facilities may not attract them. If they are not able to attend a centre, arranging sessions there would be ill-advised. Although preferences and ideas may change through exposure to new experiences or finding out that a friend is involved in an activity that was previously rejected, the starting point for planning is expressed interests. Involving interested young people in programme planning, applying for and allocating resources can develop their careful consideration of choices. The planned approach to establishing a viable group outlined in Box 5.4 should enable a youth worker to put together a case for resource allocation to relevant activities based on genuine interests and needs.

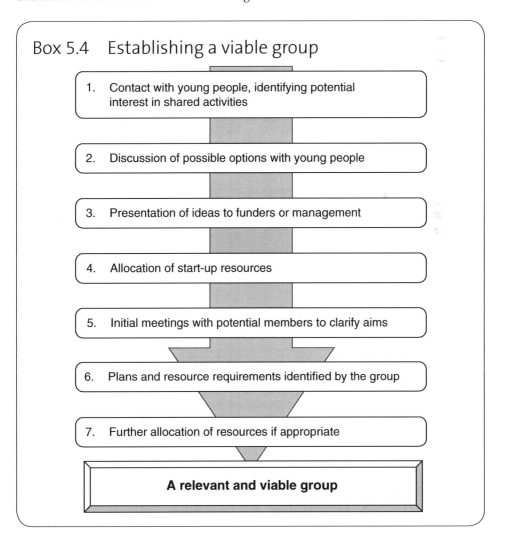

Box 5.4   Establishing a viable group

1. Contact with young people, identifying potential interest in shared activities

2. Discussion of possible options with young people

3. Presentation of ideas to funders or management

4. Allocation of start-up resources

5. Initial meetings with potential members to clarify aims

6. Plans and resource requirements identified by the group

7. Further allocation of resources if appropriate

A relevant and viable group

The common interests of the young people, community, organisation and wider society may come together to develop well-supported and sustainable youth work. However, such congruence is not always the reality. Some groups are established due to organisational or societal priorities rather than young people's needs or youth work principles. Youth workers often find that the essential steps to establishing genuine needs and interests have been bypassed. A romantic or idealistic perception of young people's needs or a social policy based on an external political agenda may direct and finance particular initiatives. Addressing targets that do not relate to the young people's concerns can result in inappropriate allocation of resources and lead to difficulties in recruiting members or maintaining participation. Attempting to establish a group without sufficient consultation and involvement can lead to problems such as a programme that is boring, an underused facility or unrealistic targets (see, for example, the figure in Box 5.5).

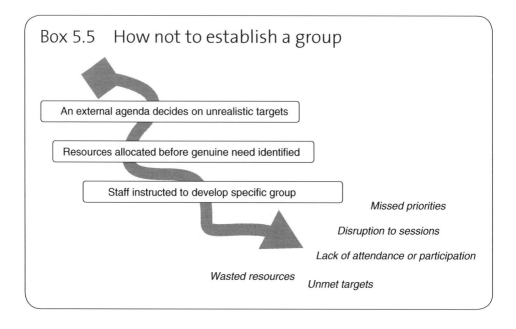

Box 5.5   How not to establish a group

An external agenda decides on unrealistic targets

Resources allocated before genuine need identified

Staff instructed to develop specific group

Missed priorities

Disruption to sessions

Lack of attendance or participation

Wasted resources

Unmet targets

Identifying needs for a group can be established through outreach, networking and getting to know a community (see Practice Example 5.1). Young people and other members of the community often suggest ideas: 'We don't get a chance to do anything with the boys around.' Young women may find it difficult to compete with boys for equipment or space so that a girls' group could ensure young women's access: 'Could we meet later on? Then it wouldn't clash with football.' A schedule that fits in with current activities respects young people's life choices, and, in this case, could encourage their continued participation in sporting activities. If the youth worker can match identified needs with existing resources or a funding opportunity, a successful group could result.

PRACTICE EXAMPLE 5.1

Identifying need through observation

A community worker enjoyed wandering around the local outdoor second-hand market during her lunch breaks and noticed a large number of young women with small children wandering around. It was apparent that neither the young women nor the children enjoyed the experience. The worker was aware that employment in the area was low, that there was a high level of debt and that loan sharks were active in the area. She also knew that there was a high percentage of young single mothers under the age of 18. The worker was aware of a brand new community facility with rooms available for community use. She publicised a parent and toddler group through leaflets distributed in the market. Response and participation levels were high.

Youth work can also develop as a result of an awareness of gaps in opportunities for young people to address their needs and interests in enjoyable activities or necessary services. Provision may be unavailable, inaccessible, unresponsive or inappropriate (see Practice Example 5.2). An awareness of community issues and the availability of sources of support for young people can help to identify whether a new activity or group is required. The information is also useful when signposting young people to other services. A needs analysis that compares expressed interests with the accessibility of existing provision can avoid duplication of activities and services. More extensive research may be necessary to prioritise needs.

PRACTICE EXAMPLE 5.2

Addressing gaps for LGBT young people

Young lesbian, gay, bi-sexual and transgender (LGBT) people living in a rural area felt isolated because they had nowhere to socialise or find out information about LGBT issues. Only by going into the regional city centre could they find venues where they felt they could be 'out'. The distance to travel and the adult facilities on offer were generally not appropriate for younger people. Their main source of relevant information was through websites, some of which were unsuitable. The 'open access' generic groups and activities for young people in the area were limited and the young people reported that they did not feel safe to be themselves in these environments. The youth workers discussed options with the young people concerned and it seemed that online support with recommended sites could be a way to make friends and gain peer support separate from the adult LGBT scene. When plans were being made for allocation of resources in the next financial year, the youth workers made sure to include LGBT young people in discussions. Meanwhile, the youth workers also began some issue-based work on heterosexism within the generic youth groups. Publicity and information was put on display and discussed.

A change in a community, such as a sudden crisis, can provoke a range of needs for youth work. Some examples could be a natural disaster, war or explosion, or the closure of a resource. Youth work can bring young people and their communities together to address short-term or longer-term changes. Discussions about trauma, addressing consequences or providing diversion can be provided through youth work activities and programmes. Youth action groups can be formed to address an issue; youth volunteers can offer services to a community; facilities for young people can be offered by youth workers (see Practice example 5.3).

PRACTICE EXAMPLE 5.3

Developing work on drug misuse

Version A: Addressing the issues

A flurry of young people's drug-related deaths galvanised young people's interests, community and political support as well as interest within a local youth centre. The youth workers involved young people in addressing the issues. Opportunities were developed to socialise without fear and to use needle exchange and advice services. The activities were well used, welcomed by the community and well supported by the organisation. The community issue focused attention on positive practice.

Version B: Conflicting approaches

In another community, conflicts of needs and interests led to disagreement about how the drugs 'crisis' should be addressed. Community leaders demanded tighter policing and curfews. When the young people asked for a needle exchange, the community was outraged. Without political support, the youth centre could not find sufficient resources for informal educational activities. The youth workers decided that developing closer links with community organisations and disseminating information about the reality of young people's lives may provide a more positive basis for future practice.

USING DIFFERENT METHODS TO BRING YOUNG PEOPLE TOGETHER

While some young people will join a group or come to a meeting through reading a notice or being handed a flyer, most will require a closer relationship with others involved prior to attendance. The figure in Box 5.6 illustrates some different ways to bring young people together.

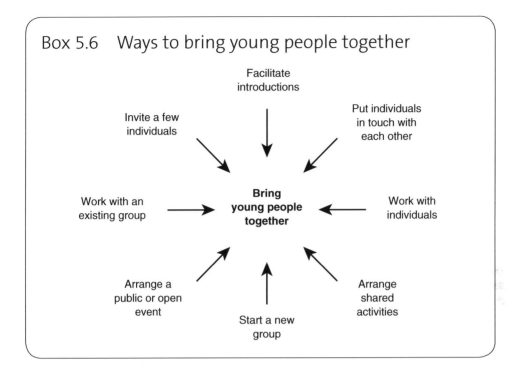

Box 5.6 Ways to bring young people together

Working with individuals

Bringing young people together may start with individuals. Conversations with potential members can build up their confidence and readiness to join a group. A young person may benefit from getting to know a youth worker first in order to be ready for the next step or to identify what the next step might be. While groups of young people can provide excellent support and learning, some young people may require additional groundwork prior to or during their participation in groups. For example, an individual may need to discuss or move on from experiences such as poor relationships with other young people. A young person experiencing certain life transitions or trauma unrelated to participation in groups may require further support. A young person may need or want to develop particular social skills, such as non-violent interactions, confidence or assertiveness and language skills prior to joining in with others (see Practice Example 5.4).

A youth worker who remembers individual young people's interests, such as a certain type of music, martial art or other hobby, can make arrangements for those young people to meet and share their interests in one-to-one meetings or independent groups. Shared experiences or circumstances may also highlight an opportunity for encouraging contacts. Depending on the age, maturity and confidence of the individuals concerned, a youth worker may need only to identify the shared interest or need, check out willingness to meet, distribute contact details and allow meetings to develop as the individuals wish. In situations where the individuals may be inexperienced or vulnerable, a youth worker could offer guidance to safety, such as recommendations for safe and neutral meeting places, getting to know each other before meeting alone or at home, or informing parents or carers about arrangements.

PRACTICE EXAMPLE 5.4

New experiences developing confidence

A youth worker became aware that a young person had been bullied in school and was reluctant to join a local youth group because of fear that the experience would be repeated. After several individual chats about 'non-serious' topics, such as favourite football teams and television programmes, the young man expressed some interest in a documentary programme about gravity. The worker remembered that an observatory in the area had advertised 'Summer Sleepovers' for young people where they would have the opportunity to look through a telescope and find out about the stars.

With the youth worker's support, the young man made some enquiries and discussed his findings. He found out that the session would consist of quite a small group, which would be unlikely to make him feel lost and under-supervised. He would be on the older edge of the age range, which reduced his fears of being intimidated by older boys. The sessions were quite structured, which would lessen opportunities for bullying. He decided that he would go.

When the young person returned from a positive experience, he felt ready to join the local youth group. The youth worker was aware of the need to keep an eye on him. However, the confidence that the young man had gained meant that he participated fully in the activities.

Putting individuals directly in contact with each other may also be a useful method of bringing young people together when developing a sustainable group is impracticable. A passion for an unusual topic or a minority interest may not naturally lead to a group activity. Individuals who live in a rural area may find it difficult to travel to a shared facility. Alternative organisational priorities or resource restrictions may mean that a youth worker is unable to facilitate these smaller groups. A self-sufficient group or independent communication between such individuals, perhaps by telephone or internet, may be more feasible and still provide opportunities for social interactions.

Facilitating introductions

Individuals may benefit from a managed meeting with an invitation to a specific time and place as a way to start building relationships. The worker may need to facilitate introductions, move the conversation on and coordinate follow-up. This approach would be useful when individuals are under-confident or need supervision because of their age or history. Sometimes the basis of the shared circumstances is a topic that the individuals find difficult to talk about (see Practice Example 5.5 of sharing experiences of bereavement).

Sharing bereavement

PRACTICE EXAMPLE 5.5

A youth worker was aware that two young people living within a particular area had both experienced parental bereavement and felt that they would benefit from getting to know each other. Without over-emphasising their shared circumstances, the worker told each individual some information about the other prior to the introduction and asked each about their interest in a get-together. The worker encouraged them to view the meeting as an opportunity to meet someone else their own age rather than primarily to discuss their bereavement. At their first meeting, the worker was more nervous than the young people and reflected afterwards that she had probably over-done her involvement in facilitating the introductions and conversation. The meeting felt rather stiff and formal. However, when the worker left the two alone to answer a phone call, she returned to find the two young people chatting cheerfully. They expressed interest in meeting again and the worker helped them to make the arrangements.

Concerns about issues related to circumstances or development, such as identity, health or relationships, may help to bring young people together but do not need to be the overt aims for a group or meeting. Involving young people in joint enjoyable activities may prove just as beneficial as exercises more explicitly related to their common concerns. For example, bringing together a group of young people who are in care ('looked-after' by others rather than their family) to play games may relieve some loneliness and lead to improvements in their relationships with others. A single parents group may benefit from socialising as much as from educational activities on child-rearing. A starting point for work with young people who are in danger of gang reprisals may be a common interest in football rather than discussions about their fears.

Recognising barriers to participation

Many young people work and play happily alongside each other despite differences or difficulties outside the youth work arena. Others find that access is fraught with practical and emotional difficulties. Youth workers attempt to enable access and participation for all young people who need or want to participate. Consideration of potential barriers or hindrances to participation can identify areas for positive action. Societal or individual attitudes, practices or policies may be at the root of some of the barriers to participation faced by some young people. Although youth work may not always be able to control, overcome or diminish exclusion, changes to practice may be able to address some of the effects.

An individual or smaller group may be prevented from participating or be unwilling to participate or contribute because of the identity or behaviour of the larger group. Involving the young people in identifying barriers to participation and ways in which they can be addressed can be a positive step. Taking part in positive action to address barriers can raise the level of young people's involvement and their confidence as well as effect genuine change. Communication with young people about the best way to address the barriers may help to find ways to enable participation.

PRACTICE EXAMPLE 5.6

Choosing the wrong location?

Another youth worker and I thought that we had recognised a good opportunity for starting a group. We had been talking with a few young men who we met in different outdoor locations and who seemed to share similar circumstances. They were all around the same age and vaguely interested in doing something different with their lives. None of them were involved in actively pursuing employment or education, but it seemed like they might be ready to do so. We thought that they would really benefit from getting together, so we booked a room in the local health centre and encouraged them to come along to discuss what we could do as a group. Although they said they would come, no one showed up. Later, I found out that young people in the area thought that using the health centre gave them a negative reputation. Anyone who went there was assumed to have an STD (sexually transmitted disease) and was ostracised. I also should have known that being comfortable talking with us individually in passing was different from having a 'meeting' or discussing their issues with peers that they didn't already know. A few months later when we booked a session in the gym, several of them came along and began talking to each other. They said they wanted to talk about jobs more than education and that they had no interest in talking about STDs! However, when we asked different members of staff from the centre to talk with the group about their jobs and how they had applied for them, we ended up having quite a conversation about sexual health and related matters.

Discussing options with young people

Checking with young people about their needs and ideas is an essential part of developing a proposal or plans for further work. For example, youth work needs to take place in a setting that can support and promote participation, the forming of relationships and learning from activities. The right environment for a group to function and grow includes a number of decisions about the venue, such as ownership, scheduling and needs in relation to facilities (see the figure in Box 5.7).

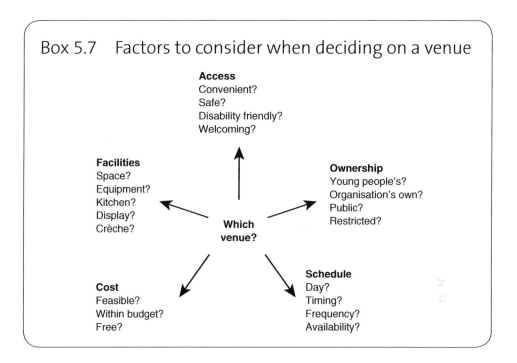

Box 5.7 Factors to consider when deciding on a venue

Access
Convenient?
Safe?
Disability friendly?
Welcoming?

Facilities
Space?
Equipment?
Kitchen?
Display?
Crèche?

Which venue?

Ownership
Young people's?
Organisation's own?
Public?
Restricted?

Cost
Feasible?
Within budget?
Free?

Schedule
Day?
Timing?
Frequency?
Availability?

The young people will have their views about the purpose of the group, who should be included and their requirements. Youth workers may need to encourage the group to consider issues for potential members as well as those currently involved, and to identify who is excluded by their decisions and whether the membership is representative of young people in the area. The discussion can be used to raise awareness of barriers and anti-oppressive practice as well as issues in the area.

Factors affecting a choice of venue can be wide-ranging and contradictory (see Practice Example 5.7). Some young people feel more confident or comfortable within their own space or peer group. Certain groups of young people may not wish to venture beyond limits defined by a school's catchment area, housing estate or other geographical features. Young people from a working-class housing estate may be reluctant to use the facilities of a youth centre situated on the other side of a main road in a more affluent area of town, and vice versa. Violence or the threat of violence within a 'gang culture' may define certain 'territories'. These boundaries may affect where the young people might be willing to go to participate in youth work activities. Many young people need strong motivation to explore beyond an existing group of friends and will only participate in an activity if others from the group come with them. Coming to an agreement or a decision about arrangements is part of the process of establishing the group and can lead to longer-term work in assisting young people to overcome any fears about going into new or different territories. (For more on working out disagreements, see Chapter 8.)

Contradictory suggestions from young people

Members of a group of young people attempting to plan the day and time for a session made the following suggestions:

- Fridays are great for me.
- I won't be able to come on Fridays because of Friday prayers.
- I have to pick up my sisters from school so we have to meet before 1.00 p.m.
- I work until 2.00 so I can't be here until 3.00.
- My parents would never let me come to this venue; it's the wrong religion.
- This is an ideal venue. My parents would be very happy to let me come.
- I can't go to that venue; it's next door to the police station.
- The bus comes nowhere near this venue. Don't you have a pick-up service?
- I don't want anyone to know I'm coming. Can you guarantee that no one will know?
- Someone needs to look after the baby or I won't be able to play badminton!
- This venue has no proper washing facilities in the toilets in keeping with Sharia law. We need clean water available in the toilets.
- This is the only venue we can afford.

We had an excellent discussion about consensus, barriers to participation, compromises, the 'bottom line' and Maslow's hierarchy of needs! (See Box 5.2.)

Once a need has been established, a youth worker meets with the young people to identify how they will address their interests. Decisions about resource requirements need to be made to establish when and how the group will meet. Certain types of activities such as cooking, gardening or sports may require specific facilities or expertise. The scheduling of meetings may also dictate availability and options. The life span (whether short-term, fixed term or ongoing) may be determined or unknown. The history and reputation of the group may also affect decisions. Clearly, funding and resources, although not always static, are a factor.

Identifying and addressing appropriate childcare arrangements and related issues can be essential for a group to thrive. Some projects aim to promote positive parent/child interactions so that offering a crèche throughout a session may not be appropriate. Other activities may not be possible for a parent whose child is present. Although a safe and well-staffed crèche may be an ideal way to enable parental involvement, resource requirements may be extensive. Alternative arrangements could include partnerships with childcare providers who may offer local or on-site services, allocating expenses for parents to pay their own childminders or creating a babysitting rota amongst the young parents themselves.

The extent to which the young people can use a particular venue and stamp their own identify onto it are important considerations when bringing young people together. Young people, as well as others, will see the opportunity to create displays, decorate or make changes to the furniture and equipment as important signifiers of power and ownership in a venue. Other users may not appreciate the images, topics and information on display that youth workers see as vital to their practice.

The formation of groups supports young people's interactions with peers, so that they can develop the skills and confidence that will enable them to make their own choices about their lives. While many youth workers value the opportunities that one-to-one work provides for identifying and addressing young people's concerns, in groups, young people can be inspired to find their own solutions and explore new options. Bringing young people together can be a beginning. The next chapter explores some of the activities that young people enjoy whilst in these groups, and, in the following chapter, we look at how to address some of the difficulties that may arise.

ESSENTIAL SKILLS FOR BRINGING YOUNG PEOPLE TOGETHER

- Recognising young people's interests.
- Having a planned approach to bringing young people together
- Using different methods to bring young people together
- Working with individuals
- Facilitating introductions
- Recognising barriers to participation
- Discussing options with young people

 ## FURTHER READING

For a detailed analysis of the process of developing and facilitating groups, have a look at Benson (2010). Handy (1999) provides an interesting overview of organisational theories that provide fascinating contrasts to work with groups of young people. For some relevant reflections on group formation for political activism, see Mullender and Ward (1991). Cohen and Mullender (2003) trace some of the relationships between feminism and group work.

6

HAVING FUN

This chapter looks at some positive and enjoyable activities that youth workers can offer. Examples of creative and sporting activities are examined to illustrate the range of enjoyable experiences, learning and action that characterise youth work. Some of the issues related to involving other professionals are also considered.

Article 31 of The UN Convention on the Rights of the Child (defined as 'every human being below the age of eighteen years') asserts the right of the child 'to rest and leisure, to engage in play and recreational activities appropriate to the age of the child and to participate freely in cultural life and the arts' and advocates that parties to the Convention should:

> respect and promote the right of the child to participate fully in cultural and artistic life and ... encourage the provision of appropriate and equal opportunities for cultural, artistic, recreational and leisure activity. (United Nations, 1989)

While youth work should be more than just a service providing activities that young people enjoy, youth work should be fun! New and challenging experiences as well as familiar and friendly pursuits provide enjoyable opportunities for learning and relaxing in the company of others. Positive feelings can develop from participation in a nurturing and supportive environment. Work with young people whose basic needs require attention can lead to a loss of focus on the enjoyable aspects of youth work. Some new youth workers may find it difficult to focus on a game of football when thinking about a young person's unfortunate circumstances. Attention needs to be paid to the benefits of providing an environment where those young people feel appreciated and can enjoy themselves. In order to avoid boredom or complacency, a youth worker attempts to find an appropriate mix of working within young people's 'comfort zones' and challenging their preconceptions about options that they may not have considered before. Involving other professionals or agencies can further extend the range and depth of activities on offer.

Simply providing a suite of computers for endless online gaming or a pool table to fight over continuously is usually not enough to maintain interest. These activities have their purpose, but offering a range of opportunities, some more demanding, is a more respectful approach to collaborative and participative practice. Youth work typically includes opportunities to socialise, dialogue and take action. The content will mirror the diversity of young people's circumstances, motivations, sensitivities, preferences and interests. Flexible and responsive programmes of activities can be developed in partnership between young people and youth workers. A youth worker attempts to adapt activities to address feedback from participants as well as identified interests from potential members. Ideas from the young people may be augmented by youth workers' suggestions or options.

Some youth workers view activities as being merely a means to an end and describe their function as a 'vehicle for delivering youth work'. Providing opportunities to keep fit, for example, is seen as a method of 'delivering' messages about healthy eating or lifestyles. Care needs to be taken that young people's interests are not disrespected; participation in leisure activities can be valued as a positive pursuit. Other youth workers focus on the activities provided and describe their role as, for example, a sports, arts or outdoor educator. Youth workers involved in this type of work may need to defend the voluntary and participative qualities of their practice, rather than engage in manipulating young people to undertake activities that do not reflect their interests or where they become passive passengers using a service. As Plato stated in around 375 BC,

> A free man ought not to learn anything under duress. Compulsory physical exercise does no harm to the body, but compulsory learning never sticks in the mind. (as construed by Lee, 2003: 269)

PLANNING OUTDOOR WORK

Planning outdoor work includes an extensive list of considerations, including location, access, staffing, activities, cost and insurance. Involving young people will have considerable educational benefit in relation to their ability to plan a project, but will also help their appreciation of the detailed work required and their resolve to make the most of the opportunity. The range of outdoor locations for youth work includes public access areas with no costs beyond possible travel or refreshments as well as private or limited access outdoor facilities, which may charge entrance fees, but also provide training and specialised insurance. Outdoor education, sporting activities or physical exercise can be organised in a local setting or accessed through excursions and overnight residentials. If a location is easily accessible, young people's appreciation and use could continue long after youth workers' involvement. Identifying potential opportunities for positive and enjoyable activities in outdoor locations can also mean seeking out options that young people would not have considered. (See Box 6.1 for some examples of youth work in outdoor locations.)

Box 6.1   Locating outdoor youth work

Nature and countryside

Orienteering, environmental projects, backpacking excursions, walks in the open countryside or near beaches, rivers and lakes, mountains, moors, woods, rock faces and caves can develop young people's understanding of outdoor environments and how to enjoy them with very little cost beyond travel. Trips to mountains, rock faces and caves may require some safety equipment and training.

Private facilities carry costs and the possibility of more controlled activities, such as visits to farms, gardens, funfairs, amusement parks, stately homes, camping grounds or trips on canal barges or boats.

Outdoor sports facilities

Low-cost activities using bike paths, nature trails, basketball courts, football fields, skateboard ramps, swimming pools, playgrounds, golf courses and tennis courts can provide opportunities for outdoor sports, games and play.

Outdoor education centres, field centres, water adventure centres, snow sports, adventure holiday summer camps and other residential facilities, camping grounds, sea kayaking, white water rafting, tubing or canoeing and gorge walking are often used to develop a group's cohesion through outings away from a usual setting.

Public 'built' environments

Detached work can take place in parks and gardens, on streets and street corners, by canals, reservoirs, fountains, bus shelters, parking spaces and spare or waste ground, particularly around other facilities, such as train stations or shopping centres.

Campaigns, public displays or fund-raising activities may also utilise these public and accessible spaces, particularly for issues related to young people in the outdoors, such as homelessness, drug use, sexual health or community relations.

Access to open spaces can be limited, for example, using a roped-off area in a park, or spaces attached to a centre (such as a field, playground, tennis/basketball courts) to hold large and public events, such as competitive sports and tournaments, or to promote, conclude or celebrate work with one-off outdoor events that are visible to the public.

Whether or not a formal assessment of the benefits, access, costs and potential risks is required by an organisation's procedures, funders and insurance, consideration of these elements and anticipating needs and events helps to plan successful outdoor activities. Although issues related to preparation can be attached to any activity involving young people, the use of outdoor locations may require extra attention, particularly in relation to health and safety. Outdoor environments tend to be less predictable and less easily controlled. If the activities involve taking young people out to new areas, youth workers' responsibilities for safeguarding the welfare and safety of the young people usually require carers to have information about the plans and to give documented consent for the young people to participate.

Access to certain outdoor pursuits can be limited to certain age groups, numbers or individuals. In open or public settings, the observations, comments or interference from passers-by may affect young people and youth workers so it is not only changes in the weather that can upset plans. Unexpected visitors, whether young people, adults, professionals or animals may make their presence known. Young people are less 'contained' so that they may be free to roam, get lost and move out of earshot. Some youth workers respond to these potential situations by increasing the structure and supervision of the activities through strictly refereed sports or well-planned and equipped projects. Others have a more flexible approach and can adapt the activities to suit the environment.

ORGANISING EXCURSIONS AND EXPEDITIONS

Going out together to a new environment can bring young people together from different backgrounds and provide a variety of new experiences and opportunities. For enjoyable activities to remain so, positive youth work practice implies change, development and learning, which are easily addressed through excursions and expeditions, whether to a local facility or a different country. Outings such as a cross-community activity or an international exchange can involve hosting as well as visiting. Through exposure to new environments or cultures, young people can learn new ways of looking at issues and widen their understanding of the world. Taking time out from usual routines also provides adventure, generally shared by the youth workers, who may find themselves joining in activities that they too had never expected to enjoy (see Practice Example 6.1 for an example of unexpected learning from a residential).

Benefits of residentials

The residential was invaluable. It brought the young people together as a group and helped build stronger relationships with the youth workers. The work we had to do on our peer education project would have been less focused and more time-consuming if we'd had to fit it in during normal sessions. The social elements helped the group to bond and acted as a reward. One of the best outcomes was unintended. The youth workers had been working for some time on challenging the overt homophobia of some members of the group, which they felt had improved gradually over many discussions. In the evening, the group started talking with another youth group staying at the centre which included some openly gay members. The groups sat up talking together until the small hours. The next day, one of the young men came up to the youth worker and said, 'You won't believe this – I've made friends with a gay guy – he's all right!'

PRACTICE EXAMPLE 6.1

Youth workers usually attempt to involve potential participants in planning and organising outings. Young people can contribute their perspectives at the same time as they learn about organising, budgeting and addressing parental or carer concerns, which can be significant factors in facilitating a successful project. Maintaining safety in outdoor settings usually means involving young people in considering the risk and safety issues (see Practice Example 6.2). Basic training in health and safety and first aid is usually required and can be undertaken by young people and youth workers together. If an activity or project necessitates limited numbers, a fair and open application or selection procedure and criteria will need to be devised. Attention to these matters should enhance young people's full contribution and cooperation (see also Chapter 11 on managing a project).

PRACTICE EXAMPLE 6.2

Planning water-based activities

A group of young people expressing interest in extreme sports contacted various water sports centres to ask about costs and preparation requirements for a range of activities including sea kayaking, body boarding, sub-aqua diving and kite surfing. Their involvement in the research generated a lot of excitement, as well as an understanding about the need for fund raising, swimming proficiency and detailed instructions from qualified staff.

Young people who were planning a day trip to the beach reviewed their own previous excursions where behaviour within the group had raised issues related to safety and consideration for others. They developed their own codes of conduct to restrict dangerous behaviour, discussed time-keeping and developed 'buddy systems' to ensure that members looked after each other.

A sub-group of the young people's summer programme planning committee organised a visit to look around a lakeside facility and decided to book some one-off sessions in sailing, canoeing or kayaking as 'tasters' to see if members' interests were genuine and committed prior to booking a full course.

Two youth workers who were working with a group planning a water-based activity carried out their own research amongst others working with young people to learn from their experience. The research enabled them to identify which facilities were suitable, potential dangers or issues arising from such activities and some handy tips on ways to address them. The youth workers were able to pass on this information to the young people.

WORKING INDOORS

Youth workers need to be aware of issues that may be defined or influenced by a venue, for example those related to access, opportunities and behavioural expectations. Although some indoor locations provide specific facilities that may be otherwise unavailable, certain venues may have regulations and established traditions which restrict youth work activities. Outreach work in premises owned and managed by other organisations may not suit young people, particularly if used by other groups or for alternative purposes. Short-term excursions and residentials to various public or private venues can provide rich and rewarding new experiences for young people, but can also require considerable organisation and preparation.

Centre-based work could take place within a youth work organisation's own venue. A youth club, drop-in advice service or football group in a purpose-built youth centre can provide a space for young people to take ownership and control. Similar services may be offered by a community association within a general purpose community centre, although attention will need to be paid to other users. Mobile provision in converted buses or caravans can be driven to particular localities, whilst temporary shelters for small groups, such as 'pods' or self-contained portable cabins, can be relocated into new areas as the need arises.

A centre that is owned and used exclusively by a youth work organisation should be able to provide a safe and warm environment. Ideally, a youth centre should be easily accessible within a locality and become a focal meeting point for different age, friendship or culture groups within a community. In this setting, the various groups can get to know each other and the youth workers well, develop the confidence to communicate their interests and needs, raise issues of concern and become involved in developing the provision and programmes. A youth centre may provide open access sessions in addition to providing certain sessions targeting groups and individuals with particular interests and needs. Some centres may be able to offer access to relevant information, services and advice, as well as facilities and equipment for artistic, sporting and educational activities. These facilities may provide darkrooms, gyms and exercise apparatus or sports facilities, music equipment, kitchens or cafés, computer suites, car/cycle/motorbike repair garages and tools, and crèche or nursery facilities. A youth work organisation promoting young people's participation can also involve young people in the management of the building.

Youth work within venues owned by others could include short-term satellite projects as well as longer-term outreach programmes. Youth work may be offered in a village hall or library, an empty shop or a church to suit a particular group, or when other facilities are unavailable or under-used. Lunchtime and after-school provision within a school setting has the advantage of proximity for a large number of young people, which can increase levels of participation. A youth worker may take a detached group to a clinic or university to increase their understanding of health or educational options, or go to a recreational or leisure centre to widen their experiences. Excursions to museums, galleries and restaurants can provide learning and cultural opportunities. A youth worker may also go out to other agencies working with young people, such as care homes, juvenile detention centres or prisons to make contact with a particular target group. Intervention programmes may take place in young people's homes, for example remedial education, intensive supervision or transition mentoring with particularly vulnerable young people. Flexibility is required to build bridges with particularly vulnerable young people who are having difficulties at school or in attending school, or with the criminal justice system or drug use.

The level of partnership with a host facility is dependent on a number of factors and stages. In some instances, a youth worker is invited in to address a particular need. Youth work may be facilitated in other organisational settings to make good use of existing facilities or to enhance the available provision of activities. During a visit to an area or site, a youth worker may identify suitable locations for outreach services. Sharing facilities can be particularly useful, especially in rural areas. A village may have only one publicly accessible facility, such as a church, a room above a shop or a school building. Identifying potential indoor spaces may require some positive and creative thinking and negotiation skills.

DEVELOPING ARTS ACTIVITIES

Taking part in performance arts, such as music, dance and drama, as well as making things such as crafts and cookery are often popular choices for enjoyable, creative and educational youth work activities (see the figure in Box 6.2 illustrating examples of arts activities). The benefits of offering arts activities can range from developing a satisfying hobby to liberating self-expression. Individuals who have not had success in educational settings that rely on verbal literacy or numeracy may show more proficiency with other methods of communication and creation. Many young people do not have other opportunities to develop or explore their artistic talents. Schools, families or communities may not prioritise these areas, perhaps preferring that young people address subjects perceived as more 'useful', such as maths and science, technology or business. Clearly, youth work has an important role to play in nurturing young people's participation in arts activities.

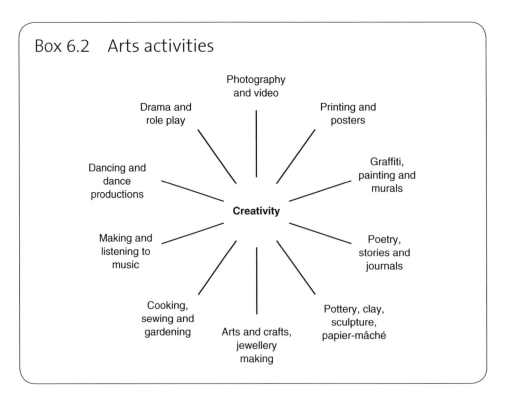

Box 6.2   Arts activities

Artistic endeavours may lead to more formal or public expressions such as exhibits, performances and competitions. Opportunities to dabble and play with materials and experiment with equipment are also valuable as a means of trying out ideas and getting used to the media. Part of the youth worker's skill is to determine when a group may benefit from the challenge of a more in-depth project. The foundation may emerge from previous work together or from a chance opportunity. Practice Example 6.3 outlines an example of how a photography project developed when an informal educator was able to match the interests of young people with a successful bid for resources.

A photography project

I was an informal educator based in a community centre, which made a successful bid to a local art gallery to create an exhibition on the theme of 'Diversity in this Town' within a six-month timescale. Discussions about the bid led to the emergence of a core and diverse group who requested suggestions from all of the groups and classes using the centre. The consensus from the 60 respondents was to produce a photographic display, a presentation book with texts, a video film of the processes involved and paintings and drawings around the theme of living in the town.

Participants were given a disposable camera and asked to photograph things about their lives. As each photograph contained an amazing story, a visual and emotional collage gradually emerged. Everyone was asked to write a short piece of text in their first language or in English to support the photographs. The design of the presentation book, the photographic hangings, the video editing, the soundtrack and the design of the exhibition stand were completed in workshops. The group handed over their precious work to a committed and interested gallery team on the deadline. Invitations were sent to families, friends, tutors, youth workers, other artists and agencies with whom participants linked in their lives. The launch day was a remarkable chance to feel the results of networking, sharing life experiences and trusting in others, as well as a chance to recognise the work of other groups in the exhibition and be recognised by visitors in turn for the commitment and creative energy the project released.

The project provided participants with a means to enhance individual skills. For example, some used their creative eye with a stills or video camera; some found the confidence to share and talk about their lives in pictures. Some enjoyed being able to express themselves confidently in their first language because they were clearly valued by others; others functioned in English with support from English-speaking volunteers. Sharing individual artistic skills, taking risks by talking with a newspaper reporter about the project and contributing to a group statement about the project involved a steep learning curve for everyone. The group experience presented challenges about ownership, communication, commitment, skill-sharing, learning to trust others in different roles, taking risks with trying new skills, negotiation and reaching a consensus, being together in new settings, being seen as a group and meeting other groups – not to mention the joy of celebrating together!

By the end of the project, participants could handle a camera with confidence, ask critical questions about what they watch on film and enjoy the public recognition of their important message to the town, which was to be kind to each other and live in peace. The project brought the individual skills and group experience alive whilst promoting participants' growth in being able to relate to others and the deepening of relationships.

PRACTICE EXAMPLE 6.3

An exhibit or performance can provide examples for young people's artistic development. Excursions to galleries, theatres or concert halls can provide inspiration, and direct attention and communication with artists through workshops is also stimulating (see Practice Example 6.4). Identifying a suitable artist to work with young people is not always an easy process. Involving young people in the selection process can help to find someone who is good at their art as well as being accessible and communicative.

Music as transformation

A group of young people that I was working with was involved in planning and organising a music festival with professional musicians playing alongside young people in a composed set of pieces. Some of the young people had never even picked up a musical instrument before. But they learned quickly! They spent months practising their parts, ringing up and emailing other groups, talking about their different pieces. It all culminated in a public performance at a concert hall attended by local government officials, parents and friends. It had such an effect on them. They got such a kick out of being on stage and it was videoed and put on the web as well. I really think that they will be much less likely to be involved in the risky and destructive behaviour that they used to get up to. It was a truly transforming experience. The project involved young people who had no access to music lessons, no experience of performance and very little contact with people outside the suburban village where they lived. Most of the professional musicians had come from an entirely different kind of background of economic privilege and high educational achievement. This festival made such a difference to both groups' understanding of the world.

USING DRAMA AND ROLE PLAY

From a discussion where a youth worker says 'imagine you had to say that to him now…' to a fully fledged film or stage play, drama is a powerful tool for youth work. Being able to take on a 'role' rather than directly talking about experience can be a liberating opportunity for a young person to explore and release emotions. Drama exercises in everyday practice (such as those outlined in Practice Example 6.5) can enable young people to develop their social and presentational skills and to practise their responses in difficult scenarios. Dramatic play may also develop their assertiveness and confidence, as well as helping them to see the consequences of certain actions.

Full dramatic productions may emerge from role-play exercises. A youth worker would need to assess a group's readiness for a long-term commitment before undertaking such a project. Considerable amounts of time and other resources are usually required, not only to organise the event, but to build up young people's confidence in performance. A partnership with an experienced individual or organisation aware of what goes into producing and directing plays or films could provide the young people with some useful guidance. Youth workers need to be clear about whether the production will be handed over to another professional's approach or will be cooperatively managed.

Drama and role-play exercises

'In the manner of a word'

We use a game to help develop awareness of body language. One person selects a card at random and has to carry out actions as requested by the rest of the group 'in the manner of the word' written on the card. The requests could be as simple as 'walk around the room in the manner of the word'. The other participants have to guess the word on the card. Examples are 'cheerfully', 'angrily', 'slowly', 'loudly', 'sadly', 'wisely' or 'rhythmically'. You have to leave enough time to discuss how to portray the more positive words, such as 'confidently', 'proudly' and 'assertively'. These are the most difficult to portray yet the most useful to them! We have enough cards for each player – or, sometimes, one team prepares the cards for the other team. You have to be careful with literacy issues though. It can be embarrassing for someone who can't read the word or doesn't know its meaning.

'Backstory' or 'What happened next?'

We have a collection of unusual photos, postcards and posters that we use to stimulate story-telling. Everyone has to say something or act out something that could happen just before or just after the picture. The images prompt thinking about situations that may be unfamiliar to them – some of them are well known but show different perspectives and identities. The game helps with self-presentation and conversational skills, especially with young people who are not used to being in the spotlight for positive reasons.

'Acting out'

We have a group that loves to develop and perform scripts based on their own lives. They form groups that take turns to act out scenes from their experiences. Then they talk about how each felt during the scene and discuss how they could have dealt with issues differently. I would only use this exercise with a group that I knew well. They need to feel that they could trust me to 'rescue' them if it got too heavy. They have looked at such a wide range of issues, from sibling rivalry to pressure to join gangs. The best thing about the approach is that they can have a laugh about some of the ways people behave, as well as trying out different responses to situations.

PLANNING GAMES AND SPORTS

Youth work offers opportunities to engage in games and sports and to provide activities that many young people enjoy that may also lead to healthy mental and physical development. Much youth work consists almost entirely of physical and sporting activities (see the diagram in Box 6.3, which illustrates some examples). Some youth workers have additional training and qualifications in specific areas, such as coaching and outdoor pursuit certificates, to enhance what can be offered. However, many youth workers undertake such activities with groups of young people despite a lack of sports training. Although 'extreme sports' and more risk-intensive activities may require proper preparation, a youth worker's lack of proficiency may provide a young person with a rare opportunity to excel, for example with a game of pool or a running race.

Some activities require a considerable amount of resources, whilst others, such as 'clap and rhyme' or 'stickball', are played in the streets without much preparation (see Rogers, 2011a for a wealth of examples). As long as health and safety issues are addressed, a wide range of sports can be organised without the 'proper gear'. Of course, certain activities are enhanced by having relevant equipment and facilities and others require the involvement of trained professionals to avoid danger. A youth worker who overcomes a fear of abseiling, however, may be a better role model for a similarly challenged young person than an 'expert enthusiast'.

Teamwork and achievement in an individual sport can both be valuable experiences for young people. Coping with pressure and disappointment as well as success are further beneficial outcomes. Most youth work may not be particularly appropriate for the development of 'serious' competitive athletes because of the emphasis on participation by all members of the group whatever their abilities. For those individuals who are able to achieve excellence in sports, youth work can provide a first step and the inspiration and direction required for further training. For all young people, participation in games and sport should lead to learning about taking responsibility, making choices and working with others as well as having a good time.

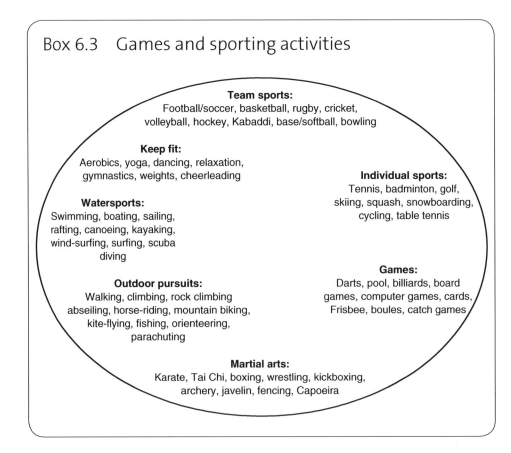

Box 6.3   Games and sporting activities

Team sports:
Football/soccer, basketball, rugby, cricket,
volleyball, hockey, Kabaddi, base/softball, bowling

Keep fit:
Aerobics, yoga, dancing, relaxation,
gymnastics, weights, cheerleading

Individual sports:
Tennis, badminton, golf,
skiing, squash, snowboarding,
cycling, table tennis

Watersports:
Swimming, boating, sailing,
rafting, canoeing, kayaking,
wind-surfing, surfing, scuba
diving

Games:
Darts, pool, billiards, board
games, computer games, cards,
Frisbee, boules, catch games

Outdoor pursuits:
Walking, climbing, rock climbing
abseiling, horse-riding, mountain biking,
kite-flying, fishing, orienteering,
parachuting

Martial arts:
Karate, Tai Chi, boxing, wrestling, kickboxing,
archery, javelin, fencing, Capoeira

Involving young people in planning for games and sporting activities can increase accessibility and full participation. The wide range of young people's skills, abilities and preferences need to be taken into account to ensure that as many individuals as possible can participate. Addressing issues of exclusion requires consideration of potential participants' needs rather than simply those of an existing group. For example, thinking about how a young person using a wheelchair would play a game can help suitable alterations to be made where required. Accessibility is usually improved by planning some cooperative and team activities as well as competitive and individual ones.

Young people will be drawn to different sports, games and facilitators, often on a personal level. Keeping an eye on whether young people are enjoying the activities is essential to youth work practice. A youth worker's enthusiasm should not cloud their judgement about the young people's level of interest. For example, a youth worker keen on basketball may participate in pick-up basketball games in the park that develop into local tournaments. Some groups develop into highly competitive teams, but this should depend on the individuals' interests. A different group of young people may prefer to carry on in their own less structured way.

Some young people are clearly motivated to be involved in physical activity and some perform well, whilst others may require encouragement and support to develop their motivation, confidence and skills. A variety of other factors can affect interest in sports, including self-image and prejudice. Young people who feel that they are the wrong size, gender or shape may be encouraged to take up physical activities through the provision of different options and role models. Issues that can arise include bullying and exclusion when a competition goes wrong or feelings of inadequacy that arise from losing. Part of the role of a youth worker is to ensure that less able or confident members are not left out or abused, to provide alternative and perhaps less typical images of individuals enjoying a wide range of sports and to support a positive approach to competition and 'having a go'. (See Practice Example 6.6 that illustrates this role.) Usually the choice of a sporting activity depends more on the young people's enthusiasm than on a youth worker's interest. Young people who have been excluded or self-excluded from participation due to negative stereotypes or poor self-image may be inspired to participate by a youth worker with a genuine enthusiasm for a sport. The experience may enable them to break free from these images and begin to enjoy the exercise and even the competitive elements.

Youth workers emphasise those aspects of activities that relate to youth work principles, such as participation and anti-oppressive practice, to enhance young people's enjoyment and self-esteem. Work with groups often requires a youth worker to promote awareness and appreciation of everyone's contribution. Physical activities and games can provide more structured opportunities for groups to interact and develop confidence. Through team sports, young people learn to cooperate and work together in planning their tactics, organising competitions and trips to other facilities. Similar benefits can emerge from the individual sporting activities undertaken as a group. Community involvement through parents and other members of the community acting as coaches, cheerleaders or uniform and transport providers can further enhance a project. Practice Example 6.7 shows how a martial arts cooperative developed to promote a youth work approach to sporting activities.

A young women's football project

I worked with a young women's group where I carried out some research and found that many young women were not engaged with sport, particularly those viewed as 'boys' sports'. They decided to hold a residential to provide opportunities for young women to try out different sports. The women-only environment seemed to make them less embarrassed. Even though many had not kicked a ball before, the most popular sport proved to be football.

A women's football project was formed and regular sessions started at the beginning, for example on how to kick and pass. Help came from professional sports coaches from the two local professional teams. Sometimes increased competitiveness and aggression lead to sexist comments amongst each other, such as 'you kick like a girl!' During the project, the young women started to challenge these and other stereotypes about 'girls' sports' and 'boys' sports'.

The group found out about an international women's football competition and decided that they wanted to go. They fundraised for nine months and held cake sales, car boot sales, karaoke and band nights, and a sponsored triathlon with cycling, swimming and a 5-kilometre run, and made funding applications with the help of youth workers. Getting a passport, flying across the Atlantic, seeing new places and feeling homesick were all new experiences for some of the members. The young women had never been outside their own city before. At the event, the team didn't win any matches but were presented with a trophy for sportswomanship.

One year later, two of the women have joined a local women's football team and two others now go to the gym regularly. Many of the young women cut down on smoking and drinking and began to do other types of regular exercise. They are producing an information leaflet about healthy eating and exercise for other young women. The group runs fortnightly football sessions and has played in some tournaments. They are also planning some sports taster sessions next year in wrestling and cheerleading! Additional benefits have been life skills and organising skills, such as getting to practice and to the airport on time, as well as a massive increase in self-confidence and a greater understanding of their own bodies and healthy living.

Martial arts for everyone

Several individuals interested in different approaches to martial arts used the same community facility to train and provide exhibitions relating to their field. Chance conversations about mutual interests gradually led to the development of ideas about how the centre could be used more effectively as a resource for young people, martial artists and martial arts educators. A vision for the centre emerged as a place where young people could explore different sports and activities within a holistic approach to assisting young people to develop into more productive members of society. The ideas developed because the martial artists recognised a potential role for martial arts that not only developed physical and mental skills and stamina, but enhanced leadership qualities and life choices.

A conference or meeting was called and parents, teachers, coaches and artists were invited to discuss core values for the centre. The themes that emerged included the need to:

- provide a space for young people to grow and mature
- focus on learning and development as well as success in competitions
- work with all young people regardless of mistakes, lack of experience or ability, or identity
- link the sporting challenges of strength, purpose and confidence, focus and dedication, time management and cooperation to all aspects of life and life choices.

The strategies were:

- to provide leadership training through mentoring youth in leadership roles
- to develop women in coaching roles
- to move away from a coach-centred model towards an athlete-centred approach aimed at helping all participants improve their performance over time.

PLAYING GAMES

As Singer (in Goldstein, 1994) says, play is valuable for a number of development areas.

I propose that children's play, with its repetitive and exploratory characteristics, represents not only fun but a critically important feature of their development of cognitive and emotional skills. Considering the various forms play takes, it is easy to identify the possible value of sensorimotor games for enhancing physical skills and even of games with rules for modelling early forms of orderly thought or even morality. (1994: 6)

Playing games also performs a number of functions in youth work: games can be fun, provide an excuse for interactions and be used to raise a number of issues. The competitive nature of sports and many games suits some young people and youth workers more than others. Some young people thrive and learn more from a disciplined approach, whilst others find this constricting or even frightening. In a similar way, some young people find much needed safety and security with a youth worker who provides a clear structure for learning particular skills and developing strength, whilst others need more freedom. Different youth workers and different activities can provide a range of options, from those who constantly alter the rules and those who have no rules to those who insist on playing by them. Valuing these differences within a team and a programme can help young people to explore and find activities that they enjoy.

A wide range of games can be used to encourage an alternative approach to play without the pressure of points, rules, winning and losing that inhibits some people's enjoyment. In some cooperative games, such as parachute games (for examples, see Le Fevre, 2007), creative thinking, participation and enjoyment are clearly valued. The competitive elements of a particular game can also be circumvented by constantly switching team members or refusing to count the score. A fiercely competitive young person playing a more anarchic game might be initially frustrated and then begin to enjoy more free play (see Practice Example 6.8).

Games with no rules

We used to have games of 'running bases' where the young people ran between two points like cricket players – but without any batting – whilst two catchers continuously threw an object back and forth. The runners could be 'tagged out' by the catcher holding the object by tagging (touching) the runners before they reached the base. Initially, the young people thought that the point was for the runners to keep score of how many runs they made and how many outs. We kept randomly adding points to some runners' scores ('there's two more points for you for running in a zig-zag line') and taking them off others ('that's minus two points for wearing a red shirt') and we never made anyone stop. So the game would last as long as they could keep running and we kept throwing. There was usually at least one who wanted to know who was winning and what score everyone had and we would just tell made-up numbers in response. The great thing about it was that if you got the right atmosphere, everyone was involved at their level and tried really hard – because there was a notion of competitiveness – but winners and losers didn't exist because we showed no interest in the rules.

Board games and computer games as well as pool tables are staple provision in much centre-based youth work. Many young people find them enjoyable and the activities are generally viewed as harmless entertainment (although most organisations will monitor internet and computer games for appropriateness). Games that can be played by several players simultaneously have similar benefits to sporting activities in relation to providing opportunities for communication and cooperation. Any arguments and disagreements, which are also part of the 'package', can be learning experiences as well. Allowing young people to find their own ways to share equipment and resources is part of youth work. The degree and type of intervention from youth workers in relation to young people's interactions and decisions about taking turns and clearing up does vary. Most youth workers will step in so that bullies are not allowed to dominate all of the time. However, some will step in simply to be a presence and play alongside the young people for a period; others may hold a discussion about ground rules (see also Chapter 8).

ESSENTIAL SKILLS FOR ORGANISING ENJOYABLE ACTIVITIES

- Planning outdoor work
- Organising excursions and expeditions
- Working indoors
- Developing arts activities
- Using drama and role play
- Planning games and sports
- Playing games

📖 FURTHER READING

Rogers (2011a) has over a hundred ideas for games to be used on the street or elsewhere. See also LeFevre (2007) and Christiano (2002).

Boal (2002) has a range of ideas for using drama games and discussion of the Theatre of the Oppressed as an approach to exploring local solutions to issues.

Collins (2010) examines sports development and looks at the different 'use' of sports in different settings/roles.

For some interesting materials about involving young people in evaluation of enjoyable activities as well as some of the benefits of youth participation, see Flores (2008). *The Art in Peacemaking* (Brunson et al., 2002) provides some ideas for using art in conflict resolution education.

7

WORKING ON ISSUES

Youth workers develop their understanding of the realities of young people's lives, particularly their experiences of unequal privilege and societal oppression in order to undertake youth work that develops young people's awareness of their options and opportunities to make changes. This chapter looks at a planned and proactive approach to issue-based and anti-oppressive practice in the immediate, short, medium and longer terms. As Buddha has been quoted 'Like a beautiful flower that is colorful but has no fragrance, even well spoken words bear no fruit in one who does not put them into practice' (cited in Cleary, 1994: 21).

Applying an understanding of oppression to practice enables youth workers to promote transformations in attitudes, practices and structures.

IDENTIFYING OPPRESSION

Ongoing anti-oppressive practice and issue-based youth work attempt to address the effects of inequalities by focusing on specific issues or targeting particular groups to support changes in young people's lives and in society as a whole. The values and principles of youth work mean that practice aims to challenge and change attitudes and practices that limit young people's lives and to offer opportunities that otherwise may be unavailable. Youth work can address some of the effects of inequalities arising from the often unearned privileges enjoyed by some individuals and groups that are denied to others. Perceptions of difference can lead to prejudicial attitudes, negative discrimination and oppressive practice by individuals and groups in powerful positions over others who are excluded from equal access to opportunities. Perceptions of identity are particularly contentious, although lifestyle choices, as well as other events outside of an individual's control, can also be misconstrued as indicators of worth. Oppressive forces, such as the examples in

Box 7.1, can prevent basic needs from being addressed, such as safety, security and love (discussed in the previous chapter). Working on issues in youth work means that the profession aims to have a transformative function in young people's lives and communities to address oppression on a range of issues.

Box 7.1   Examples of oppression

Individual, societal, and structural oppression can negatively discriminate in relation to:

- identity, such as class or caste systems, sexism, racism, heterosexism, ageism and ableism
- ethnicity, such as xenophobia and nationalism, certain religious groups, speakers of other languages or people from other countries
- certain lifestyles, perceived by powerful individuals and social structures as anti-social, such as single-parent families, young parents, large families, street workers, communal living
- difficult circumstances, including individuals who are:
  - o asylum-seekers, refugees, economic migrants
  - o homeless, residents in a particular area or in temporary or inferior accommodation
  - o in poverty, on low wages or having low economic status
  - o in care, in prison or in a remand centre
  - o with high levels of health, drug and alcohol problems or substance users and abusers
  - o experiencing mental health problems, such as low self-esteem, tendencies to suicide and self-harm, and anorexia or bulimia
  - o sufferers of physical illness, i.e. those who are chronically ill or have mobility problems
  - o less successful in relation to academic achievements.

Youth workers develop clarity about the oppressions that marginalise certain groups in society through reflection on power. Unless individuals are supported through wealth and/or political power, the effects of their negative perceptions of others would rarely extend beyond their immediate circle. Their oppressive power would be restricted to personal oppression of known individuals, through, for example, domestic abuse or bullying of peers. Societal and institutional oppression involves power being exercised in discriminatory ways that affect the opportunities, experiences and self-esteem of individuals from marginalised groups. Discriminatory attitudes and practices are embedded in and promoted through legal, political and educational systems that create and oppress marginalised groups throughout society.

Recognising oppressive practice and distinguishing situations where individuals may be able to exert more control can assist youth workers and young people to understand and make choices about their responses to oppression. Identifying when and how their actions may be able to make a difference to how they are perceived or treated can assist them to make life choices that are both positive and practical.

Thompson's (1993) 'interactive' model of overlapping circles illustrates how cultural, structural and personal oppressions are interrelated as well as distinct (see Box 7.2 for an example of how this can be applied). Structural oppression is exerted by society's powerful institutions, such as legislation, the media and global economic forces. Cultural oppression arises from social attitudes generally accepted by populations and communities. Although political lobbying or democratic elections may be examples of how cultural consensus can effect changes in legislation, the oppressive strength of structural oppression is generally more significant. Some aspects of personal or individual oppression relate to structural and cultural forces; some are due to individual experiences. Box 7.2 provides an example of the relationship between sources of oppression where an individual experiencing personal oppression through domestic abuse from a violent partner may also be culturally oppressed by a consensus notion in the community that 'blames the victim', and be structurally oppressed by the lack of alternative housing or protection. Taking personal responsibility to counter oppression may need to take into consideration the varied forces at work.

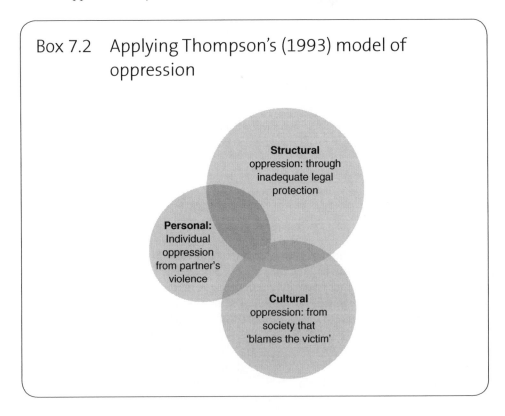

Box 7.2   Applying Thompson's (1993) model of oppression

Structural oppression: through inadequate legal protection

Personal: Individual oppression from partner's violence

Cultural oppression: from society that 'blames the victim'

Applying this analysis could involve looking at the effects of 'culture' or social attitudes in communities and the structural oppression of discriminatory legislation or political policies on young people. Identifying the relationship between certain negative experiences and social constructions can assist young people to construct alternative perspectives based on new interpretations of what is going on around them. For example, a young woman unhappy about her appearance may find it helpful to consider the media's role in defining very limited notions of beauty. Listing the powerful women who do not conform to these notions, including celebrities, politicians, business executives as well as mothers, youth workers and good neighbours, can be illuminating. Highlighting media practice as oppressive and sexist can support the young woman's further research to find out how women overcome this structural oppression. The process should be facilitated so that young people do not feel hopeless about oppression and its effects, but use their new understanding of reality to take appropriate responsibility for addressing the consequences.

The challenge for youth workers is to bring an anti-oppressive perspective to their practice without resorting to one-way communication that undermines their relationships with participating young people or colleagues. Youth workers aim to be involved in mutual learning, not teaching or training, and share information rather than tell others what to think. Finding effective methods of not colluding with discriminatory attitudes or practice often requires an alternative perspective to be presented. While some youth workers can adopt another persona and 'take off their hats' when associating with friends and family, most find that ignoring racist jokes or tolerating homophobia becomes impossible whether they are on or off the job. An anti-oppressive approach generally becomes part of all interactions, whether with young people, members of the community, other youth workers, managers or funders, other professionals, friends and/or family members. Retaining a positive, participative and anti-oppressive approach to practice must be part of the process of addressing issues. Having a range of possible responses, some of which may be more appropriate in specific situations than others, can be helpful.

WORKING AT DIFFERENT LEVELS

Just as oppression operates at different levels, anti-oppressive practice includes work with individuals, groups, organisations and societal structures, as well as work on the youth worker's own professional self-development (see the table in Box 7.3 for some examples). Although prejudices will be similar, varying levels of power and control mean that anti-oppressive practice will depend on the level of work being carried out. For example, a youth worker's capacity to affect a change of attitude within young people could be quite straightforward. Welcoming and involving someone from a group that has been traditionally excluded from participation can challenge young people's misconceptions about individuals from that group. Meeting someone whose identity, lifestyle or experiences they had negatively stereotyped and observing the youth worker's actions can transform young people's attitudes. A model of practice for young people, colleagues and the organisation could be quickly provided. On the other hand, anti-oppressive practice to create sustainable change in the organisation or society as a whole generally requires more in-depth or long-term strategies. The organisational and societal culture may exclude individuals from that group from employment opportunities or decision-making processes. Changes at organisational level would require other youth workers to be involved as well as external agencies; whilst structural changes would need campaigns and other forms of political support.

Box 7.3 Anti-oppressive practice at different levels

	Examples of anti-oppressive practice
Individuals In the community, members of groups, colleagues, other professions	Reach out to new members; target marginalised, detached or excluded individuals; raise awareness of issues and provide alternative perspectives; promote positive images and role models; recognise contributions and alternative experience; discuss options and support participation in new experiences.
Groups Of young people, community groups, working groups	Initiate, support and develop accessible and welcoming groups; reach out to under-represented groups; enable participation of marginalised individuals in groups; facilitate communication, stimulate thinking about issues and develop issue-based activities; respond to oppressive language, attitudes and practices; pass on information about marginalised groups, establish anti-oppressive ground rules, promote interactions (excursions, sporting events, festivities) with other groups to widen experience.
Organisations Employing agencies, networks, forums	Initiate and value responses and challenges to oppressive and discriminatory attitudes and practice; develop targeted provision and allocate resources; ask questions, debate and make proposals; develop inclusive anti-discriminatory policies and procedures, widen participation in decision making, promote representative staffing, promote and provide awareness-raising information sessions for staff, share experience and joint work with other organisations representing different identities; encourage participation and feedback from a wide range of perspectives.

Social structures Educational, political and criminal justice institutions, the media, housing providers, commercial bodies and employers or religious bodies	Campaign, inform, challenge oppressive attitudes and practice; promote and provide alternative images and perspectives of marginalised groups; support young people's participation in decision-making organisations, particularly those from marginalised groups.
Own professional development	Discuss, read, use supervision, undertake training, attend conferences, network, seek out information and critical feedback from a range of sources and perspectives.

WORKING WITH INDIVIDUALS

One-to-one conversations with young people experiencing the effects of oppression can provide them with strengths to value themselves and their lives. When young people are listened to, they begin to articulate their genuine interests, goals and life plans. Young people are individuals with varying experiences and may benefit from different methods of raising their confidence and self-esteem. Some simply require that their aspirations are taken seriously and need information about potential options.

Some may be better able to deal with the 'slings and arrows' (Shakespeare's description of oppressive attacks) after exploring methods of handling themselves, including self-control and focusing on a goal. Others may benefit from seeing the differences between minor difficulties or short-term setbacks and more serious or longer-term problems. Two-way conversations and some flexibility can help youth workers to find an approach that works well with a specific individual.

Youth workers also work with individuals who have absorbed or internalised oppressive attitudes that they then impose on others. Youth workers are often well placed to form positive relationships with individuals who have been misled or have fallen into negative patterns of behaviour. Individual conversations can be a powerful way to find out what is behind a young person's discriminatory views and address some of the causes. Ignorance is a frequent cause of oppressive behaviour and many young people are not aware of the origins or meaning of the language or opinions that they express. Relevant information may change some young people's ideas or deter them from continued use.

A different approach may be required for work with individuals who are not ready or willing to change their entrenched views. Some individuals recognise and enjoy the power of their negative views or actions and may not be prepared to give them up. Many youth work organisations ban young people who become involved in fascism, gangs or other kinds of violence. Some youth workers will simply 'draw the line' at certain behaviour – either refusing to work with young people acting in certain ways or not allowing them to express their views. These approaches may protect other vulnerable members and could effectively control those individuals motivated by a desire to participate. Such acquiescence could be a positive exercise in self-control rather than evidence indicating a new position on oppressive behaviour.

Positive practice requires a range of approaches to address individual needs. Getting to know people from a wide range of backgrounds and experiences, enjoying the company of people who were previously unknown or feared, and learning about different histories and cultures can be effective tools for perspective transformation. Individual conversations with open and honest discussions about where certain negative ideas come from may also serve to open a young person's eyes. A young person may not recognise issues related to oppression until the opportunity to identify their own experiences of bullying or abuse, lack of opportunity or prejudice has an impact. Some may benefit from the knowledge that their reactions to situations, such as abuse, domestic violence or bereavement, may be common or expected. Recognising the effects of direct and indirect discrimination on marginalised groups may help to illuminate issues that may not have been clearly linked previously. Young people who experience stress, difficulties in pursuing educational and career opportunities and low self-esteem may appreciate opportunities to discuss them.

Anti-oppressive practice means working with young people in various situations so that they can identify their own, often difficult choices about managing changes in their lives. However, youth workers need to recognise the reality and extent of the changes that some individuals would need to make in their lives for this exercise to have any meaning. Having aspirations for alternative pathways and the wherewithal to take them may require individuals to completely change their circumstances. Some may need to move to a different area, find new friends, get a job, study for qualifications, escape addiction and/or face retaliation from a gang to make a fresh start.

DEVELOPING ONE'S OWN UNDERSTANDING OF OPPRESSION

Youth work that attempts to address these oppressive practices needs to be based on an understanding of oppression gained through analysis of experiences, observation and reading. Continuous professional development through supervision, critical feedback and research can assist youth workers to continue to develop their awareness and practice related to oppression. Youth workers who are not directly affected by issues may have to work hard to identify the implications and fully understand what young people who are directly affected are saying. To use Macpherson's (1999) description of 'unwitting' racism: 'unfamiliarity with the behaviour or cultural traditions' of individuals and groups by a youth worker whose 'lack of understanding, ignorance or mistaken beliefs' can lead to 'well intentioned but patronising words or actions' (Macpherson, 1999: 6.170). Considerations of identity in relation to the various oppressions as well as anti-oppressive practice need to be part of 'locating self' (see Chapter 4). Professional practice requires recognition of how identity affects thinking and perspectives, as well as how others perceive them. Unless proactive efforts are made to recognise an issue, learn more about it and address it through policies and practice, youth workers can become part of the problem rather than the solution. As Eldridge Cleaver said in his 1968 speech as a Black Panther, 'What we're saying today is that you're either part of the solution, or you're part of the problem' (1969: 32).

Recognition of the lack of positive images and knowledge of different groups can provide a particular arena for practice. Individuals from both dominant and oppressed groups are often deprived of the rich and varied knowledge of cultures that are different from the mainstream. Young people and youth workers may not know much about marginalised groups whose history and cultures are not taught in schools, represented in the media or valued by political and social leaders. Some youth workers undertake research with young people to find out about diverse groups and to address gaps in educational systems or individuals' learning from those systems. Mentoring may also provide relevant informal education and role models.

Separate lives and experiences can also create divisions between different groups that youth work may be able to address. Fear, enhanced through lack of contact and negative images, can divide communities, inhibit 'cross-cultural' communication and prevent mutual understanding. Inappropriate actions or ignorance of customs can also cause unintended offence. 'Cultural competence' or confidence in cross-cultural interactions or a 'valuing diversity' approach that accepts and respects differences are potential frameworks for practice in these areas.

Youth workers who focus on oppression and the effects of personal, cultural or societal prejudices may not gain a true or real picture of the actual experiences of specific individuals or groups. In youth work practice, identifying the potential effects of discrimination means developing openness to others' experiences and an awareness of societal and cultural influences rather than seeking out disadvantage or inferiority. Information about a particular group's 'lack of achievement' in education is recognised as a consequence of various factors rather than any direct result of inadequacy. Generalising about the experiences of 'oppressed' or 'oppressing' groups due to concerns about unfair treatment could in itself be prejudicial. Recognising the existence of oppression, the strength of oppressive practices and then the specific contexts in which oppression takes place is not the same as having low expectations, which can lead to further discriminatory practices.

ADDRESSING SOCIETAL OPPRESSION

Individual youth workers have different experiences of social and political inequality and sometimes have conflicting ideas about ways to address these realities. Some youth workers become involved in campaigns for legal rights or arguments about changes to the law or organisational policies. Many youth workers find themselves challenging other organisations to improve their services for young people, particularly in relation to individuals who do not seem to be receiving adequate attention. Others believe that attempts to adjust an oppressive system are exhausting or even counter-productive. Some believe that although they may not be able to make systemic changes, working for individual success or improvement is worthwhile. Many youth workers have political or philosophical beliefs that underpin their work. For example, a belief that only conflict or revolution will enable everyone to benefit from global and social resources might sustain one youth worker, whilst another may have a religious vocation.

The natural impulse of caring adults is to protect children or young people in difficulty. The realities of oppressive and unequal circumstances mean that even well intentioned steps do not always have the desired results. For example, it is not uncommon for abused and neglected young people to find themselves further abused in foster 'care'. An innate sense of responsibility and legal requirements for ensuring young people's safety often mean that professionals attempt to take positive action when young people reveal issues related to basic human needs, such as safety, hunger, homelessness or burdensome care responsibilities. Youth workers sometimes need to recognise the boundaries of their practice and the limitations of their role. Working with young people to consider their options is the role of a youth worker, and unless there are very good reasons for an alternative approach, the young person should make the decision about which route to take. (See Chapter 9 for more discussions about different roles.)

HAVING A PLANNED APPROACH TO ISSUE-BASED PRACTICE

Issue-based practice requires youth workers to develop appropriate responses to issues that arise through action and reflection. Applying Lewin's (1946) spiral process provides a structure for a planned approach (see Box 7.4). Practice starts with a general idea about the need to address a particular issue. The issue is examined carefully and researched to devise an overall plan. The next step is deciding on appropriate action or actions, for example putting certain policies and/ or practices in place. Immediate, short-, medium- or long-term action is undertaken. Monitoring and evaluation of the action could identify further issues requiring a response. So the spiral of steps: planning, action and evaluation, continues. Involving participants and individuals directly facing the issues assists the practice in maintaining relevance.

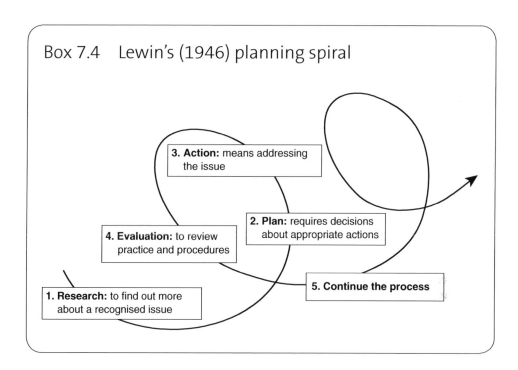

Box 7.4 Lewin's (1946) planning spiral

3. **Action:** means addressing the issue

4. **Evaluation:** to review practice and procedures

2. **Plan:** requires decisions about appropriate actions

1. **Research:** to find out more about a recognised issue

5. **Continue the process**

Appropriate responses to evidence of oppressive attitudes or practices will vary according to the situation and individuals concerned. The context and severity of oppressive attitudes, practices or policies, will affect decisions about whether an immediate response is necessary and/or whether a longer term action would be more effective or relevant. Some issues or incidents demand a quick remark, question or discussion. Alternatively, a different time or place may present a more appropriate opportunity to make a point that will be heard fully. An appropriate response may require some further thought. The effectiveness of an intervention might be enhanced through prior research to check facts, discussion in supervision and/or design of a relevant argument or exercise. Some work would require a longer-term project or strategy to be developed, for example informal education to raise awareness of a particular issue or collective action to demand change. Youth workers need various ideas and strategies to take the initiative for a proactive approach to promote anti-oppressive awareness and understanding.

RESPONDING IMMEDIATELY

A situation for immediate action might be one that could be dealt with quickly. Perhaps the attitudes displayed are not overt or have not had significant impact on anyone present. A quick response that clarifies the youth worker's position or that indicates their disapproval may be sufficient to lessen or remove the effect of what has been said. Responses could include a snappy one-liner to contradict what someone has said, a short outline of a different viewpoint or perspective, or a joke; or a question to provoke alternative thinking. A response can be delivered in a humorous or thought-provoking manner rather than as a negative put-down. Apt examples could be collected as a 'tool kit' ready for use the next time a similar situation arises and may prove flexible enough to be used with young people, members of the community, other youth workers, managers and other professionals, as well as friends and family. Through trial and error, research, discussion and evaluation, an experienced youth worker collects a sizeable range of responses to access in response to different situations. Similarly, an increasingly sophisticated set of 'templates' to diagnose a situation that may call for a particular response is developed (Boreham, 1988). Box 7.5 contains some examples of different types of immediate responses that could be made to oppressive remarks or behaviour.

Box 7.5   Examples of immediate responses

Thought provoking	How would you react if...?
	What if I told you that...?
Opinionated	In my opinion...
	I think that you'll find that...
Probing	Why do you think...?
	Do you really think that...?
Signposting	You could have a look at this leaflet that explains...
	Why don't you have a talk with so and so? She used to think the same way as you.
Humorous	That's an interesting point of view. I'm not sure I've heard that said before. Tell me more...
Direct challenge	If you really think that ... then ...
	You need to re-think that statement again carefully.
	Imagine what you would do if someone said that about you.

Whilst humourous and thought-provoking responses might be used in any setting, the opinionated and probing ones may be more effective once mutual respect has been established. Sign-posting is useful when someone has begun to listen. A decision to challenge directly may be based on recognition of the severity or power of an individual or event. Varied responses, such as those in the examples in Box 7.6, may also be more effective than a 'broken record', which can lose meaning.

> ## Box 7.6   Responses to heterosexism
>
> Heterosexist attitude
>
> Lesbian and gay people could just keep it to themselves. They don't have to tell everyone what they do.
>
> Possible responses
>
> - So you think that a young person would volunteer to get a hard time from their friends?
> - Straight people talk about their boyfriends or girlfriends, kiss in the street, dance, get married, go on holiday together. Why should lesbian and gay people have to hide?
> - Most lesbian and gay people do keep their relationships and sexuality to themselves – and this kind of self-denial leads to high levels of suicide, drug use, dropping out of school, homelessness...
> - Most people know about their sexuality when they are 5 years old. Do you really think a 5-year-old shouldn't be able to talk about this?

CHALLENGING LANGUAGE

A lack of clarity about oppression means that some youth workers fall into a trap of thinking that anti-oppressive practice is just about challenging young people's use of language. An inordinate amount of time is spent rebuking young people for using 'oppressive' words, whilst simultaneously worrying about the negative effect that this constant 'challenging' may have on developing positive relationships with the young people. Sometimes the terminology that offends the youth worker is not recognised as offensive by the young people, nor is it intended to be. Even the 'victims' being referenced do not perceive it as offensive, as the language is common parlance in the communities in which they live.

A typical situation facing youth workers is an expectation to challenge language. Young people, colleagues and society as a whole use words and phrases that convey prejudicial attitudes through offensive labelling that demeans and belittles. Rather than challenging everyone every time certain language is used, youth workers need to find a range of responses to suit the particular terminology, its use and the speaker. The offensive nature and the power of particular words to offend changes over time and can be quite subjective, depending on the setting or the identity, personal circumstances and lifestyles of the individuals involved.

A youth worker who recognises that some young people frequently use a word that is offensive is likely to find that being challenged every time they use the term would be ineffective and possibly counter-productive. The youth worker would need to identify whether the young people are aware of the word's meaning and effect, as well as their underlying attitudes towards the group that is apparently being labelled. What might be clearly a pejorative term to some people may be everyday language within other groups. A group that is aware of the meaning and is using the term to abuse or create an effect would require a different approach than a group that uses the word as a form of speech in a thoughtless manner or without intention to target a specific group. Appropriate responses could include pointing out its oppressive nature, raising the profile of the group being labelled, asking the group for appropriate alternative words and challenging the underlying attitudes.

Youth workers need to find ways to address oppressive practices that challenge thinking, raise awareness of the effects of oppression and support positive action. An intervention that points out or contradicts an oppressive remark or action requires considerable calm and confidence. Simply pointing out that something is offensive can create additional problems, such as defensiveness. Explaining why something is offensive may be difficult to articulate and may not come easily if the situation causes feelings of upset, anger or fear. Expecting others to recognise that their own actions have been oppressive can be rather ambitious. Putting someone on the spot to admit responsibility or guilt may not have a positive result. An analysis of the dynamics or causes of what happened can lead to a more appropriate response.

CHALLENGING BEHAVIOUR

The stress caused by experiencing oppression can lead to very challenging behaviour. Ideally, the respect that a youth worker shows young people will result in mutual respect, and the positive environment will foster engagement and participation rather than acts of rebellion, more common in highly structured and 'controlled' situations. Discussing and clarifying boundaries to behaviour and the reasons for any rules can reduce lack of compliance. A mix of calming and exciting activities can utilise energy positively. Sufficient staff to anticipate situations escalating and defuse arguments can also be helpful. However, young people can get involved in behaviour that is intentionally or unintentionally antagonising, particularly when external factors are affecting them. Youth workers generally develop a 'tough skin' and are not upset by the vocabulary that young people use or by what young people say if the words are addressed to the youth worker. Interventions would be initiated if the words humiliate other young people who are present, but, otherwise, responses may depend on circumstances and impact. Other behaviour may be unacceptable, such as fighting or illegal activity. Occasionally, a young person needs to be stopped from engaging in behaviour that is dangerous. Physical contact is best avoided.

A number of tools might be used to deter young people from behaviour that leads to exclusion from a centre or organisation, but temporary or permanent exclusions are possible 'last resort' sanctions, used as little as possible in order to increase the contact with young people who are experiencing difficulties in their lives. An immediate response might involve a change of activity to divert attention and energies elsewhere, particularly for the young people not directly involved. This presents more opportunities for focus on the individuals at the centre of the difficulty. Other options include taking an individual to one side for a chat about why their behaviour is getting out of control. Talking through the situation may help to identify possible causes and alternative interpretations. Some organisations have reparation and restitution procedures, where individuals are asked to make amends to anyone they have hurt or give something back.

Youth workers sometimes 'challenge' young people to understand the implications of their actions or to change their ways in order to reach their goals. Inevitably, a challenge establishes disagreement with what a young person is doing, so an explanation of the reasons for challenge is positive practice. Generally, challenges are made to maintain safety, raise important issues and promote changes to behaviour. Noticing risky or anti-social behaviour, for example, a youth worker may challenge the action rather than seeming to agree or collude by ignoring it. Challenging usually introduces a different perspective to a situation, but may also be a reminder of a previous conversation about ground rules or expectations of members. (See Box 7.7 for some advice from youth workers about challenging young people's oppressive behaviour.)

Box 7.7   Challenging behaviour

If you get to know the young people first, you will know when to intervene and what they will hear. Recognise that it is not always possible to change a young person's behaviour; it's a real achievement to get someone to stop and think for a minute. That has the potential for a long-lasting impact. And you don't need to challenge every instance; choosing to walk away is an option on both sides.

- Don't collude; you can express your choice not to be involved.
- Don't preach; you need to be heard.
- Get to know the young people; don't judge them.
- Don't over-react to behaviour; most young people are inclined to take risks.
- Separate the behaviour from the young person; you can react to the behaviour as wrong/risky/rude rather than label the young person as such.
- Choose your time and place for raising an issue. You can't challenge everything they do.

DESIGNING AN ISSUE-BASED PROJECT

Counteracting the negative messages that young people may have absorbed from the media, family and other social structures may require more planned attention. The alternative perspectives presented by a youth worker can transcend this restricted social conditioning with issue-based practice. Passing on information about other perspectives, such as feminism, a black perspective or social model of disability to colleagues or members of the community can begin to counteract societal and institutional negativity. Some youth workers may focus more on young people's practical needs arising from particular issues such as poverty or exclusion, whilst others focus more on raising awareness of individuals who perpetuate oppressive attitudes.

A short-term plan could include designing an activity, session or project to address issues that have been raised or that a youth worker has noticed. Engaging in relevant games, such as stimulating role plays or bingo and quizzes that reveal facts that challenge perceptions, can raise awareness and change attitudes. A young person may only require a piece of information from the youth worker or an opportunity to think through some options. In some settings or projects, a youth worker may only have a short and fixed period with an individual or group. Devising an activity or small project to raise awareness may be all that a youth worker can do. A typical reactive short-term plan to address an issue is to first listen and show interest, encourage analysis of options and then 'leave the door open' for further discussion. (See Practice Example 7.1 which illustrates a short-term response to oppressive practice that could have real impact on a young woman's experience.)

PRACTICE EXAMPLE 7.1

A short-term response

A young Muslim woman said that she was being harassed at school for wearing a niqab (a face-covering veil), so she was too distressed to go to school. The teachers seemed unsupportive and asked her to remove the garment, especially during science and PE classes. The youth worker allowed the young woman to tell her story and express her views whilst attempting to offer a listening rather than a judgemental ear. The youth worker encouraged the young woman to consider and evaluate various issues arising from her account, such as motivation, practical steps and their consequences. By the end of the conversation, the young woman was still planning to attend school despite her distress and said that she had a number of options to address her concerns.

The following week, the youth worker asked the young woman how she was and gave her the opportunity to talk more. The young woman indicated that she felt less distressed about attending school. The worker gave her some relevant news articles about students' experiences in challenging school policies and also about different types of religious dress. She also made sure that the young woman knew she could return to talk with her about these or any other topics.

Youth workers can play a proactive role in raising issues and do not always wait for young people to bring issues to their attention. A youth worker may provoke a discussion or plan an activity that is designed to raise a particular issue, particularly if it is known to be a local concern. If young people in the area are victims and perpetrators of crime, failing their school work or having difficulty finding employment, a youth worker cannot ignore these issues. While youth work activities may provide a safe haven from external dangers, young people's defences and alternatives also need strengthening.

A youth work project may be set up to develop young people's resilience, for example an anti-bullying campaign, a clean up the environment scheme or a project looking at self-image. Involving young people in discussions of issues that affect them provides opportunities for young people to share problems from a perspective of equality. Within a group of young people, shared experiences can be identified and discussed in order to develop understanding as well as options for ways forward. The 'solutions' can be based in a young person's reality and thought through from their perspective. Youth workers may have never experienced the issues faced by the young people with whom they work. What they can do in a particular situation is act with the authority and skills gained through experience.

A multi-agency response can be an effective way to address certain issues, particularly when other agencies or services have relevant resources. A multi-agency approach can allow each organisation or professional to contribute their particular area of expertise. Rather than, as is sometimes the case, 'straight-jacketing' youth workers to carry out services that might be better addressed by others, a multi-agency organisation that supports youth work to contribute their strengths may provide a worthwhile partnership (see Practice example 7.2).

A multi-agency approach

A youth worker was employed within a youth work organisation to work with young people on the issue of domestic violence. Research had identified that organisations in the area were dealing with a high number of cases of abuse and sexual exploitation and that they felt ill-equipped to work on the issue or discuss options with young people. After making contact with different groups of young people in schools, on the streets and in youth centres and networking with other agencies, the youth worker decided that a multi-pronged approach to the issue and its effects was required. Awareness-raising sessions were planned within the local schools and youth centres. A drop-in session for young women was developed at a local health centre. Girls and women-only sessions were held in the youth club. A programme for work with young men was developed with other youth workers. Partnerships with other agencies were established to share information and highlight good practice.

PRACTICE EXAMPLE 7.2

RAISING AWARENESS OF OPTIONS

Young people's prospects can be limited by their lack of awareness of different options, as well as by internalised oppressive attitudes that mean their readiness to take up certain options is undermined. Youth workers raise awareness of options through challenging prejudices and providing new experiences, which can prepare young people to widen their understanding of what may be available to them. Knowledge of potential opportunities and the practical steps that may need to be taken to learn new skills, gain employment or access better housing can stimulate both interest and action. Youth workers encourage young people to consider jobs or roles that they may not have envisioned for themselves. If necessary, young people can be encouraged to identify different ways to tell their friends, parents, employers or teachers about any mistakes they have made that have prevented them from attending so that returning to school or work is more feasible. Similarly, a criminal record, gaps in employment or failed exams are presented in applications or interviews as learning experiences. Youth workers need a range of ways to widen horizons to suit different needs and interests. (See Box 7.8 for some varied examples from different youth workers.)

Box 7.8   Ways to widen horizons

- Ask why certain jobs are associated with a specific gender, class or age group and ensure that examples of positive and 'non-traditional' images appear in materials, displays, information about jobs, careers, lifestyles and families.
- Network with other organisations to provide access to alternative resources and experiences, particularly those that challenge stereotypes.
- Discuss the source of attitudes and stereotypes, such as the influence of the media, education, friends, parents, community or individual choices.
- Express the point of view that the experiences or aspirations of parents, carers and communities do not necessarily need to define their choices.
- Find ways to introduce issues related to equality of opportunity in conversations about television programmes, local issues and national politics.
- Establish targeted work with particular groups to build confidence and promote discussion that might be stifled in mixed groups.
- Visit prisons and universities, art galleries and homeless shelters to experience at first hand what some options provide.
- Arrange mentors with shared experiences to provide alternative pathways.
- Focus on building specific skills to develop confidence through work experience, teambuilding and training.

A proactive approach to anti-oppressive practice is essential to youth work practice and can make a difference in young people's lives as well as to society as a whole. Addressing issues as they arise also requires attention to relationships in groups, which is addressed in the next chapter.

ESSENTIAL SKILLS FOR ANTI-OPPRESSIVE PRACTICE

- Identifying oppression
- Working at different levels
- Working with individuals
- Developing one's own understanding of oppression
- Addressing societal oppression
- Having a planned approach to issue-based practice
- Responding immediately
- Challenging language
- Challenging behaviour
- Designing an issue-based project
- Raising awareness of options

FURTHER READING

Read Thompson's (2011) analysis of the development of anti-discriminatory practice. Joseph et al. provide an excellent suggested list of reading:

> From Gandhi we can learn about non-violence, self-determination and political organisation; from Kwame Nkrumah we can learn about the independence movements, national youth movements and Pan-Africanism; from the Rani of Jhansi we can learn about leadership and resistance; from Martin Luther King we can learn about civil rights; from Mary Seacole we can learn about dedication and compassion; from Marcus Garvey we can learn about the principles of organising in the Diaspora; from Augusto Boal we can learn about the techniques and methodologies of art and theatre in tackling oppression. (2002: 26)

For an outline of Gandhi's views, see Brown (2008) and for Nkrumah, see his own collection (1964). Devi (2010) tells the story of the Rani of Jhansi. Carson (1988) has collected autobiographical writings by Martin Luther King, Jr. Seacole (1857) tells her story in her 'Wonderful Adventures'. Garvey (2005) has collected his speeches and writings and Boal (1998) outlines his analysis of the 'theatre of the oppressed' and using performance in a book about 'legislative theatre'.

8

SUSTAINING GROWTH
IN GROUPS

Working out disagreements, making decisions and addressing barriers to participation are ways of building cohesion and strength within groups and individuals so that they continue to grow and develop. This chapter looks at different ways to enhance communication and shared decision making that can create positive group work experiences that enable young people to enjoy, learn from and effect changes in their lives.

RECOGNISING GROUP PROCESSES

An understanding of group processes can assist a youth worker to recognise when to intervene in a group and when to step back. Some examples of group functions and how they might be tackled to support positive relationships are provided throughout this chapter, for example establishing agreements, making decisions, working with conflict, challenging attitudes and practices and reviewing group development and progress. The simple group process illustrated in Box 8.1 shows a cycle of debate and discussion that characterises most functioning groups. For some groups, the cycle can be smooth. A group may come together around an issue, question or interest and begin to establish the 'basics', i.e. their way of working by defining options or making planning decisions. The group may become more cohesive as new experiences are shared together. 'Bonding' may establish the group so that group members can confidently explore new territory or experiences, even when disagreements are part of their journey. When necessary, they can go back to group 'basics' to discuss how the group should work, roles and planning decisions, which enables them to review what took place and take on further new challenges. Returning to the 'basics' provides a reminder of group aims and purpose, an opportunity to make sense of any differences, incorporate any learning or simply find some basis of agreement. Some groups continue this cycle with minimal intervention.

Other groups or experiences may face or provoke greater fragmentation and disagreements. Members may respond to new ideas at different rates so that any new territory brings a greater challenge to the group identity. New experiences can expose uncertainty and conflicts. These groups may need to go 'back to basics' with greater frequency – perhaps every few minutes or every few sessions – to discuss 'ground rules' or their interactions. The group can then settle into working together to identify what the differences are or what the next steps should be. Working together may give them greater confidence or allow them to progress so that they can explore different perspectives in the next round of the cycle.

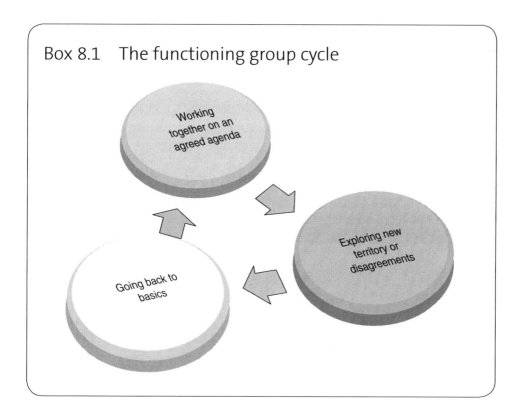

Box 8.1   The functioning group cycle

Working together on an agreed agenda

Exploring new territory or disagreements

Going back to basics

Poole (1981) likens group process to intertwined threads developing at the same time but at various rates. When the group is involved in the analysis of problems and solutions, gathering information and choosing solutions, a 'task thread' is being followed. When the issues and arguments are focused on the content of the group activities, the group is following a 'topical thread'. Concerns about inter-personal relationships between the group members means the group is concentrating on a 'relational thread'. 'Breakpoints' occur when a group switches focus from one thread to another through normal changes of topic in the conversation, adjournment or postponement, delays caused by going back over previously settled matters, or disruptions caused by conflicts or failures in communication. When the group develops in a coordinated way on all three threads at once, problems are identified and addressed. When the threads are not coordinated and the focus shifts repeatedly, an analysis of the process may assist the group to progress.

When changes occur, such as when challenges are made or new ideas are discussed, a group can be less sure about what to think or expect and has to explore new territory. This period can include great creativity, confusion and conflict. A youth worker may simply observe group changes and development, which is often an ongoing feature as new members come and go. Alternatively, the youth worker may provide a 'nudge' into the next stage or part of the cycle so that a group does not become 'stuck'. A residential, for example, could be used for a group to explore new experiences and territory together, or to have a meeting to discuss basic group functions and plans. Group interventions could include providing suggestions for the next stage, initiating opportunities for a change or facilitating an exercise to move a group on. Proactive youth work, such as finding out about interest in a new activity, allocating some funds for a day trip or bringing out some materials to stimulate a discussion, can motivate a group to take on a new challenge that they may not have considered previously.

Being able to identify patterns and changes in groups enables a youth worker to anticipate development and support positive change – as well as to decide when or whether to intervene. Tuckman (1965) describes stages of group development that typify cooperative teams (see Box 8.2 for Handy's (1999) interpretation of this). His theory was that if groups did not explore the stages fully, teamwork and achievements would be limited. The definitions can provide a useful framework for a group to consider when identifying and reviewing how they are feeling both about the group and the relationships in that group.

DECIDING WHETHER TO INTERVENE

Many youth workers will look out for opportunities to contribute ideas, assist negotiation or support individuals so that the group continues to develop. Some only intervene when asked or when information about the organisation needs to be shared. Others work more intensely, encouraging members to participate in project development and drawing out the quieter members. A group of young people that works well together knows what to expect from each other and from a youth worker so that relationships of trust can develop. Deciding when to intervene in a group depends on a range of factors, including the individual worker's style (see also Box 4.1 in Chapter 4) and the context of the group. For example, a drop-in group's relationships with each other and with the youth workers are generally looser than the more team-like bonding associated with a fixed term project, which may also be more closely facilitated by the youth worker. Many youth workers have a light

Box 8.2 Tuckman's (1965) stages in groups

Stage One: Forming

Some 'looked after' young people living in different types of care residences are invited to join a weekly session. Although more a set of individuals than a group, the young people follow the youth worker's lead in setting the scene. Disagreements may flare up but tend to be over quickly. Generally the members agree to talk fairly superficially about the purpose and content of future sessions, the name for a potential group and who should be invited to join. At this stage, the majority of members allow the more confident individuals' contributions to prevail.

Stage Two: Storming

The group goes through a period of more outspoken disagreements as members feel 'safer' to reveal themselves and previous unspoken rules about not delving into personal circumstances are challenged. Some personal hostility arises between young people who are in the care system due to court orders resulting from police arrests and those who are there due to family emergencies. The youth worker encourages mutual listening and respect so that the storming leads to greater honesty between members and more realistic norms. Storming can play a significant role in not only testing, but building levels of trust and acceptance in the group

Stage Three: Norming

The group settles into a regular pattern of working and is able to discuss and make decisions about appropriate levels of participation and what is expected from members in relation to openness, trust and confidence. Individual members continue to test the responses of others to their ideas and feelings and the youth worker may need to offer additional support to them. Generally, the group is in a period of growth and development that accommodates new challenges, such as new members, without being unduly disturbed.

Stage Four: Performing

As the Previous stages have been successfully completed, the group is at full maturity and is able to be fully and cooperatively productive. The members work together well to produce a booklet of 'arrival' stories – their first days in care – to share with new members. The youth worker provides information about resources and opportunities that continue to inspire and challenge the group to evidence how far they have come.

Stage Five: Mourning? Adjourning?

The group begins to break up as individuals become ready to move on and deal with new life challenges: some to new fostering or adoption arrangements, others returning to their families. Some members are unable or not ready to do this and stagnate – still needing the group for support. The youth worker encourages recognition for what has been achieved to engender and celebrate a positive ending for the group.

Source: Based on Handy's (1999) interpretation of Tuckman

touch in relation to getting involved in group relationships and development, and tend to encourage participation and sharing of ideas through example rather than instruction. Unasked-for interventions may be limited to responding to need, for example reminding a group about any previous agreements about bullying or oppressive behaviour, preventing harm or halting a fight. Most youth workers see a need to intervene when a group is unable to work together, negative behaviour is in danger of becoming a pattern or more vulnerable members are persistently excluded.

Establishing agreements

Whether group agreements about acceptable behaviour are unspoken or displayed on the wall, most youth workers communicate information about boundaries through their responses to young people. Some youth workers rely on self-presentation and the creation of a positive environment for practice. Others facilitate discussions about issues arising to establish 'ground rules' or group agreements. The process of agreeing 'do's and don'ts' can be a useful tool for stimulating thought and debate amongst a group of young people about how the group should work. The discussions can be used to start a group or referred to regularly as part of the ongoing process of group development. The agreements can play a key role in the induction of new members, fostering group relationships, planning the content of future sessions and establishing and reviewing the aims and objectives of the group (see Practice Example 8.1 for an example of some ground rules established by a group).

Youth workers often negotiate agreements with and between young people about the ways in which a group works and plan activities together. This consultation and cooperation provides young people with a positive stake in the activities and involves them in maintaining youth work aims and values. As youth work practice is informal and participatory, agreements are usually oral rather than written, flexible rather than rigid, and negotiated rather than imposed. Issues and practice are discussed and any actions are agreed upon by consensus. The process means that members understand and participate in group decisions and their implications.

PRACTICE EXAMPLE 8.1

Group 'ground rules'

- **DO** listen to each other
- **DO** allow others time to express themselves
- **DO** maintain confidentiality outside of the group
- **DO** think about what you are saying and doing
- **DO** let others know if you disagree
- **DO** include others in the discussions
- **TRY** to remain calm and don't over-react to comments
- **DON'T** think that someone else will do all the work
- **DON'T** expect everyone to agree with you

- **DON'T** be upset if all of your suggestions are not taken up
- **DON'T** interrupt or criticise
- **DON'T** be aggressive
- **DON'T** ignore other members of the group
- **DON'T** allow others to do any of the above without saying something

Agreements can be useful at different points in the life of a group. Some youth workers always start a new group or project with a discussion of ground rules so that members are included in the identification of how the group will function. The discussions can be used to establish boundaries of acceptable behaviour, such as defining appropriate relationships or interactions between members. A project-oriented group could identify issues related to timing of sessions, coffee breaks, keeping to agreed agendas, and what to do if missing a session. Some youth workers and groups keep the ground rules on display and refer disruptive members to them. More indirect reminders of the discussions and agreements that have taken place can work well with some individuals. Reviewing the guidelines both individually and collectively, especially when new members join, can keep agreements current and is a good basis for monitoring how the group is getting on. A review at the end of a group project can help to identify learning outcomes or group development.

Discussions of issues affecting participation are important exercises for developing a group. The support of the group in condemning certain behaviour and supporting rights to participate fully can be a powerful method of developing young people's confidence. Sharing experiences or opinions about issues such as bullying, abuse and assertiveness can strengthen the bonds between young people. Sometimes the issues have more relevance outside of the group. Young people may face racist abuse at work or their home life could be affected by alcoholism. Having the opportunity to discuss appropriate behaviour can be liberating (see Practice Example 8.2 for an example of a group agreement).

A group agreement

Everyone should welcome new members.

We don't have to agree with someone else's opinions.

We do have to respect each other as people.

We don't use abusive language or bullying behaviour.

We can each decide what we want to talk about in the group.

We all take turns washing up.

PRACTICE EXAMPLE 8.2

The process of establishing guidelines may be more important than the specific outcomes or rules themselves. Working with a group of young people to establish ground rules is a way of enabling participation and raising issues. Discussions about issues affecting participation and ways to address them can enable individuals to express their hopes and fears and establish a group identity. A ground rule may clarify human rights issues such as rights to privacy, to participate, to be free to express themselves or to be free from oppressive behaviour. Drawing up the guidelines is a useful way to discuss feelings about a group or programme and to develop a sense of common purpose. The process actively encourages participants to take responsibility for the direction of the group, the level of challenge taking place and the support that may be necessary (see Box 8.3 for some methods for establishing agreements).

Box 8.3   Establishing group agreements

- Provide a good example for members of the group in relation to listening, negotiating, sticking to agreements and fulfilling responsibilities.
- Facilitate discussions about ground rules.
- Discuss issues such as confidentiality, appropriate behaviour and relationships, rights and responsibilities.
- Ask the group to share their hopes and fears.
- Encourage young people to talk about their experiences of non-participation.
- Have everyone answer the question: 'How could I ruin a session for the members of this group?'
- Ask the group to identify barriers to participation and consider ways in which the group could address them.
- Organise role plays of situations in the group that members have found difficult to handle and discuss ways to address these.
- Promote bonding in the group through team activities, group or line dancing and cooperative games. Healthy relationships within the group enhance regard for others' feelings and rights.
- Review the aims and objectives with the group and talk about what hinders progress in relation to them.
- Break into smaller groups to make proposals that are then discussed in the larger group.
- Provide sheets of paper on a 'suggestions wall'.
- Ask individuals to draw up lists of 'I would like this group to ...' and 'I would not like this group to ...', and then share them.
- Have the group consider their rights and responsibilities as members.

When negotiating agreements with a group, it is important to distinguish any imposed rules made by the venue or organisation from those established by the group. Drawing up agreements about ways of working may be a useful time to highlight any regulations that already exist due to legal or organisational constraints. Some organisations deny participation rights to someone under the influence of illegal or prohibitive substances or carrying weapons. Fixed rules such as these are often imposed to protect staff and other members. In most organisations, these rules are stated as non-negotiable. Youth work organisations need to look carefully at any rules, particularly in relation to their target groups, to make sure that any restrictions are genuinely required or essential. Unnecessary statements that insult, irritate or suggest negative behaviour are clearly counter-productive and may interfere with good youth work practice (see Practice Example 8.3). A useful way to determine which rules are superfluous could be to consider what, if anything, might happen if a rule was breached or non-existent.

Boundaries to detached youth work?

I find that rigid restrictions saying that I shouldn't work with someone who is under the influence of drugs or alcohol can get in the way of good practice as a detached youth worker. While I agree that there is no point in carrying out a discussion with a young person who is out of control or unable to carry out a conversation, there are situations where I don't feel I can walk away. I feel that I have to consider the options available before I signpost a young person who needs safe refuge. If a young person is experiencing difficulties with dosage or dealers, I would want them to come to us rather than be deterred. If our target group includes alcohol or drug users, we have to be able to make contact with them. The right time and place to reach certain young people to discuss these issues, such as harm reduction or appropriate housing and health services, sometimes means being in the midst of a group that includes young people 'under the influence'.

PRACTICE EXAMPLE 8.3

RECOGNISING DIFFERENT WAYS TO MAKE DECISIONS

The ways in which decisions are made are part of the process of developing group and individual autonomy. Procedures, policies and practice may be discussed and decided upon by a whole group, part of a group or by one person (see the table in Box 8.4 for some examples of different types of decisions). Ideally, decisions would be by consensus and members would discuss their decisions so that all agree. However, varying levels of confidence and interest mean that not all members will participate in all decisions. A group may not even recognise that their actions are decisions or that individuals have been excluded from the process. Sharing an analysis of the group's methods for making decisions can provide opportunities for members to suggest improvements to both the process and the outcome. Alternatively, an intervention may be called for if a youth worker notices negative patterns emerging.

Box 8.4   Types of group decisions

Non-decisions	Decisions are avoided, ignored and/or left to someone else.
External decisions	Decisions are made by someone or a body outside of the group.
A leader's monopoly	One person makes the decision.
Minority decisions	A smaller group makes decisions from within a larger group.
Majority decisions	A decision is made on the basis of which option has the most support, despite other views being expressed.
Democratic decisions	All members have an equal right to participate.
Unanimous decisions	Everyone agrees on the decision made.
Consensus	Individual differences are thoroughly explored and negotiated to arrive at an agreement.

A decision-making process can be complex and contain elements of more than one type of decision. A youth worker needs to observe who is participating in discussions and whether minority interests are considered or understood by the group. In some groups, a decision which appears to have been made unanimously may actually have been engineered by a powerful bully or a loud-voiced minority. Dissenting voices, which could help decisions to be fully informed, may not be heard or encouraged. An analysis of membership participation and compliance can assist a youth worker to identify what is really going on in a group and how to intervene.

The process by which a group of young people makes and takes responsibility for decisions can be facilitated or supported by a youth worker. The degree to which a youth worker becomes involved will vary depending on the particular young people and the type of project. While a group of young people left to their own devices could make and learn from the same mistakes as any other group, in a youth work setting, a youth worker observes the process of decision making and will sometimes facilitate, intervene or mediate to move the group on. The aims are to enhance the learning experiences for the group and to make sure that youth work principles are addressed. For example, a youth worker may intervene to assist a group to make decisions with an inclusive approach rather than developing elitist factions or adopting bullying tactics. (Practice Example 8.4 outlines some groups' decisions and the youth workers' interventions.)

Deciding where to go

PRACTICE EXAMPLE 8.4

No decision? Or a decision to 'leave it to someone else'?

A group discussed at length which date would be best for an outing but was unable to agree which option was the best. Eventually the youth worker realised that the group could not handle the conflict or responsibility involved in making the decision and made the selection for them. Over the following weeks, the youth worker helped the group to develop their communication and negotiation skills through smaller decisions about the outing, which increased their confidence.

A minority decision or a unanimous decision?

An experienced group of members said that a particular activity was a good idea and the others 'went along with the flow'. Everyone seemed to agree that this was the best option, although only the more confident individuals contributed to the discussion. The youth worker recognised that the decision was far from unanimous and that a small group had felt pushed into compliance. The worker planned to make sure that sufficient opportunities were provided for the less confident members to participate in future discussions and decisions.

Is this a majority or a minority?

The members of the group discussed the benefits and drawbacks of several destinations and then voted on three options. Option 'C' had the most votes so the group was about to book to go to this destination. Then one member of the group complained that the majority had disagreed with this choice. The group realised that although option 'C' had the most votes, more members had voted for the other options – so the majority of the group had decided *not* to choose option 'C'. The worker used this opportunity to talk about the implications of voting as a method of making a decision and encouraged the group to think about the benefits of more discussions in order to develop a consensus.

A minority option that becomes a majority decision?

A group decided to vote on which residential venue to use. After the vote, one venue had a clear majority (over 65%) but a significant minority of the group supported one of the other options. When the minority pointed out that they would be unable to go on the outing if the majority option was selected, the others agreed to forgo their first choice. The group realised that a majority decision ignored the minority interests. In the end, they reached a consensus to choose the 'minority' option so that everyone could go. The worker did not need to intervene in this discussion and recognised the maturity of this group's development.

Consensus or chance?

A group spent a long time exploring different options and felt that a number of possibilities were viable and of interest. Some options were preferred by certain members of the group, but there was no clear majority. The group decided to select the option by rolling a dice – assigning an option to each of the possible numbers. The decision to use chance was agreed by consensus. Although the option was selected by 'chance', the method was agreed upon unanimously. Even if their preference was not selected, everyone went along with the outcome. The worker pointed out that this process had worked because members were prepared to be flexible about the outcome.

MOVING DECISIONS ON

Most groups need to experience some form of agreement on process or goals in order to make any progress in planning. The example of a group attempting to plan publicity for an event without having established agreement on how they are going to work or where they are going (see Box 8.5) illustrates how these questions will continue to get in the way of making any further decisions. Rather than progressing through decision-making stages (as indicated in the left-hand column), the group continuously returns to the 'basics' without any real advance to agreement or exploration of new territory. A youth worker may allow these circular discussions to continue or suggest that the group go back to stage one to establish some goals so that the group can progress. Helping a group to move on to make a decision could also include a reminder about time constraints (if applicable) or re-structuring the group by setting up a smaller sub-group to make the decisions. Thinking about the structure of the group can temporarily divert attention away from the questions that a group is finding difficult and is an alternative form of 'going back to basics'. While not recommending that groups always be diverted from difficult decision making, sometimes a break from a broken record is welcome.

Box 8.5   Not making decisions

Possible stages	Examples of incomplete decisions
1 Establishing goals: Okay, should we look at the plans for publicity now?	• Do we need publicity? I thought we were going to have a fun day just for us. • There's no point in planning any publicity until we know what the budget is. • I think we should make a start on what we want to do for publicity – then we'll know how much we need for the budget.
2 Clarifying objectives: So, who do we want to attract to this event?	• Do the numbers matter? It's no good if just a bunch of parents come – isn't this just for kids? • We need more members. Anyone who comes can get word around to somebody who may want to come.

Possible stages	Examples of incomplete decisions
3 Identifying and discussing options: So what are some of the ways you would like to attract people to the event?	• If we use leaflets, it's bad for the environment. • Should we see if we can get something on the buses? • It's a waste of time putting up posters; no one reads them. • I think we should use text messages and blogs. • Let's just have a go at designing some kind of logo that we can use in different ways.
4 Deciding on a way forward: So, what's next?	• Let's vote on it! • Voting's stupid. We don't have to have just one way to do publicity. • All we ever do in these meetings is just argue.

WORKING WITH CONFLICT

Assisting young people to find ways to deal with conflict and disagreement are important areas for youth work practice. Issues of power and control can be difficult areas for young people to comprehend or handle. A youth worker may work with young people to assist them to understand the sources of conflict, to articulate their point of view and to find ways to cope with the reality of inequity. Youth workers can provide young people with opportunities to gain a better understanding of their own ideas and perspectives as well as others' positions. At the same time, a youth worker needs to ensure that their own practice is clear, fair and equitable.

Recognising the difference between conflicts and disagreements can assist young people and youth workers to find ways of working together in groups. When the source of a conflict is a clash of principles, a continuous battle for limited resources or contested power where neither party will back down, resolution is generally impossible and needs to be recognised as such. Unless either or both parties are willing to give up or give away their side of the argument, which is unlikely in a conflict over values and principles, a conflict cannot be 'won'. Progress is generally only possible through avoidance or some form of accommodation, such as an agreement to disagree. In such situations, cooperative working will require an alternative focus away from continued battles over issues that are not possible to resolve.

Disagreements, on the other hand, may be worked out to arrive at some form of genuine cooperative progression. Negotiation, sharing information and improved relations can all help to move participants towards agreement or shared understanding. While a conflict involves opposing principles, disagreements can arise about issues, a situation or a relationship based on a misunderstanding, negative patterns or experiences. These patterns may dissipate with more positive interactions, better communication or different circumstances. Often, the various parties find that their positions are not such polar opposites and manage to find common ground.

LOCATING ONE'S 'DISAGREEMENT COMFORT ZONE'

Youth workers are individuals who react differently to arguments and disagreements. One youth worker with a high level of tolerance may perceive a particular incident as 'usual horseplay', whilst another might sense a potential for a violent outbreak. Some prefer to negotiate a resolution to any arguments that arise, whilst others have a more laissez-faire (leave it alone) approach. Experience and temperament clearly play a part in the type of response a youth worker decides to take, although understanding the sources of conflict (see the table in Box 8.6) can assist the development of a more calm and considered approach.

Box 8.6   Sources of conflict or disagreement

Area of difference	Possible causes	Possible ways to address
Perspectives: groups that refuse to cooperate with each other, individuals that constantly fight	• Conflicts between value systems, religions, ways of life, ideologies, beliefs • A lack of understanding or knowledge of the other's perspective • A history of interpersonal conflicts and disagreements, such as membership of opposing gangs	• Create an inclusive environment that welcomes all values and perspectives • Allow parties to disagree; point out that resolution on certain issues is not possible or necessarily desirable • Identify areas of commonality and don't focus on differences • Explore differences without judgements about right or wrong • Concentrate on interests rather than positions • Discuss the origins and effects of prejudice and stereotypes • Encourage working together on an agreed and common goal
Interpersonal relationships: individuals who don't like each other and refuse to work cooperatively, fighting	• Previous arguments • Differences in style, preferences, interests • Competitiveness • Misunderstanding • Disagreements about decisions	• Encourage members to accept that friendships are not essential for cooperative work • Listen to both sides; encourage them to listen to each other; encourage both to focus on what is being said rather than who is saying it

Area of difference	Possible causes	Possible ways to address
Interpersonal relationships *(Continued)*		• Identify whether the positions are misunderstood, conflicting or just different • Use ground rules or group agreements to govern the group • Provide alternative activities, such as games, that can build and develop communication between members • Find other avenues for cooperative working, such as physical or artistic activities • Encourage the group to identify and address the issues • Discuss the effects of being misunderstood or stereotyped
Intrapersonal dilemmas: an individual's repetitive negative behaviour, such as withdrawing or domineering	• Individual insecurity or inability to communicate • A history of abuse or abusive relationships • Lack of opportunities to exert power elsewhere • Personal crises or uncertainty	• Use exercises that build up individual confidence rather than expect group cohesion • Provide opportunities for individuals with similar concerns to meet and find common ground • Identify whether the behaviour is a 'cry for help' by providing opportunities for one-to-one conversations
Structural barriers or inhibitors: such as competition over actual or perceived unfair treatment	• Unfair treatment • Unequal distribution of resources or ownership • Lack of transparency about decisions and decision-making; • misinformation, different interpretations of information • Organisational culture or procedures	• Clarify procedures and information and find ways to share information and enhance communication • Alter the roles within power structures or assign roles to new individuals • Provide suggestions for changes in the ways that decisions are made • Widen the group's knowledge of opportunities and access to alternative resources • Provide a change of environment or experience to enable change to roles and patterns

THINKING ABOUT EXTERNAL INFLUENCES

An awareness of external forces or influences and how they can affect individual and group behaviour, as well as interactions, can assist a youth worker to anticipate disagreements or physical demonstrations of stress. A range of external events and changes in individual families, as well as in the community as a whole, can lead to disruptive behaviour in a group. A new leader may take charge of a group of bullies; unemployment in the area could increase; a family member may be imprisoned. The effects of these external events can reverberate in youth groups. In organisational analysis, such external changes in political, economic, social, technological, legal and environmental issues, coined 'PESTLE' forces (a framework outlined in Thompson, 1997 and illustrated in Box 8.7), demand attention in the form of organisational change and adaptation. In youth groups, the 'PESTLE' forces are similarly significant. An awareness of how external change can influence young people's moods and situations can assist a youth worker to recognise signals indicating that trouble could be brewing – and to take action to address the situation.

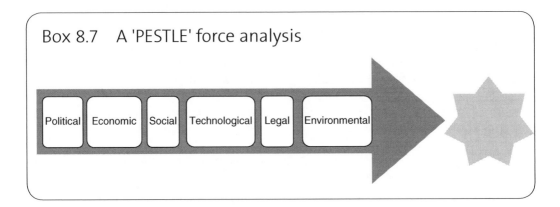

Box 8.7   A 'PESTLE' force analysis

Political | Economic | Social | Technological | Legal | Environmental

DEALING WITH VIOLENT DISAGREEMENTS

Many youth workers are worried about losing control of a situation that turns violent. The possibility that young people in their care or themselves will experience injuries can be a real concern. Anticipating danger is often a matter of 'reading the signs', a skill that develops through reflection on experience. The skill depends on an understanding of the dynamics of conflict, knowledge of the individuals and setting and an ability to recognise the potential for danger. Youth workers need to develop their understanding of situations or exchanges that could inflame an argument, incite violent reactions and deepen conflict. Getting to know young people and their individual 'boiling points' and stresses can take time. Unfortunately, some young people demonstrate their anger and frustrations both verbally and physically before a youth worker has a chance to get acquainted. Gaining an understanding of the cause of certain behaviour generally takes even longer. A useful method of identifying warning signs and the ingredients is reflection on events in supervision and discussions in team meetings (see Practice Example 8.5).

Responding to a fight

PRACTICE EXAMPLE 8.5

Two members of a group each wanted a turn on the pool table and started a fist fight. Even though the session still had nearly half an hour to run and clearing up usually only took about ten minutes, one of the workers stepped in and shouted at everyone to 'Clear up, it's time to go home – show's over – we can't have any violence here!'. The worker then put a hand on each protagonist's shoulder and said: 'Come on – apologise to one another or I'll knock your heads together – and we'll have to ban you.' This produced some mumblings from both parties. The two did not seem to be hurt and both seemed to be consoled with a free packet of crisps. The groups mostly dispersed and took extra time to clear up so that the session actually finished at the usual time. After the session, the team of youth workers reviewed the session to identify what had taken place. The other youth workers said that they would not have put their hands on the young people or used the same language. The group agreed that a greater presence around the pool table would be useful to review whether the young people wanted to initiate a different system for taking turns. They also discussed some options about what they should do in the future should a fight break out, and came up with the following list:

- Make sure that other staff members are aware of the situation.
- Keep calm.
- Depending on the level of violence and physical strength of the young people fighting, two youth workers might be able to step into the middle of the scuffle and tell everyone to disperse.
- A couple of individuals said that we should ignore the fight as the individuals needed to vent and express their anger. Unless it escalated and lead to injury, some rough play was perhaps harmless.
- When tempers were less high, each party could be asked to calm down and apologise to each other for their bad behaviour.
- Although the group agreed that closing early and exclusions should be avoided if possible, excluding one, both or everyone from the session either temporarily or permanently was a viable option.
- If the fight was not too involved, we could remind all concerned about the centre's ground rules about sharing and non-violence.
- If the incident was serious, a group investigation could be held into what had led up to the violent behaviour – either immediately or later on.
- The two individuals could be taken out of the situation, either together or separately, to discuss a way forward.
- In the slightly longer term, the group liked the following options:

- o Initiate some 'anger management' discussions about triggers, consequences and outlets for anger, either in the immediate, short, medium or long term.
- o Involve the whole group in a discussion about allocating time on the pool table, the ground rules or which of the above options to take.

ANALYSING THE 'INGREDIENTS' OF AN ARGUMENT

A confident youth worker recognises the benefits of discussing disagreements and conflicts. Although conflict is often portrayed as divisive or dangerous for a group, a good discussion about an argument or a conflict can assist recognition of important issues and help to bring a group together. The outcomes of such discussions in relation to a group or individual may depend on the factors that contributed to the differences being expressed. The discussion about deciding where to go in Practice Example 8.4, for instance, could have erupted and created irreconcilable differences between the young people and the staff. Evaluation and team supervision can lead to issues being handled more confidently. Identifying the 'ingredients' of an argument or a conflict can help to determine its nature and potential for benefit or harm (see Box 8.8 as an example).

Box 8.8   Analysing an incident

If you see an argument between some young people:

- Don't say too much. Listen to what is going on. Move towards the people arguing and present yourself calmly. Communicate with body language, tone of voice and a few words that you are interested in and respectful of the person(s) as people.
- Find out what's going on through observation. Don't ask too many questions and don't say anything unless you really know what's going on. It would be useful to notice:

  - o who is involved
  - o how they see the situation
  - o what seems to be in their way.

- Don't get involved or caught up in the conflict. If you must say something, share your own thoughts or observations, for example saying quite calmly: 'I can see that you are feeling quite angry at the moment.'
- Identify and consider a range of possible options, for example:

  - o acting, speaking, responding or doing nothing
  - o approaching the situation positively. You could tell them what you would like to happen, for example: 'I would like us all to still be here tomorrow having a conversation about our favourite football team.'
  - o getting them involved in a solution, for example: 'What would you do if you were in my shoes?'

- o changing the focus slightly: 'Right, so if we focus for a minute on the ideas here rather than the people, what do you think the other person(s) is saying to you?'
- Don't expect the argument to be resolved right away. A lot of arguments have all kinds of elements that may not be immediately obvious. The argument may be temporary or have deeply conflicting roots. Your objective is to enable the participants to express themselves without physical violence. This might be difficult in the short term.

REVIEWING GROUP PROGRESS AND DEVELOPMENT

Individual members' learning and group development occurs when a group learns from their experience; recognising these changes can help a group to feel positively about the group. Kolb and Fry's (1975) experiential learning cycle could provide a useful method of analysis of learning experiences whether by a youth worker or the group. Following a new experience, observations and reflections help to make sense of what has taken place. The shared experiences and reflections can help a group to come together. Articulating what has been learned can help to form new concepts for application to new experiences or experiments. In youth work, this could occur through planning, monitoring and review. The role of this process in working out differences, changes and learning can be invaluable in work with groups, whether or not the cycle is referred to overtly. The figure in Box 8.9 applies to Kolb and Fry's cycle to a group's reflection on their planning for a residential that went wrong when members did not identify sufficient funding for their trip.

ESSENTIAL SKILLS FOR DEALING WITH DISAGREEMENTS

- Recognising group processes
- Deciding whether to intervene
- Establishing agreements
- Recognising different ways to make decisions
- Moving decisions on
- Working with conflict
- Locating one's 'disagreement comfort zone'
- Thinking about external influences
- Dealing with violent disagreements
- Analysing the 'ingredients' of an argument
- Reviewing group progress and development

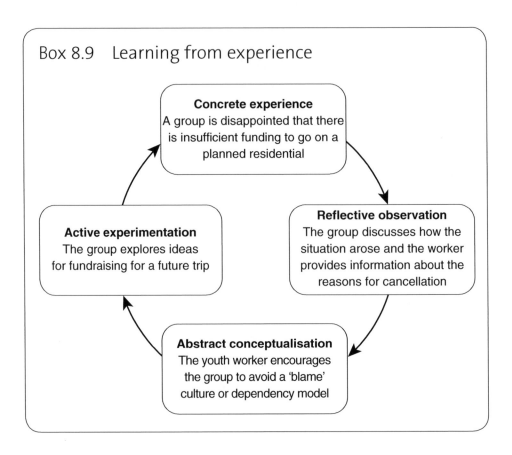

Box 8.9   Learning from experience

Concrete experience
A group is disappointed that there is insufficient funding to go on a planned residential

Reflective observation
The group discusses how the situation arose and the worker provides information about the reasons for cancellation

Abstract conceptualisation
The youth worker encourages the group to avoid a 'blame' culture or dependency model

Active experimentation
The group explores ideas for fundraising for a future trip

 FURTHER READING

Chambers (2002) and Rogers (2011b) have some useful tools for establishing ground rules in groups. MacBeth and Fine (1995), as well as Feinstein and Kuumba (2006), provide a range of tools to use with groups in conflict with communities and each other. Hope and Timmel (1984) present training materials to use with groups to enable transformation. Belenky et al. (1986) provide some interesting reflections on the different perspectives of women on learning which may provoke some further thinking about what goes on in groups.

9

ENHANCING YOUNG PEOPLE'S PARTICIPATION

Young people often have limited control over many of the decisions that affect their lives. This chapter looks at ways of facilitating young people's participation that provide opportunities for them to develop skills and confidence in making their own decisions and to participate in decision-making processes.

FOCUSING ON PARTICIPATION

Youth work promotes young people's participation in decisions about issues that affect them, from relationships with their families and friends to environmental pollution, globalisation and world peace. Youth workers provide opportunities for young people to have a voice and a positive impact on the ways in which decisions are made. Young people's participation can improve existing services or make demands for new services to address community needs. Through youth work, young people express themselves socially, artistically and politically in ways that can make a difference. Young people who are brought together to learn from each other can find ways to improve their lives. Youth work practice aims to enable participation at different levels: with young people, with communities and with services and organisations. (Box 9.1 outlines some examples.)

Box 9.1 The aims of participation and related practice

Aims of participation	Work with young people	Work with communities	Work with services and organisations	Self-development
Young people have more control over the decisions they make about their lives	Providing opportunities to develop confidence and responsibility	Raising awareness of community issues with young people and enabling them to influence these issues	Enabling young people to feedback and contribute to the decision-making process and decisions that are made	Learning from young people and involving them in relevant research
Young people's services become more accessible and appropriate	Developing and promoting opportunities for young people to become involved in evaluation and development of services	Raising awareness of young people's needs for accessible services	Developing structures and opportunities for young people to affect service development and management	Networking to develop multi-agency links and services; developing an understanding of the barriers and shortcomings of services
Society develops positive attitudes towards young people	Developing their awareness of others' perspectives and any impact they may have on how they are perceived and treated	Raising awareness of young people's positive actions	Challenging negative and oppressive attitudes and practice, and enabling young people to do so	Researching to understand power, oppression and social structures
Young people are able to participate in decision-making processes	Involving young people in cross-generational work; enabling young people to develop the skills and knowledge required for participation	Providing opportunities for young people to be heard	Developing structures for participation and enabling young people to participate in existing decision-making structures	Researching to identify relevant issues, resources and opportunities for participation

According to Max-Neef's (1991) list of interdependent human needs (simplified here in Box 9.2), participation is fundamental. If young people's needs for participation are not satisfied, the effects can interfere with other aspects of their lives. For example, if young people are disempowered or alienated, the sense of belonging and self-esteem that comes with identity can be adversely affected. On the other hand, if young people participate and have the opportunity to behave responsibly, they can be empowered in other ways. The skills and confidence developed through cooperative action or being able to dissent could have positive effects on their ability to understand others within their social groups, families, schools, communities and employment. Practice Example 9.1 provides an example of how participation in planning projects and activities can enhance young people's confidence and address a range of other human needs.

Box 9.2 Max-Neef's (1991) fundamental human needs

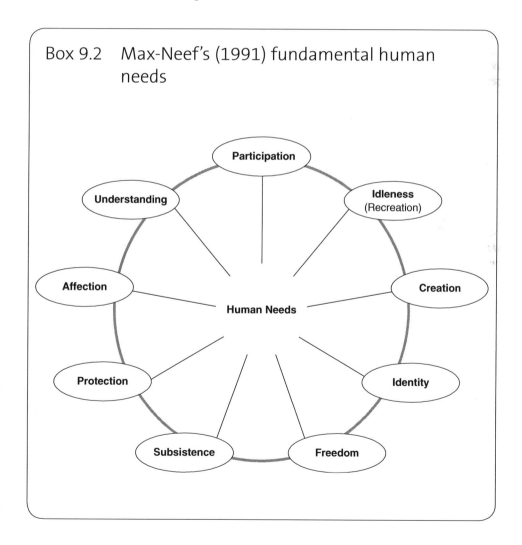

Developing skills through planning a camping trip

A youth worker's report identified that young people learned the following skills whilst planning and organising their camping trip:

- **Research:** identifying preferences in relation to destination, activities and food; finding out about accessible and available campsites and transport; learning about insurance, parental permission and risk assessment requirements.
- **Negotiation:** with local shopkeepers for donations of supplies, with campsite and transport for a good deal, with parents for permission, with each other to make decisions.
- **Fund raising:** organising sponsored activities, seeking out donations.
- **Budgeting:** planning and recording expenditure and resource requirements.
- **Cooking and healthy eating:** identifying ways to address individual diets and health requirements, preparing meals, clearing up.
- **Planning:** the registration process, the journey, the activities, the menus, the paperwork.
- **Teamwork:** sharing tasks, joint decision making, keeping each other informed, addressing responsibilities.
- **Critical reflection:** evaluation of the project, of their learning, of whether they want to be involved again!

Addressing the barriers between young people and those in positions of power can involve youth workers in a variety of roles (see Box 9.3). Acting as an intermediary or advocate, youth workers can create links between young people and decision-makers. Youth workers need to be cautious about getting in the way of direct communication between young people and decision-makers and speaking on young people's behalf rather than enabling them to speak for themselves. Passing on second-hand information, although clearly a second-best option, may be the only opportunity for young people's views to be heard. If called upon to be such a go-between, youth workers need to present young people's views as accurately and as fully as possible.

Successful campaigns for organisational or structural change to enable participation may require a youth worker to undertake a range of different roles. Some youth workers prefer to advise other organisations on ways to involve young people whilst others focus on being advocates for young people. Youth workers engaged in networking and research seek out opportunities for young people's participation whilst an activist is involved in challenging those in power. Challenging organisational or societal ways of thinking or acting can provoke negative reactions. Pushing or overextending the boundaries of a remit or job description to increase young people's involvement needs to involve others within the organisation. Otherwise, should employers disapprove, this activist role can leave a youth worker unsupported. Some situations benefit from a strategy that builds good relations with those in power. Providing viable suggestions for change that can be clearly understood may address or pre-empt resistance or backlash.

Box 9.3 Examples of roles to develop participation

Role	Examples
Advisor	I enable young people to participate by making sure that organisations know about different ways that young people could contribute to their decision making. I have a number of proposals to address barriers to participation: structural changes, challenges to attitudes and examples of good practice.
Advocate	I enable young people to participate by making a point of acknowledging young people's contributions, ensuring that young people's views are taken into account and supporting young people in expressing their views. I always pass on young people's ideas to people who make the decisions and support or present proposals for structural changes that mean they have a greater say. For example, our organisation recently developed some procedural changes that delegated budgetary decisions 'downwards'. Enabling face-to-face youth workers to have greater control over their budgets means that young people have more direct access to decision making.
Networker	I enable young people to participate by building links between organisations and groups of young people or organisations. I seek out organisations who wish to take account of young people's opinions and match them with youth-led organisations who wish to have their voices heard. I make sure that young people know about meetings, conferences and training events.
Researcher	I enable young people to participate by consulting with them about their aspirations and interests, involving them in research to identify resources and funding, and making sure that they bring a global perspective to their planning, such as taking into account environmental issues and linking with young people from other countries.
Activist	I enable young people to participate by developing informal networks and forums that enable them to influence and share in decision-making processes. I support young people to challenge those in power, for example in their campaigns to influence decisions. I structure my own practice so that young people have a direct say in decisions such as staff selection, organisational priorities and resource allocation.

RECOGNISING LEVELS OF PARTICIPATION

The level of power and control that young people experience ranges from passive recipients to active decision-makers. Various yardsticks to identify different levels of participation can be used (such as Arnstein, 1969; Hart, 1992) to identify young people's roles. (See Box 9.4 for a figure illustrating Hart's 'ladder'.) While acceptable levels of participation do not require young people to be managers in control all the time, young people need to know where they stand. Clear identification of roles and communication can protect against false expectations.

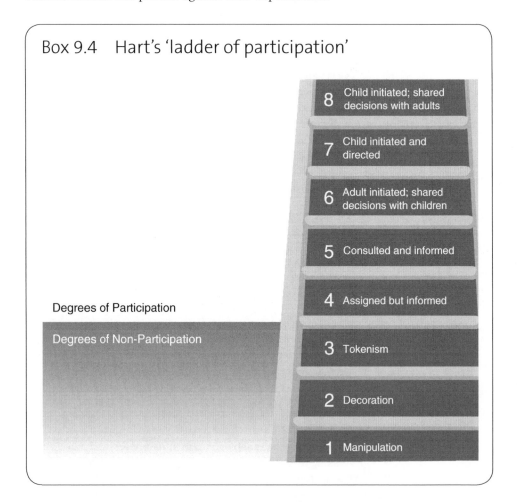

Box 9.4   Hart's 'ladder of participation'

8   Child initiated; shared decisions with adults

7   Child initiated and directed

6   Adult initiated; shared decisions with children

5   Consulted and informed

4   Assigned but informed

Degrees of Participation

Degrees of Non-Participation

3   Tokenism

2   Decoration

1   Manipulation

An important factor in young people taking control of a project or activity is the commitment of the young people, the youth workers and the organisation. Support for the development of participation may come from the organisational culture and individual staff members, as well as from positive policies and procedures. Providing the right level of support at appropriate times without being overly directive is critical although not always easy to gauge. The degree of participation that young people are able to exercise may depend on the particular activity or organisation, or on what Shier (2001) defines as 'openings, opportunities and obligations':

> At each level, an *opening* occurs as soon as a worker is ready to operate at that level; that is, when they make a personal commitment, or statement of intent to work in a certain way. It is only an opening, because at this stage, the opportunity to make it happen may not be available.

> The second stage, an *opportunity* occurs when the needs are met that will enable the work or organisation to operate at this level in practice. These needs may include resources (including staff time), skills and knowledge (maybe through training), development of new procedures or new approaches to established tasks.

> Finally, an *obligation* is established when it becomes the agreed policy of the organisation or setting that staff should operate at this level. It becomes an obligation on the staff that they must do so. Working in a particular way, enabling a specific level of children's participation, thus becomes built in to the system. (Shier, 2001: 110)

Communication between youth workers and young people about the issues concerned in having a voice or making a difference needs to be regular and informative. Young people's understanding of the degree of influence or difference that their participation can make is often bluntly accurate. Experience of exclusion and being patronised, through ageism as well as other oppressive attitudes or practices mean that young people's cynicism about participation cannot be ignored. A 'map of participation' (such as in Practice Example 9.2) or other means of communication can assist young people to identify and communicate information about their experience and the level of their participation, whether that is being excluded or having a leadership role.

A map of participation

We use 'maps of participation' to let young people tell us and other members of the community where they feel that they can make a difference and where they feel excluded. We use a large map of the area that shows the community centre, school, shops and their homes. Sometimes it's just a rough drawing – other times a printed one. For a group, we make one as big as the table. The young people decorate the map with symbols to highlight the places that are significant to them. Colours can show positive or negative feelings about certain areas. Sometimes we use stickers – a picture of a lion to be placed where they feel they can be leaders or a sheep where they feel like followers – although usually they decide on their own symbolism. Logos or graffiti 'tags' are put on areas that are 'theirs'. The map gives them a powerful way to compile information about experiences and a basis to work from to address the issues raised.

PRACTICE EXAMPLE 9.2

PROMOTING POSITIVE ATTITUDES TOWARDS YOUNG PEOPLE

Young people recognise that adults and their social structures tend to treat young people differently from mature adults. They experience the fact that adults generally have more political, social and economic power, which can be exerted over them to their benefit or detriment. Mutual mistrust between younger people and adults is often a result of reciprocal ageism, or generalised negative assumptions about different age groups. Ageism might be insignificant or oppressive, somewhat related to a truth or completely false. For example, assumptions are often made about the ignorance of a particular age group in relation to what is going on around them despite evidence to the contrary. If these assumptions lead to unfair or unequal treatment, abuse, exclusion or ridicule, then the ageism is discriminatory or oppressive.

The involvement of young people in local organisations or community activities can effect change in relation to ageist attitudes and practice. In certain communities, young people may be seen as problems and youth work as the solution or at least a form of problem intervention. Meanwhile, the young people may feel misunderstood and unclear about how to address their negative image. Developing the participation of young people in partnership with communities can enhance the recognition of young people as individuals and build positive relationships.

A youth worker can work with communities and agencies to support the participation of young people as individuals with certain perspectives. At the same time, work with young people to build on their strengths and seek out their ideas, encourage their questions, respond to their energy and enthusiasm and support their creativity can build up their confidence. All parties can emerge from a project (see Practice Example 9.3) with a very different and more positive image of the young people's capabilities.

PRACTICE EXAMPLE 9.3

Promoting positive attitudes

A new community facility was being planned in an inner-city area. Initially, the planning committee was managed by local political leaders and representatives from certain services mostly related to primary healthcare. A group of young people came by the building site one day when one of the members of the planning committee happened to be visiting. Following an animated conversation about the plans, the young people were invited to come along to a meeting to present their views. The young people were able to present a few ideas and ask a few questions related to the plans. The enthusiasm, ideas and creativity displayed by the young people impressed the committee, who were able to see the benefits of involving the young people in planning the facility.

While it did not seem appropriate to invite a random group to participate fully in the planning meetings, the committee decided to ask the local youth services to find a way to involve young people. The youth service recommended that a subgroup of the planning committee be set up as a forum for young people to discuss their ideas for presentation at future planning meetings. This meant that the young people's views could be contributed – without having to sit through all of the 'boring parts'. The planning committee acknowledged the value of the young people's contribution to the planning process.

DEVELOPING YOUNG PEOPLE'S CONTROL

Different types of youth work provide different opportunities for young people to develop their capacity for taking responsibility and working with others (see the table in Box 9.5). In a 'young people's project', young people are in control. 'Youth work activities and projects' have different degrees of control depending on the level of their involvement, whereas a 'youth service' may involve young people in participative youth work activities and projects or simply offer options from which young people select.

Through participation in youth work activities and projects, such as discussions and negotiations to make group decisions, young people develop clarity about the world and find ways to articulate and assert themselves. The previous chapters provide examples in which young people are involved and develop a range of social and team-working skills. Being listened to and seeing the results of their contributions can be very positive learning experiences. For many young people, these opportunities to demonstrate capability provide useful and sometimes unique transitional experiences into adulthood and affect their confidence in other aspects of their lives.

Box 9.5   Working on participation

Participative roles

Organisation	Young people's role	Relevant youth work practice
Young people's projects	A group of young people decide on possible project options, select from them and carry out the work required.	A youth worker is in a supportive role, providing information, advice and access to resources, as well as encouraging the development of the project so that it is inclusive and accessible to others.
Youth work activities and projects	Representative young people are involved at various levels of organisation to inform planning and management.	A youth worker consults with young people and encourages their participation. Decisions are made in partnership to provide options based on young people's expressed needs and interests.

(Continued)

(Continued)

Organisation	Young people's role	Relevant youth work practice
Youth services	Young people select from options designed by others and feed back their views.	A youth worker provides a programme of activities and information, listens to young people through monitoring and evaluation, and makes reasonable adjustments to the programme.

Non-participative roles

Setting	Young people's role	Other work with young people
'Care', entertainment, diversion	Young people are involved in activities that they do not understand.	The worker has control, designs a project and allocates the young people to certain activities.
Training	Young people are told what to do.	The worker instructs the young people without identifying their previous knowledge or interest.
Coercion (court order, compulsory education)	Young people have no say in the activities.	The worker requires compliance for the project, which may also have enforced attendance and record-keeping.

Youth workers encourage young people to pass ideas and information between themselves to develop and manage projects. Role conflict can arise when the drive for participation comes from external funding criteria or organisational aims rather than the young people concerned. Attention needs to be paid to the aim of youth work, that is, to address their needs and interests and to the reasons for enabling their participation: to enable them to have more control over the decisions they make about their lives (see the previous Box 9.1 on the aims of participation). Merton et al. (2004), for example, define some functions of work with young people, which can conflict with youth work aims and values (see the table in Box 9.6). 'Participatory' projects can be more about *socialisation* and control than young people's interests. Such projects may enable young people who enjoy taking on responsibilities to flourish whilst others feel excluded because managing a project 'is just like school'.

Box 9.6   Merton et al.'s (2004) functions of work with young people

Function	Application to work with young people
Integrative youth work	Is concerned with the socialisation of young people and introducing them into 'social norms, expectations, roles and institutions as preparation for the adult world. Seen in this way, social institutions remain broadly the same and it is the task of the young people and those working with them, to fit into what is expected of them' (Merton et al., 2004: 29).
Reflexive youth work	Recognises that local, incremental and individual instances of social change are necessary as 'social structures and systems may serve to exclude and disadvantage certain groups and individuals, and that one of the purposes of youth work is to ensure that the perspectives of young people are better accommodated within these institutions' (Merton et al., 2004: 30).
Redistributive youth work	Is concerned with social justice and social capital (e.g. Putnam, 1995) and 'counters disadvantage, by raising the sights of young people and directing resources to those least likely to receive them' (Merton et al., 2004: 30).

IMPROVING SERVICES FOR YOUNG PEOPLE

Decisions taken within a range of relevant structures, services and systems have widely varying expectations with regard to young people's participation, yet young people are affected by their decisions in most aspects of their lives. Assisting young people to identify where the power lies, how procedures work and how to participate in their decisions can be part of a youth worker's role. In particular, youth workers support young people in dealing with the effects of inequalities. Youth workers who are able to identify how power operates within society and its institutions, employing organisations, families and social groups can assist young people to find their way through these various arenas and enable them to participate more fully in decisions. Youth workers also need to be aware of their own power to identify whether their practice addresses or promotes oppression or liberation.

The ideas and perspectives of young people could usefully inform the design, development and implementation of services that they might use. When young people participate in management and evaluation, activity resources might be more sensibly allocated. Services might become more accessible and relevant. In addition, young people could develop more of a sense of ownership and responsibility for the services. Practice Example 9.4 (below) provides an illustration of the type of contribution that young people can make to a planning group, in that they could foresee a range of issues that may not have occurred to an adult planning group. In addition, they were able to make suggestions that were more feasible and interesting to the particular target group. Taking their ideas into account can give the young people a sense of pride that can precipitate their further involvement in maintaining a facility. If they had not been involved, the development may have been unused, dangerous and expensive. Their participation not only improved provision, but had the potential for benefits throughout the community. Through involvement in a socially responsible activity, young people can provide a positive image to their peers, families and community, which could have far-reaching effects.

This model of young people's participation can be seen as 'market research' and lead youth workers and others to lose sight of the purpose of participation. While improvement in services may be a worthwhile by-product, youth workers need to focus on enabling young people to have more control over the decisions that they make. Enabling participation is meant to be liberating for young people, not providing more restrictions.

PRACTICE EXAMPLE 9.4

Young people's participation improves a park

A committee involved in re-designing a park involved some young people in discussing the plans. The young people pointed out that a skateboard facility under discussion would:

- be unlikely to interest the target age group unless certain design features were included
- only accommodate a limited number of young people at a time
- only accommodate one proficiency level at a time
- require access to expensive safety equipment, which was beyond their means
- need supervision to prevent younger children or alternative activities getting in the way.

The input of these young people meant that the plans were changed and the resulting facilities were well used and safe.

INVOLVING YOUNG PEOPLE IN ORGANISATIONS

An understanding of organisational structures, roles, relationships, power and decision-making processes can assist a youth worker in identifying relevant practice to increase participation. Practice Example 9.4 demonstrates how a project can fall through with a lack of clarity about relationships and who has the power to make decisions.

Young people are duped

A board of directors for a youth organisation decided to set up a management group for a project made up solely of young people that would have responsibility for redecorating the youth centre, including the design and budget allocation. The project group put a lot of effort into considering different ways in which to involve other young people in the project. The final design included a mural with contributions from different groups using the centre. The centre was redecorated with a high level of participation by young people. A grand reopening was planned by the project group and the organisation's board of directors was invited. Several key members of the Board, who were also funders of the organisation, were offended by the content of the mural. At the next board meeting, it was agreed that the mural would be painted over.

A youth worker could have made a difference to Practice Example 9.4 outlined above. Pointing out ways to enhance young people's participation at all levels of the project could have lead to more positive outcomes. For example, an experienced youth worker could have ensured that the board of directors fully discussed the implications and consequences of the brief prior to establishing the group. The Board's discussion might also have been enhanced by the participation of young people as representatives or members on the board of directors, which could also have improved communication and relationships between the two groups. Continuous representation from the project group on the board of directors would have helped to keep them informed about the development of the project. A youth worker or young person may have sought clarification from the board of directors about whether the project group's designs would need approval. Although this would limit the young people's power, a revised brief would more accurately reflect the views of the board. The project group would also have been clearer about the consequences of their decisions.

A youth worker may also have been able to suggest a different approach to the way in which the board handled the disagreement. For example, the board of directors could have informed the project group about their concerns and asked them to come up with alternative proposals. A youth worker taking on an advocacy or networking role may have suggested that the board of directors keep in touch with the young people to be in tune with their interests, styles and attitudes. Relationships could have been based on two-way communication. Then the young people's views may have been valued and the board may have been able to communicate their own values to the young people.

The example highlights a number of issues about enabling participation. For participation to be positive, young people need to be treated with respect. In this example, the young people may have known that the mural was offensive yet have gone ahead in order to antagonise the board or to highlight the bogus power on offer. Alternatively, they may not have known that the mural was offensive and have been denied the opportunity to put the situation right. Youth workers need to question who has the right, the power and the access to knowledge and who makes the decisions over who will have access. This analysis of groups, organisations and society will assist in the identification of meaningful participation.

While conflicts about power can be inevitable, a number of structural changes could enhance young people's participation. Identifying different structures and different ways in which young people can participate on committees can provide options for organisations looking to increase young people's participation. A youth worker may be able to advise young people about effective contributions in committees and provide an understanding of the implications as well as the limitations of various roles. Participation in committee discussions from the initial allocation of funds to a project may enhance all of the members' understanding of possibilities and limitations. Or young people's ongoing participation on an advisory committee could contribute a relevant perspective to policy development.

A youth worker can also set up structures to enable young people's participation. Relevant structures could be based on informal youth groups or more formally constituted groups and committees. The aim will usually determine the levels of formality and young people's influence – although sometimes the history of the group is also significant. The remit and procedures of a group established by young people are likely to be quite different from an adult group that young people join. For example, young people on a youth council would set the agenda themselves, whereas the contributions of young people invited to attend the board meetings of a housing trust may well be limited to certain agenda items. An understanding of the specific roles and responsibilities that members undertake when joining a committee can provide clarity for both young people and the committee. A youth worker can suggest different types of committee structures as options (see the table in Box 9.7) to enhance the decision.

Box 9.7   Types of committees

Type of committee	Role of committee
Boards of directors **Management committees**	• Provide direction • Be responsible for projects or organisations • Manage staff and budgets
Advisory boards **Policy committees**	• Give feedback and advice • Have no responsibility for management • Discuss issues; develop proposals • Present findings
Task forces **Working groups** **Action forums** **Subgroups**	• Develop short projects with a specific purpose • Report to another body • Meet outside of the decision-making body
Youth councils **Youth forums**	• Network to discuss issues • Disseminate information • Attend other bodies as representatives

ENABLING YOUNG PEOPLE TO PARTICIPATE FULLY

Young people who feel involved in decisions and are able to contribute to the process and outcomes of decision making can be a great asset to any organisation that works with young people. Certain circumstances can encourage or enable individuals to participate fully, such as an understanding of the topic, the potential choices being made and the implications of the decision. Young people also need information about the decision-making process and how they fit in (see the table in Box 9.8 for some examples). Simply adding young people as members to an existing adult committee without any thought to how they might be received or how either party might feel about the culture and procedures is not usually a very successful way to enable participation. Usually both the existing committee membership and the new younger members need some induction and training as to how to proceed.

Box 9.8   Young people's rights on committees

Rights	Potential roles
Voting and speaking rights	Chair, Secretary, Treasurer
	Full member
	Appointed member
	Worker or volunteer
	Representative of subgroup or other group
Speaking rights but no voting rights	Chair, Secretary, Treasurer
	Worker or volunteer
	Representative of subgroup or other group
	Contributing member
No voting rights and restricted speaking rights	Representative of subgroup or other group
	Invitee to discuss specific topics or make presentations
	Consultant
	Advisor
Right to attend only. No voting rights and no speaking rights	Observer
	Representative of network or forum
	Shadowing member or officer
Receive minutes and/or reports; no voting rights, no speaking rights and no right to attend	On mailing list

Honest and open discussion about participation and answers to questions (such as those outlined in Box 9.9) are important. If a youth worker is unsure about whether a young person will be listened to when attending an adult committee meeting, this needs to be honestly communicated. Encouraging a young person to go to a committee meeting without knowing what to expect could lead to disappointment and a lack of tangible outcomes. At the very least, a discussion of possible scenarios is advisable. Preferably, young people attending meetings should be prepared with clear explanations of their roles and the procedures of the meeting.

Box 9.9   Do I want to be involved in this decision?

Factor	Questions raised
Relevance	• Do I understand the topic, the discussion, the decision and its impact? • Am I interested in this topic or the decision? Do I care? • Will the decision make any difference? • Will my participation affect anything?
Purpose	• What is the purpose of the decision? Is there another agenda? • Is a decision being made? What is it? What are the choices? What are the implications of the different choices? • What are the potential impacts of this decision? Will this decision have effects other than those intended? • Do I want this responsibility? Do I have concerns about being involved in this decision (e.g. reputation, other repercussions, lack of confidence)?
Process	• Do I have sufficient information on which to base a decision? • Can I ask about this? Will my questions be answered? Will the options be discussed? • Is there too much information? Are too many decisions being made? • Do the others making the decision with me understand me or my perspective?
Power	• Will my opinion or decision be listened to? Respected? Implemented? • Do the mechanics of the process or culture of the organisation enable me to agree or disagree with what is being decided? • How will my involvement be perceived by others?

ESSENTIAL SKILLS FOR DEVELOPING PARTICIPATION

- Focusing on participation
- Recognising levels of participation
- Promoting positive attitudes towards young people
- Developing young people's control
- Improving services for young people
- Involving young people in organisations
- Enabling young people to participate fully

FURTHER READING

Read about Arnstein's (1969) and Hart's (1992) ladders of participation. Driskell (2002) provides a wealth of ideas about ways to involve young people in community development. Wates (2000) outlines tools to use to develop participation. Ledwith and Springett (2010) examine a theoretical approach to participatory practice. Conger and Riggio (2007) discuss leadership and ways to develop young people as leaders. Hudson's (2009) book on managing third sector organisations has a wealth of examples about organisational structures that can be used to train young people and other managers about participation and responsibilities.

PART C

SUSTAINING DEVELOPMENT

Sustainable communities, as Roseland says, are 'not merely about "sustaining" the quality of our lives – they are about improving it' (2005: 2). Part C is designed for youth workers who are keen to ensure that their professionalism and practice continuously develops and improves through proposing and managing relevant projects and supporting professional development through work placements and supervision.

Chapters 10 and 11 are interlinked. Chapter 10 outlines a structure for project development based on research that engages stakeholders to plan projects that address genuine and sustainable interests. Chapter 11 explores the relationship between youth work values and management of people and programmes. In Chapters 12 and 13, the sustainability of the profession is addressed by supporting youth workers who are new to the field as well as experienced practitioners. Chapter 12 looks at placements from the perspectives of the student and the host organisation. Similarly, Chapter 13 examines best practice in using supervision for professional development from the vantage points of both supervisor and supervisee.

10

DEVELOPING A PROJECT PROPOSAL

Involving young people in developing projects for relevant and accessible activities can make a real difference to the sustainability of interest and relevance. This chapter outlines the skills involved in project development through staged and participative research. The chapter focuses on more formal or structured research for the purposes of identifying the need for youth work rather than on the informal methods of research, such as networking, that were explored in Chapter 2 of this book. At the end of this chapter are some suggested headings for a proposal.

IDENTIFYING A POTENTIAL PROJECT

The need for a project may be identified through the variety of information and sources that informs everyday practice about relevant issues and young people's interests. Through listening, conversations and more formal discussions, a picture is compiled of individual and group concerns based on 'grounded knowledge' of the community and the area that can inform the identification of a relevant project. Although informal and regular interactions with individuals and groups of young people in the community continuously stimulate responsive practice, patterns may emerge that indicate an interest in a more substantial and new development. Ideally, a student project would also be able to build on local youth workers' knowledge to maximise the relevance and usefulness of their projects. This process of ongoing formative evaluation that informs practice may provide sufficient information to identify suitable aims and plans for a small project proposal. The information also provides a context for more formal research that may be required for a substantial project proposal to an external funder. (See also Chapter 5 on how ideas for groups emerge.)

Defining the general topic area for a project, such as a target group or issue, allows participants to identify whether a project is of interest and to consider what type of proposal might be appropriate. Further discussions with stakeholders can clarify the scale of the project, for example whether the project will need substantial external funding or can be carried out 'in-house'. Some examples of such 'ball park' statements about the type and scale of a possible project that could be used to aid explorations of potential interest and support are listed in Box 10.1.

Box 10.1   Project summary statements

- A trip to the seaside with 300 local young people
- A three-month project to engage with young people congregating in particular areas
- A six-month pilot for targeted support for young people in residential care
- A resource development project for ideas and materials to support work with girls
- Organising a conference for 100 young people on computer gaming
- Building a youth centre in the neighbourhood
- Putting together an induction pack for volunteers
- Developing a new organisation to bring young musicians and poets together

---

Designing a statement or short definition of the core purpose of the project can assist the project in becoming more focused and is useful for communication with others. The statement should identify the nature and purpose of the project, what it intends to do, how this relates to any underlying principles and how it may differ from other services, provision or work with young people. The statement should be quite short, easily communicated and motivate or inspire. Full participation by stakeholders (i.e. young people, other local community members, staff within the organisation and other relevant agencies) in the design of a mission statement could be a difficult process to manage, but feedback on the statement could ensure that the language and purpose are appropriate. The process could also be a useful exercise for establishing agreement amongst stakeholders about a project's purpose. (See Box 10.2 for some examples of mission statements.)

Box 10.2   Project mission statements

The 'XYZ project' is committed to involving young people in the organisation of enjoyable, educational and inspirational activities that will assist their transition into mature, caring and committed adults.

The 'ABC youth group' will promote the development, well-being, rights and participation of young people by ensuring that they are able to enjoy themselves whilst making meaningful contributions to planning and organising activities and making informed choices about their futures.

The '123 Scheme' will create opportunities for change in the lives of young people and their communities through participation in environmental improvements and intergenerational relationships.

A project proposal is an outline of information about a planned piece of work, whether a specific activity or a whole programme, that can be used to apply for funding, agreement or support from others. The proposal needs to include information that indicates clearly what the project sets out to do, the resource requirements and how they will be met. The process of putting together a proposal can assist the planning needed to take the project forward. Compiling the information with potential participants can also enhance project relevance and accountability. A youth worker may put together a proposal for a piece of work to gain feedback or agreement from young people or colleagues. Students may design a project for a work placement for approval by host organisations and tutors. The amount of information and research required to put together a proposal will vary according to the size of the project and the audience. A proposal for a small project, such as an excursion for an existing group or a one-off event that does not require a lot of additional resources, may consist simply of the aims, objectives, a timetable, a list of resource requirements and risk assessments. Practice Example 10.1 is an example of a student whose successful proposal provided the opportunity to manage a small project. For larger projects, particularly one seeking significant external funding, a proposal may need to include sufficient research data to evidence viability and details to confirm planning. Suggestions for the content of a project proposal appear at the end of this chapter (see Box 10.11).

Student project proposal

I was interested in facilitating some sessions on sexual health because I knew that some of the young people had talked about getting into difficulties when mixing alcohol and relationships. I also wanted to have the experience of managing a project during my student placement so I could talk about initiating work and carrying it out in future job interviews. When I put this to my placement manager, she was not so keen. However, after I discussed the idea with some young people, found that they were keen, identified a suitable time and room, put together a draft programme and wrote it up as a project proposal, she was really pleased. She could see that I had given a lot of thought to the sessions and gave us the 'go ahead'. (Student on placement)

PRACTICE EXAMPLE 10.1

UNDERSTANDING THE ROLE OF RESEARCH IN PROJECT DEVELOPMENT

Although most projects will involve some form of research, the type of research will depend on the information that is needed and at what stage the research is being undertaken. Research can inform the project priorities, feasibility, development and evaluation. For example, if some young people express an interest in a new facility, a wider survey could identify potential take-up and capacity requirements. Research can also be a useful method for involving young people and others in the community in identifying the issues that affect them. Instead of simply providing a project to deliver a service, a ready-made and planned programme of activities or solutions to perceived problems, young people and their communities can be involved in participatory and emancipatory research where they identify their own questions and interpretations of data. (The table in Box 10.3 contains some examples of the links between different types of research and the questions that the research aims to answer.)

Box 10.3   Types of research

Type of research	Aims of the research	Sample questions
Exploratory research	To find out about something unknown, e.g. when a youth worker moves into a new area and wants to identify priorities for project development.	What's going on? Who is here? What do they want? What services are available to them? Why is this happening? What are they interested in?
Feasibility study	To identify whether a project will work and what resources are required, e.g. to put together a project proposal.	Is this project possible? What resources would we need to make it work? If we did this, who would be interested or involved? What are the necessary steps to make this happen? What are the consequences?
Baseline research	To establish a starting point for comparison during and at the end of the project, e.g. current attendance, crime statistics.	How will we know when or if the project is effective? What is going on now so that in the future we can identify what changes are taking place?

Type of research	Aims of the research	Sample questions
Experimental research	To try out something new, analyse its effects and evaluate its use, e.g. to evaluate a pilot project.	What happens when we do this? How does it compare with when we do that? How effective was this? Should we do it again?
Evaluation	To identify the outcomes, quality and effectiveness of a project or to identify ways to improve its effectiveness or appropriateness (during or at the end of a project).	How could we improve this project? What was the impact of this work? On whom? How do the results compare to our aims and objectives?

INVOLVING YOUNG PEOPLE IN PROJECT DEVELOPMENT

The early stages of project development are an ideal time for involving young people. Young people can be involved as consultants, researchers or managers of project development. Their interests and concerns can provide clarity and purpose for the project as well as the motivation to research and put together the proposal. The level of interest in the proposal may also be an indication of the level of interest in the project itself. A committee or group of young people can identify whether a potential project is useful and interesting, or simply a diversion of resources to unnecessary or unwanted activity. (Some examples of involving young people in project development research are listed in Box 10.4.)

Box 10.4 Involving young people in project development

Type of research	Examples
Peer-led research: young people manage the project	• Young people design a quantitative survey to identify interests developing an inter-generational community garden.
Peer research: young people representing the 'target group' are the researchers	• Young people interview other young people who use drugs to develop an information pack about the consequences of drug use.

(Continued)

(Continued)

Type of research	Examples
Participatory or emancipatory research: young people affected by the issues are managers and researchers	• Young people design and carry out research making their own analysis of findings and evaluation of how to utilise available resources.
Action research: young people carry out research alongside youth workers	• A group of young people identify, implement and evaluate a project with a youth worker. • Young people from a different area or organisation work with a local group to provide ongoing feedback and guidance on their project.
Participatory evaluation: young people evaluate the project to inform ongoing development and future projects	• The young people network and discuss their projects with other groups of young people through forums, exchange visits and conferences. • The young people participating in the project compile written, oral and multi-media displays and reports of projects for evaluation and discussion with others.

Any constraints on project development (if known) should be communicated to the young people and/or interested communities so that false expectations do not arise. Potential constraints, such as budgets, timescales, type of project and long-term sustainability, may be determined by the organisation or funding stream to which the proposal is being made. Personnel, whether students or paid staff, may have limited time to offer the project. The timescale for a project is significant; the turnaround for a proposal and any completion dates for the project will affect the aims of the project being proposed as well as whether extensive research is required. Project development that takes too long to address the issues raised could be counterproductive. Young people who are consulted through research may move on or change their minds before the project proposal is completed, not to mention the project itself. The results of their recommendations may not be ready until the next 'generation' of young people – who may prefer quite different facilities or activities. Instead of addressing the issues, this research only raises false hopes. The experience of being a part of project development should benefit the young participants and be conducted using youth work principles.

CARRYING OUT RESEARCH TO IDENTIFY NEED

Larger projects may require structured investigative research, such as a community audit or profile, which involves data collection and analysis to identify the need and feasibility of projects. The reasons for selecting or prioritising certain issues are underpinned with up-to-date information about young people, their interests and available resources. For example, an audit could identify any barriers preventing young people from accessing existing services or changes that could enable or encourage take-up. The findings may generate ideas for improvements to existing services or evidence a need for new ones. Reports of the research incorporated into the proposal communicate this evidence to others who may be able to offer support for relevant projects to address the identified gaps. (Practice Example 10.2 is a relevant example.)

Research to identify a need

A group of young people complained to a youth worker that there was 'nothing to do around here'. The youth worker encouraged them to find out about existing leisure facilities. The research could either corroborate their views about gaps and accessibility or identify under-publicised activities that they could become involved in. The youth worker pointed out that in either case, their views could be fed back to service providers. The youth worker also provided advice and guidance, use of a phone and stationery and took their views seriously. The complaint, in the form of a research report compiled by the young people, was forwarded to the leisure services department. The area manager invited the young people to make a presentation to the board. Soon the young people were involved in decisions about allocation of resources for young people in the area.

PRACTICE EXAMPLE 10.2

Research can provide a context and evidence of the need for a project. Identifying research questions for representatives of a target group can enable a project to be based on genuine need. Elements of quantitative as well as qualitative information are useful. Quantitative research could provide the statistics from responses to closed questions or numerical data, whilst more descriptive information can be gathered from the qualitative research that seeks out views and opinions or observes experiences and actions. Usually youth workers can obtain first-hand information from primary sources through direct contact, observation or involvement of those experiencing an issue. Many young people and youth workers have existing relationships with individuals and groups facing the issues concerned. In general, the strength of youth work research relates to such 'privileged access'. In addition, youth workers tend to have a wide range of contacts and networks within an area that can be called upon for suggestions and advice about relevant primary and secondary sources. Statistical analysis of 'hard' information, such as numbers of individuals indicating preferences for a particular activity, combined with evidence of young people's points of view, such as direct quotes, can be a powerful combination. (See the table in Box 10.5 for some examples.)

Box 10.5   Identifying research questions

Potential project	Sample research questions
Work with street-based youth	Why do they congregate on the streets? What do they gain from this activity? Are they satisfied with this activity? What prevents them from accessing current youth work provision? What are their hopes and aspirations? Do they need more information about how to pursue their interests?
Educational needs in relation to drug use	What type of drugs are the young people using? Are they legal or illegal, expensive or inexpensive, inhaled, swallowed or intravenous? Do they know about safe use or consequences of use? What would deter young people from misusing these substances? Do some groups have higher levels of drug use or use of particular drugs?
Gaps in services for young parents	How can we access this group? What services do they access? What ideas do local young parents have about their needs? Are they interested in meeting other parents, money advice, parenting advice, educational development?
Arts project feasibility study	How do we find young people interested in this project? Where are young people currently involved in dance, drama and participative arts? What are the existing facilities in the area, for example performance space, short-term projects or full-time schools? How much would such projects cost? What are some of the common factors in the success of other projects? How do these relate to the young people, services and support for a project in this area? How did other projects get off the ground?

ENSURING RESPONDENTS' INFORMED CONSENT

When individuals are the subjects of research or the sources of information for project development, ethical and often legal constraints may require their 'informed consent'. Individuals or groups who are observed, interviewed, involved in discussions or asked to fill in a questionnaire that will appear in a project proposal need to know about the researchers' aims, methods and plans for disseminating the results. This information enables participants to make informed choices about whether they wish to be involved. An ethical approach involves taking steps to address the safety, rights, dignity and well-being of respondents. Care and attention needs to be taken with data and methodology if respondents' circumstances or views are included in a project proposal, particularly when participants are young or potentially vulnerable or when the topics are sensitive. The age, abilities or circumstances of a respondent may mean that others, such as a legal guardian, would be responsible for providing consent to participate. A legal minor, someone who may not be deemed competent or someone who is dependent on the researcher may be perceived as too 'vulnerable' to provide consent. In order to provide consent, participants or guardians should be told what will happen with personal data during the project development and in any dissemination. Questions about anonymity, whether individual details are linked to responses and findings, as well as how and whether their contribution will be recorded and published, are key issues to be resolved and communicated clearly. (See Box 10.6 for some examples of ethical ways to involve young people and protect informed consent.)

Box 10.6   Ethical practice in project development

1   Project development should:

- be for the benefit of young people whether directly or indirectly
- be based on positive, participatory and anti-oppressive practice
- be clear about the aims and what happens to the results
- involve voluntary and informed consent that incorporates the right to withdraw
- include an assessment of risk
- avoid asking invasive questions that could cause mental suffering or embarrassment
- where possible, involve young people in design, management, steering and/or researcher roles
- include participatory evaluation
- be discussed with stakeholders.

2   A clear outline of research procedures for participants and stakeholders should include:
- methods for collecting data and what will happen with it
- how to withdraw and any timing constraints on withdrawal
- the commitment required, for example the timing and schedule for participants and for the project
- potential risks, consequences and outcomes.

3   Confirming respondents' consent requires checking out whether an individual:
- is being or feeling pressured to participate
- has any questions about the research
- is able to take responsibility for a decision to participate

(Continued)

(Continued)

- needs an adult's consent
- understands the information being provided and the implications or consequences of participation, such as recording methods, the form of publicity or dissemination of findings
- has any objections
- wants to participate and agrees with the procedures.

DEFINING PROJECT AIMS AND OBJECTIVES

An analysis of research findings and recommendations or discussion with participants in a project planning group can be used to define project aims and objectives. Specific aims and objectives can further clarify the direction of the project and the intended outcomes and help to plan the programme. The aims convey the changes that a project hopes to achieve, whilst the objectives outline the activities that will be undertaken or the services that will be offered to bring about these changes. (See Practice Example 10.3 for an example of some aims and objectives.)

PRACTICE EXAMPLE 10.3

A project's aims and objectives

The 'Transitions to Independence' project
    Overall purpose: to improve the life chances of 'looked-after young people' through specific projects carried out during their transition from living in 'care' to independent living.

Specific aims

- To increase life skills and knowledge
- To provide appropriate support structures
- To enable the location of suitable housing and employment
- To develop financial literacy and household management skills

Objectives

- To make contact with looked-after young people who are about to leave care
- To develop appropriate relationships with them as individuals
- To bring them together and facilitate a support group
- To discuss issues arising during their transition from care to independence
- To provide information and advice on housing, financial and household management and job-seeking

PLANNING THE PROJECT PROGRAMME

A more detailed plan or programme based on the objectives leads to allocation of tasks and responsibilities. Some proposals require details of each stage of the project, including the activities, time frames and resource requirements. Involving participants in project design can enhance viability. Estimates of the time, staffing, equipment and expenses required are much easier when the individuals who are going to carry out the work have some input. For example, the plan may list the number and destinations of journeys that will be required, the length and amount of reports to be printed, or the size of rooms and the facilities that will be needed. Greater detail in the plan allows for more accurate budgeting in the next stage, although some flexibility will be needed for necessary changes or unforeseen expenses. The table in Box 10.7 contains a possible format for such a plan, whilst Box 10.8 provides a rough example.

Box 10.7   A format for project planning

Aims	Objectives	Stages and timescale	Resource implications	Milestones
Overall aims	The steps that will enable the aims to be reached	The programme or activities that will enable the aims and objectives to be reached	Personnel, equipment and funding needs	Indicators for monitoring development

Box 10.8   A sample project plan

Objectives	Stages	Resource needs	Milestones
1 Carrying out research to identify potential members and interests	Jan to Feb • Identifying key staff • Planning the staff timetable • Identifying contact points • Making contact with target group via outreach and detached work	Part-time pay for three staff @ 15 hours each for 12 weeks	Staff allocation; weekly programme for staff established; contact with 150 young people; interest from at least 30 young people

(Continued)

(Continued)

Objectives	Stages	Resource needs	Milestones
2 Forming a group	March to April • Developing promotional material that explains activities • Involving young people in an excursion	Part-time pay for three staff @ 15 hours each for 12 weeks; coach hire, refreshments for a day	At least 12 members start attending; promotional material on website and social networks; one excursion
3 Developing and facilitating a programme of activities	May to July • Holding weekly sessions on a range of topics	Part-time pay for three staff @ 15 hours each for 12 weeks; money for activities	Weekly activities planned and carried out; minimum attendance target of 12 young people per session
4 Involving members in promoting the work to others	• End evaluation/ celebration • Inviting key stakeholders	Refreshments; poster printing	Dissemination via website and social networking

Although some funders may require a detailed programme prior to funding being allocated, not all projects lend themselves to this level of planning. Commissioned projects for a focused project may expect specific information about issues, context or targets that could only be identified through more extensive research. A proposal might designate the research as the first stage of a larger project or propose the research itself as a feasibility project. Project development, as well as the project itself, needs a firm empirical foundation in the reality of young people's experiences and perceptions. The involvement of young people, in peer-led research or as peer researchers, can assist youth workers to retain a youth work perspective through an 'Appreciative Inquiry' (Cooperrider and Whitney, 2005) that builds on strengths in the young people and the community. Project proposals should be based on positive anti-oppressive practice rather than on having a deficit model of young people or their communities. Practice Example 10.4 demonstrates how youth work values can inform the identification of an appropriate approach.

Identifying appropriate aims

Our team was concerned about young people's involvement in gangs but didn't want to sensationalise what was going on – it didn't seem like that would be helpful. Obviously there are problems with violence and drugs in the area and related gang activity goes on. Our research wasn't about highlighting this. We wanted to hear from young people about their experiences. We wanted to see if we could understand and identify what pressures, if any, led to their participation or membership of gangs; maybe what they gained from being involved in a gang. We wanted to avoid negative labels and we didn't want to demonise their actions. We didn't want to deduce from certain evidence that they belonged to a gang. We used their definitions and their perceptions and used their language. We didn't even want to use the word 'gang' ourselves unless a group was clearly involved in illegal behaviour. As street-based workers, we also wanted to make sure that the information we collected did not lead to the arrest of individual young people. That wasn't the point of our research. We just wanted to hear what the young people thought so that we could work together to address their real situations.

PRACTICE EXAMPLE 10.4

DESIGNING A BUDGET

Designing a budget necessitates identifying the income and expenditure that will be necessary to meet the estimated resource requirements for the planned programme. This aspect of a proposal is not just about acquiring funding; the discipline required to forecast resources helps to focus planning decisions and to deal with the reality of the scale of the project. The resources required for carrying out a research project may come from additional funding, reallocation of existing resources or from contributions. Discussions with others about the budget are useful at this stage as multi-sourcing can make projects more viable and different ideas about procurement, such as borrowing, donations and sharing, can release pressures on financial income requirements. Existing staff may be able to carry out the work as part of their usual job description. Resources may be made available from multi-agency partners, and in-kind contributions and partnership arrangements can be discussed. One agency could coordinate a project whilst another provides supervision, a third the expenses and the fourth the access to interested young people. Experience and varied perspectives can also help to identify additional expenditure requirements and potential problems in realising planned income.

Compiling a budget requires estimates of requirements and research to establish actual costs. Attention to detail will lead to more accurate entries. Capital expenditure, such as the purchase of computers, vans, office or sports equipment, can often lead to further costs, for example insurance and maintenance or replacement. Participant contribution to budget planning can enhance the detailed nature of the plans, as well as a more general understanding of budgetary constraints, effective use of resources and adherence to any financial control and record-keeping requirements. (See Box 10.9 for an example of the headings that might appear on a budget for an organisation. Further information about fully costed-out budgets appears in the next chapter.)

Box 10.9   A budget framework

Income	Examples of what to include and how to calculate
Membership fees	Expected number of entrances × fees.
Grants	Any grants received, committed, pending, to be submitted.
Donations	Any donations received, committed, or aimed for.
Fundraising	Number of activities × expected income from each .
In-kind contributions	Volunteers' time, pro bono (donated) work, goods or services.

Outgoings (expenditure)

General operating costs (overheads)

Staffing	Include calculated costs for managers, project workers, administrative and ancillary staff working for the project. The pay for sessional or temporary staff may be listed as number of staff × rate × time (hours/days). Salaried staff may be listed as a percentage related to the time they work for the project (salary × %).
Management overheads	Staff and volunteer management/supervision and support may be estimated at a percentage (such as 4%) or separately costed at hourly rates.
Other staffing costs	Staff time and costs for recruitment and selection, tax, insurance, benefits, such as pensions, auditors.
Staff training	Training costs or allowance for conferences, courses + related travel costs.
Premises	Rent/mortgage, upkeep, maintenance and safety checks, insurance.
Equipment (capital expenditure)	Photocopier, computers – include purchase price + depreciation, maintenance, insurance.

Consumables	
Telephone	Identify options for payment schemes or include office running costs as a percentage of budget (usually 5–10%).
Office supplies and printing	Stationery: numbers of photocopies/reams of paper/ pens/folders × cost.
Postage/delivery	Estimate the number of letters per week or month.
Utilities	Heating/lighting: electricity, gas, water (check previous bills or research).
Project or activity costs	
Project staff	Staff engaged solely for this project (see staffing above).
Travel	Mileage, train/taxi/bus fares × number of journeys × travelers or coach/mini-bus hire.
Expenses	Number of meals × reasonable cost, fuel: journeys × miles × rate.
Volunteers' expenses	Number of volunteers × donation to expenses.
Volunteers' benefits	Number of volunteers × equipment/training provided.
Overheads	Could be calculated as a % of overhead costs included above.
Equipment	Purchase price, depreciation, maintenance and insurance or hire costs.
Additional consumables	E.g. arts materials, clipboards, games, books.

PUTTING THE PROPOSAL TOGETHER

A proposal that presents a clear outline of intentions is a useful tool for involving others and gaining consent for plans. The criteria for acceptance of a project proposal may be clearly outlined in a funding application or the organisation's procedures for planning new work. Alternatively, an informal or internal proposal may have more flexibility. Box 10.10 contains some suggested headings for a project proposal. A student may also use this structure to put forward a proposal to a placement organisation to ensure that all parties understand and agree to the plans (see also Chapter 12).

Box 10.10   A framework for a project proposal

About the proposed project (or piece of work):

1   Overall project description: a short summary of the type of project, e.g. core activities and target group.
2   Context: why the project is needed, how the need for the project was identified and how the project will meet this need.
3   The aims and objectives of the project: what the project hopes to do and how it will benefit the relevant young people, communities and/or organisation(s) and how it will be done.
4   Project plan: the stages of the project with the planned activities and any expected milestones for review.
5   Planned outcomes: the anticipated hard and soft project outcomes and how they will be monitored and evaluated.
6   Participants: who will be involved in the project, who are the target group/beneficiaries, how they will be identified and the methods to ensure that they are able to participate fully.
7   Responsibilities for the project: the governing body or management committee and/or named individuals responsible for managing and organising the project activities and finances; job descriptions and CVs of staff are also involved.
8   Monitoring and evaluation: recording and reporting – how often? What information?
9   Risk assessments: any ethical, financial or safety issues and how any risks or unforeseen events will be managed and addressed.
10   End and exit arrangements.

About project costs

1   Resources: a fully costed-out budget proposal including overheads, staffing, running costs, expenses and equipment, plus any costs incurred for additional training, supervision and development of staff or volunteers. If there is any income, details of the source and amounts, e.g. fees or grants, should be included.
2   Costings: explain how the above costings and resources were identified and calculated.
3   Existing resources: identify which of the elements in the resources are already accounted for and which can be contributed to the project without additional cost.

Project setting

1   Organisational aims and legal standing.
2   The main sources of income and funding for the organisation.
3   A summary of the organisation's recent accounts: total income and expenditure for the last financial year, surplus or deficit at year end; savings or reserves at year end.
4   Tax and charitable status.
5   Insurance coverage.

ESSENTIAL SKILLS FOR DEVELOPING A PROJECT PROPOSAL

- Identifying a potential project
- Understanding the role of research in project development
- Involving young people in project development
- Carrying out research to identify need
- Ensuring respondents' informed consent
- Defining project aims and objectives
- Planning the project programme
- Designing a budget
- Putting the project proposal together

 FURTHER READING

Bell's (1999) outline for carrying out a research project is a clear and easy to follow guide. Kindon et al. (2007) have some very interesting examples of participatory action research projects. Burton (1993) and Hawtin and Percy-Smith (2007) provide introductions to community profiling or audits. Wates (2000) has extensive guidance on 'community planning events' which can be used in collaborative projects. Whaley (2007) outlines various stages in applying for grants which support community organisations in the UK. Pakroo (2011) has detailed instructions on starting a 'non-profit', and Eastwood and Norton (2010) is a 'plain English' guide for funding applications.

11

MANAGING A PROJECT

Project management may be taken on by youth workers at any level, from a student undertaking a project in a work placement to a manager of a large organisation. This chapter provides an overview of some of the skills required to manage a project, including management of self, finance and people. As Niebuhr implies, perhaps the most significant of these is the management of self:

... the grace to accept with serenity the things that cannot be changed, courage to change the things that should be changed, and the wisdom to distinguish the one from the other. (1987: 251)

APPLYING PRINCIPLES TO PROJECT MANAGEMENT

Managing a project often highlights differences between the theory and practice of youth work, as the reality of limited resources or organisational capacity may interfere with hopes and expectations. Some managers experience conflicts between their innate idealism and their organisation's more pragmatic requirements. Ethical decision making whilst prioritising where resources should be allocated and maximising their effectiveness requires considerable thought and professionalism. Having the grace, wisdom and serenity (see the Niebuhr quote above) to make appropriate decisions does not come easily in all situations or to all managers. Managers attempting to promote positive change in their organisations need to develop confidence and clarity when managing their professional principles and the reality of individual, organisational or societal expectations and assumptions.

Focus can be maintained by promoting participation by young people and staff in difficult decisions. For example, deciding whether to accept certain constraints imposed by a funder in order to secure resources for a project may be clearer when youth work values are applied. A manager may decide not to apply for funding offered for projects that control or contain young people. Another may decide that the potential benefits for young people outweigh any limitations on how the project is run. While either decision could be defensible, most youth work managers would choose to involve others affected by the consequences of the decision in the decision-making process so that the implications are understood and agreed. Sharing power rather than imposing compliance can improve the quality of the decision and agreement with the outcome.

The job title of 'manager' generally indicates that an individual is responsible for some direction and control of operations and resources. The level of their responsibility can depend on whether an organisation has established lines of accountability and codes of practice, as well as good communication between 'top level' decision-makers and managers implementing their policies. If a manager is following a set of established procedures, both the organisation and the manager are protected from problems resulting from unsanctioned decisions. Moreover, the development of appropriate policies, procedures and codes of practice can help to provide a positive environment for practice for youth work, young people and youth workers. Involving staff and young people in this process can help to create a 'learning organisation' (Senge, 1990), which could benefit all concerned. On the other hand, procedures that restrict professional decision making can inhibit the development of youth work projects.

BALANCING INTERESTS

A participative approach to management may require the balancing of a number of different interests and influences. Young people, members of the community, workers, employers and funding bodies can each have particular needs, demands or opinions about a project. Effective management usually requires consideration of the needs and interests of these stakeholders; deciding on priorities can be more difficult. Giving equal weight to each or finding general consensus is not always possible. Managers may need to negotiate a creative compromise or settlement that balances various influences, including the interests of young people, communities, the funder and the organisation. In addition, finding an approach that is feasible within resource constraints may require further compromise.

When organisations depend on external funding linked to specific positive project outcomes, the pressure for results and related evidence that follows can often be quite restrictive. The completion of certain targets and tasks to address funders' interests may become more important than the process of participation. Insufficient or unreliable funding may lead to less of a long-term commitment to young people or staff, a lack of development work or sustainable practice. Having clarity about the aims of short-term projects can help youth workers to maintain youth work principles in their practice and avoid the pitfalls of such projects.

Some youth workers attempt to prioritise projects based on young people's expressed interests or self-identified needs, only to find that the employing organisation's aims, objectives or targets conflict with young people's preferences. At other times, a manager may find a community's priorities are expected to take precedence over young people's needs. A planned project may require staff to work to schedules they are unwilling or unable to adopt. Finding solutions that satisfy many interests often requires imaginative approaches, some of which may be identified through discussions between participants.

A 'successful' project is often one in which all of the interested players are equally satisfied or involved in management or design. An example could be that the young people in the area express interest in an outdoor basketball court; their parents think that's a wonderful idea and the community is happy to have the facility erected in local waste ground; the youth work organisation says that the tidied-up area fits with their priorities to be involved in environmental projects; the funding and expertise are available and so the project works well. Many youth work projects do not naturally emerge with such congruence. Some require considerable attention to conflicting needs to avoid running into difficulties that can affect future work. The concept of a Venn diagram (see Box 11.1), a simple, yet effective method of finding common ground, may help a 'third way' to be identified. Rather than compromising interests, identifying where interests overlap and disregarding the areas of difference, can help to plan a successful project.

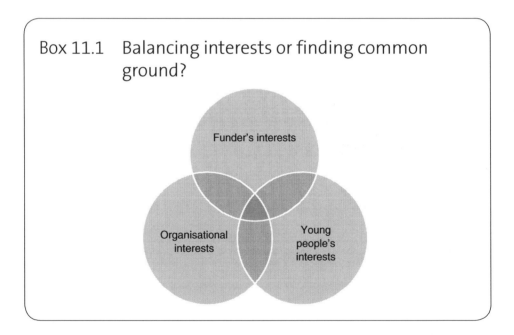

Box 11.1   Balancing interests or finding common ground?

Funder's interests

Organisational interests

Young people's interests

MANAGING SELF

Although 'management of self' may be a concept more usually associated with individuals learning to cope with difficulties in life, aspects of managerial responsibilities that relate to self-management are important areas for reflection (see the diagram in Box 11.2). For example, the ways in which individuals present themselves can affect how an organisation is perceived, as well as how staff respond to them. The impact of health-related issues on practice, including balancing work/life time and attention, mental health and ensuring sufficient physical activity to provide energy and enthusiasm for work, is very relevant. Issues such as alertness, which may be affected by alcohol consumption or fatigue, are also significant in managing self, whether a youth worker is engaged in managing a project or day-to-day interactions with young people. Managing self-presentation could also cover a range of areas that may be open to debate, such as dress, manners, methods of communication and levels of openness. While individuals vary in how they present themselves, an awareness of the impact made by self-presentation probably warrants occasional reflection and evaluation. Punctuality, reliability and alertness are also key areas. The realistic identification of strengths and gaps in knowledge and experience through 'location of self' can assist an individual in seeking support when necessary and in avoiding over-extending responsibilities and workload.

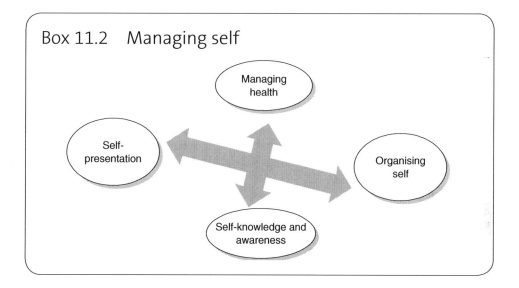

Box 11.2   Managing self

Managing a project often requires a considerable amount of organisational and administrative work. Liaising with external organisations to make bookings, scheduling appointments by telephone and email, and double-checking arrangements require communication skills as well as organisation. Maintaining accurate records and files demands either a good structure or a good memory, preferably both. Acknowledging correspondence, confirming details and circulating information widely can help to create a programme that fits together. (Box 11.3 has some examples of others' 'tips' for good practice in this area.)

Some managers may have the luxury of delegating administrative duties or working in a supportive team that offers help. Individuals need to be aware of the implications of delegation in relation to time and organisation. Keeping on top of decisions that are delegated elsewhere can be time-consuming. Delegation also requires the manager to be organised, know what assistance is required and how to pass on their responsibilities. If someone is used to making random notes on scraps of paper surrounded by piles of files, passing on responsibilities can be problematic. Even when managers are able to make sense of their own complex array of arrangements, a 'system' that others cannot follow will inhibit support and participation by others. On the other hand, when an organised manager appears to have everything under control, colleagues in the team may not see that any assistance is needed. Clearly, developing transparent record-keeping systems is beneficial to good management.

Box 11.3   Simple record keeping

- Keep a running notebook or log to record the substance of phone calls and conversations.
- Maintain a diary to record events.
- Have a contact list ready so it is clear who to call when something goes wrong.
- Have a sensible naming system for files, folders and documents.
- Organise electronic files in computer folders following a standard structure.
- Agree protocols for files, e.g. how draft documents will be labelled.
- Maintain a back-up system for your computer.
- Think about paper filing in relation to access: short term, medium term and for the archives.

A manager or project can combine the need for relevant support structures with accountability. Involving others in providing advice or reviewing decisions can be enhanced with a mechanism for regular feedback. Some projects will be supported by an organisational line management structure; others need to be developed by the project manager. Box 11.4 has some examples of such structures. Ensuring that stakeholders, particularly young people, have a say in how a project is run has also been addressed in previous chapters, particularly Chapter 9.

Box 11.4   Organisational support structures

- **Peer review**: individuals, including young people who have carried out previous similar projects, could provide critical perspectives.
- **A steering group,** with 50% membership from young people in the area, could meet regularly to monitor and evaluate the project.
- **An advisory group** made up of young people, colleagues, potential participants, members of the community, management, funders, academics and other agencies, could meet regularly to discuss the issues raised by the research project.
- **Supervision or consultancy** for the manager could provide a regular sounding board for discussion of ongoing practice and professional issues arising.

MANAGING FINANCE

Managing the finance of a project has several components: applying for funding, managing budget controls and keeping accounts, managing cash flow and monitoring expenditure. Clarity about the management of finances will assist a project to involve all participants in efficient and transparent systems. The involvement of young people in budget design has a range of benefits, including their perspective on resource and spending requirements. For example, a project planning an international exchange may not have considered that some young people may be financially excluded from participation unless a budget allocation is made to provide them with the necessary resources to purchase a passport, suitcase and/or suitable clothing for an alternative climate. Additional benefits include their awareness of the resources available, of any constraints and of the financial literacy skills they can gain that will be useful in many arenas.

Applying for funding

Securing financial support for activities and operating costs generally depends on an accurate prediction of requirements, addressed in the previous chapter. Applications for funding may be made internally or to larger charitable or government bodies. Successful applications generally require an understanding of a project's financial requirements, gained through designing a budget, careful research to know what a potential funder is looking for and a well argued and evidenced match between the two. A project budget is also a useful method of planning, monitoring and disseminating information about resource requirements, use and evaluation.

Differentiating between different types of costs can help with devising appropriate funding applications. For example, identifying capital expenditure, which covers the purchase of new items such as buildings or equipment, and running costs, such as postage, stationery, rent, heat and electricity and revenue or income, identifies 'one-off' and ongoing costs. (See Box 10.10 in the previous chapter for a budget framework.) Fully costing a project, that is identifying all of the costs needed, including a percentage of the ongoing overheads, can provide a better picture of requirements for sustainability. Distinguishing the core costs required for organisational survival from the optional activities can also lead to more informed choices about resource allocation. The figure in Box 11.5 provides a tool undertaking an analysis of activity costing that recognises the core elements that could contribute to an optional activity. Identifying those resources required for maintaining an organisation's core programme provides an opportunity to review whether the status quo is affordable or desirable. For example, a sizeable proportion of resources may be allocated to the upkeep of an expensive building. Recognising that this is the case could lead to the consideration of alternatives, such as charging a percentage of the core costs to specific projects (the shaded areas of the diagram).

Box 11.5   Core and activity costings

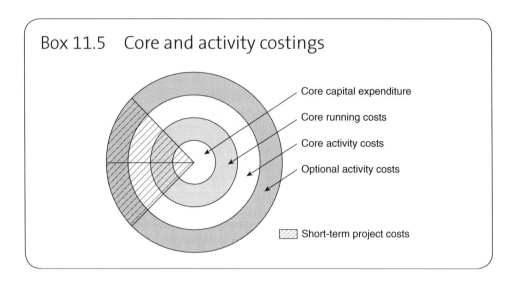

Making a successful application may mean recognising gaps as well as overlap between the resource requirements and any potential sources of funding. An individual source may only provide funding for certain aspects of the project, such as running costs rather than core organisational overheads. Contributions from a host organisation may be required to secure the funding. Access to some sources may only be available to certain types of organisation. Putting together an application could mean developing a partnership with an organisation that meets the criteria. Discussions about whether sources of funding are suitable can assist the development of an appropriate funding plan. Decisions need to be made about whether or not an application is worthwhile; Practice Example 11.1 shows how inappropriate funding can impact on practice.

PRACTICE EXAMPLE 11.1

The 'wrong kind' of funding

We applied for funding for a project because we thought it would enhance the work we were doing with young people in the area. The funding was for projects with a very specific brief to reduce conceptions amongst 11–16 year olds. We were aware that the number of conceptions in this age group was high and it seemed like a project on this topic would be relevant and useful. However, the funder's monitoring requirements really restricted our work. In order to receive condoms or sexual health information, the young people had to give their names, ages and addresses, which created difficulties for some. Any work utilising the funding had to be directly linked to the project outcomes. Activities became specifically target-related whilst other useful activities that did not label young people as 'at risk' were under-funded. We found that we could not 'justify' work with younger children, who often came to the sessions because they were being looked after by their older siblings. Interactions with young people on non-sexual health matters were not recognised or valued by the management team.

Managing budget controls

Allocating responsibilities and methods for controlling income and expenditure in relation to a planned budget and then checking that the procedures are being followed means that a manager can keep an eye on the financial viability of a project. Even a project with a small budget needs to have a method for making payments for items such as expenses and equipment. Maintaining records and control can avoid problems such as unexplained debts or withdrawals. Systems for requesting and authorising expenditure can range from simple measures such as using cheques that require two signatures to more complex tracking systems for invoice requests and purchase orders. The system should provide an opportunity to confirm that a payment is coming out of the correct budget and is allowable under the terms of the budget. Spending according to the budget is more likely to happen when all concerned are aware of the procedures. Practice Example 11.2 illustrates what can go wrong when projects do not conform to usual procedures.

Accurate records of payments both in and out of accounts assist a project to maintain budget controls and to keep track of progress on expenditure. An understanding and awareness of spending and its relationship to the planned budget means that appropriate responses can be made to any changes in plans. Accounts should enable a record to be kept of how much funding is left under each heading and how much money needs to be kept aside to address planned expenditure. Keeping track of what happens to cash, cheque books, credit and debit cards is necessary to manage a project's cash flow. A clear account of the movement of money helps to avoid temptation, missing cash or unexplained losses. Ensuring that all participants collect receipts and that there is a system for submitting and organising receipts provides evidence for payments and a record of transactions.

Learning about budget controls

Our project involved allocating money to participants to spend on presenting their work via a medium of their choice: video, photographs, posters, etc. We thought it would be a good learning experience for the individuals to have control over their own funding. It turned out that our organisation didn't have a mechanism for withdrawing cash and invoices were required for any payments. Most of the participants didn't have bank accounts and couldn't pay up front. As they weren't employees of the organisation, claiming for expenses wasn't possible anyway. The project timescale was nearly finished before we found a way to pay for the materials, but, unfortunately, we couldn't just distribute cash, we had to go by receipts, which meant that spending didn't conform to the exact amounts we expected and it was difficult to keep track of how much money had been spent overall. By that time, some of the participants had given up, whilst others had lost their receipts. After insisting that everyone be careful not to overspend, we ended up with an overall under-spend. Meanwhile, all of us had learned more about budget controls than we expected.

PRACTICE EXAMPLE 11.2

Checking the project accounts against the planned budget can identify over- or under-spending. Inflation may have an effect, and changes or differences may arise that will require amendments to plans. In some instances, the transfer of costs to different headings (known as virement) may be permitted to manage over- and under-spending. A manager will need to consider when funders should be informed about any questions, discrepancies or major difficulties. Sufficient time may also be needed to implement alternative strategies.

MANAGING PEOPLE

Decision making that takes into account the power relationships within organisations can result in effective and strategic resolutions. Analysis of the assumptions that can govern beliefs and contexts for choices and behaviours (Hammond, 1998) may also help to illuminate a way forward. An authoritarian and task-oriented 'Theory X' manager (McGregor, 1960) assumes that 'the average human being has an inherent dislike of work and will avoid it if he can'. A participative, process-oriented 'Theory Y' manager believes that individuals are capable of creativity and naturally accept work and responsibility. According to McGregor, managers need to be able to identify their own and others' standpoints on these theories.

> Every managerial act rests on assumptions, generalizations, and hypotheses – that is to say, on theory. Our assumptions are frequently implicit, sometimes quite unconscious, often conflicting; nevertheless, they determine our predictions that if we do a, b will occur. Theory and practice are inseparable. There is, in fact, no prediction without theory; all managerial decisions and actions rest on assumptions about behaviour. (1960: 8)

Organisational culture and experience may limit change and development. Individual staff members who are accustomed to working with a manager who regularly takes responsibility for issues that arise may not know how to change; others may see no need. Teams may be reluctant to raise or discuss issues through fear of exposure or blame. Hierarchical systems may exclude the majority of staff from participating in decision making. Established practice may deter certain groups from accessing resources so that individuals may not trust a manager to be non-discriminatory.

The management of a project includes a range of duties and responsibilities for ensuring that appropriate individuals are able and motivated to carry out required tasks with sufficient resources. Staff could include paid professionals, volunteer activists and trainee young people. Members of a group may carry out the project themselves. Whether the individuals are paid or unpaid, members of a project group, or staff, the responsibilities can be similar. Good working relationships and communication are obviously important in relation to participants' experiences. The success of a project can depend as much on goodwill and individual energy as on structured job descriptions and task allocation.

The management of paid and unpaid youth work staff can start or significantly change at any of a number of points in a cycle of work and responsibilities. (The diagram in Box 11.6 illustrates some of the responsibilities that can be incurred when managing people). The definition of a job or task could be seen as an ideal starting point for this cycle, although new projects often develop or emerge through ongoing work rather than having a clear beginning. Reviewing previous experiences can inform the development of an appropriate plan for a new task description.

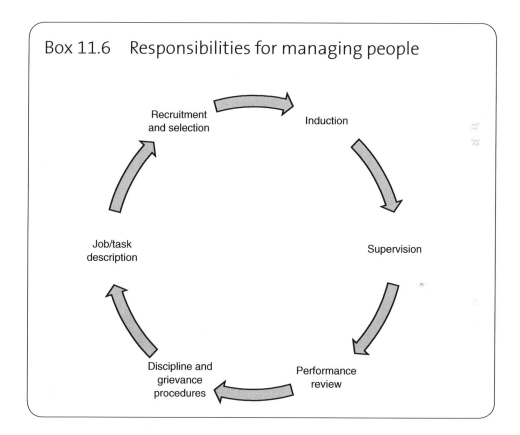

Box 11.6   Responsibilities for managing people

Designing a job or task description

A critical part of managing a project is defining and communicating the work that needs to be carried out. A job description can be a useful vehicle for defining work objectives, whether the individual is an employee, volunteer or young person. Any difficulties in carrying out the work can be more easily addressed through managerial supervision when clear job and task descriptions provide an organised and defensible basis for performance review. The table in Box 11.7 includes some suggestions for key elements in a job description. Using a job description as a basis for discussion can provide valuable opportunities for input as well as guidance and feedback on specific duties and responsibilities.

Box 11.7   A framework for a job description

	For employees or volunteers
Job title	• Rank or job title
Task title	• Name of the project or piece of work
Setting	• The department, base and organisation • The base or area of work
Level of the post	• Payment or salary scale • Whether full-time or part-time (and how that relates to the pay, such as pro rata or hours worked) • Whether the job is permanent or temporary • Whether job shares are welcomed or possible • Probationary period
Aims of the post/position	• A short summary of the main purpose of the job and why the position has been set up • If applicable, relevant information about the history of the post, such as whether the position is new, to cover temporary leave, why the position is vacant
Responsible to	• Reporting relationships and to whom the postholder is accountable • The individuals or groups responsible for providing overall direction, line management and/or day-to-day support
Main duties and responsibilities	• The main duties listed first from the essential to the non-essential, from most to least important or from the most to least time-consuming • The specific tasks or required outcomes • Any physical or mental demands • 'Other duties as required by the project' (see also the disclaimer below)
Working conditions	• Describe the general physical environment or surroundings and any potential conditions related to physical or mental health or access

	For employees or volunteers
Person specification	• The minimum requirements for an individual to do the job competently, the essential criteria, and the desirable points • Practice or educational experience • Qualifications or certification • Skills • Knowledge • Personal attributes or qualities • The ways in which the points can be evidenced and/or assessed in the selection procedures [Note: A project may wish to prioritise the involvement of individuals with experience of living in the community or awareness of certain issues over others with more 'professional' skills to promote community involvement and development]
Disclaimer	• *This job description is not exhaustive and may be added to in the future depending on the needs of the project*, or • *The list of job elements, responsibilities, skills, duties, requirements, or conditions is not intended to be comprehensive*, or • *The project reserves the right to revise the job description or require that other tasks be performed when the circumstances of the job change (for example, emergencies, funding issues, changes in personnel, workload or technical development)*, or • *Other duties as assigned*
Date	• A record of the date of preparation or approval of this version of the job description

Recruitment and selection

A job description can provide the focus for communication with prospective applicants during recruitment and selection. Accurate information about the position, including management and support structures as well as duties and responsibilities, can help potential applicants to decide whether the job is for them. Information about the criteria that will be used in selection, which provide a structure for the questions during selection, may also help to narrow the field to appropriately qualified candidates. Ideally, a panel trained in equal opportunity policies and practice would be involved to reduce unfair discrimination and questioning. The panel would be responsible for ensuring that the job is advertised appropriately and the procedure is carried out fairly.

Providing support and direction

Providing support and direction for project participants means making sure that individuals are clear about what the work entails and where support is available. There needs to be a balance between direction that is spoon-fed or is so laissez-faire as to leave participants feeling unsure about what to do or unsupported in their decisions. Regular discussions about progress and project team meetings can assist with project monitoring and planning. Engendering a sense of cooperative working can start with an induction, where participants are introduced to each other and roles are clarified.

Individual managers and projects exercise widely varying levels of control and monitoring of projects and project workers. Relationships with and between staff, working with colleagues, team working and leadership are all issues that can arise and are handled differently by individuals. Some project managers place a high value on conflict avoidance, meet regularly with each member of staff and provide precise directions for handling issues as they arise. Others leave the project workers to address issues in their own way and make their own mistakes – only dealing with conflicts that impinge on their horizon. Clearly, there are a number of approaches in between.

Preparing an outline of a task can be a useful basis for a discussion about expectations of participants, such as anticipated outcomes, ways of working, roles and allocation of responsibilities. Box 11.8 provides a plan for the specific work that needs to take place. The list could be used with young people, staff members, volunteers or a project management group. Discussions of the outline can elicit suggestions as well as agreement on what needs to take place.

Box 11.8   Planning a specific task

Task title	An appropriate name for the task or project could be identified by those planning the task and redefined by those carrying it out
Summary	A short summary of the project/task
	Aims and objectives
	Relevant background information
Those responsible	Names and roles, such as members of project management team, project workers
	Contact details
Timescale	Start and finish dates
	Any scheduling information, such as estimated or planned stages
	Approximate number of hours

Setting	Base for operations, contact details, access issues
	Resources available, for example desk, phone, photocopier
Benefits	Whether any educational award or certificate of participation will be made
	Any expenses that can be claimed
Responsible to	Reporting relationships, for example to the project management group, the youth worker
	Who provides overall direction and day-to-day support and contact details
Main duties and responsibilities	Specific tasks or required outcomes
Requirements	Criteria for participation and/or selection, for example availability on the required dates
	For young people: parental permission if necessary, plus any criteria dictated by the organisation or funder for targeting purposes, such as gender, age range, situation
Disclaimer	*Details may be subject to change*
Date	A record of the date of preparation of this version

Handling disciplinary matters

A project establishes what is expected of individuals involved through discussions about what constitutes unacceptable actions or activities. Where paid or unpaid staff are involved, task or job descriptions, recruitment and selection procedures, ongoing training, guidelines or codes of practice, supervision and project meetings are used to establish expectations about behaviour. When young people manage a project, discussions about ground rules may be a better tool. Managing a project includes defining which actions are considered to be misconduct and what, if any, penalties can be expected for differing levels of misconduct. For example, gross misconduct may lead to a recommendation for dismissal, whereas other instances of misconduct, incompetence or negligence may lead to a series of measures to improve the situation. Generally, an organisation is responsible for providing clear guidance on disciplinary matters, on which a manager should be able to advise staff. A well designed disciplinary scheme will include a clear definition of what constitutes misconduct and the consequences as well as the procedures that will be followed, including opportunities to present responses to 'charges' and fair and impartial grievance resolution (see the table in Box 11.9 for some examples of staff misconduct).

Box 11.9   Staff misconduct

Misconduct, incompetence or negligence	Gross misconduct, incompetence or negligence
• Poor timekeeping • Absenteeism • Not following procedures, such as health and safety, dress code, publicity approval • Unauthorised use of facilities or equipment, such as vehicles, computers, telephone, post • Poor performance of duties • Acceptance of gifts or bribes • Conduct outside work that affects the organisation's reputation in a fairly minor way	• Theft, fraud or deliberate falsification of records • Physical violence, serious bullying or harassment, particularly in work, but often outside of work as well • Deliberate damage to property • Criminal activities, particularly those leading to conviction and incarceration for violent crimes or those of a sexual nature • Serious insubordination or failure to maintain work responsibilities • Misuse of an organisation's property or name • Bringing the organisation into disrepute • Serious incapability whilst at work through use of alcohol or illegal drugs • Serious negligence which causes or might cause unacceptable loss, damage or injury • Serious infringement of health and safety or other policies and procedures such as confidentiality

---

Any disciplinary and grievance procedures that are developed as part of the management of a project will need to comply with legislation protecting the rights of employees and young people. Providing opportunities for due process and accurate reporting and recording structures are important when dealing with matters related to complaints or discipline. Having a named individual with whom employees, volunteers or young people can discuss grievances or appeals is generally considered to be good practice. An individual's wish to be represented or supported by a peer, colleague or union official should also be respected.

MANAGING PROJECT EVALUATION

A project can often offer participants a new experience, and frequently includes professional development, whether informal 'on the job' learning or through more 'formal' training courses. More structured projects often culminate in a celebration or event, such as an artistic production, exchange visit or achievement award. Distinct projects can provide tangible outcomes attractive to both young people and funders. Identifying and addressing areas of learning or professional development needs before, during and after the project can be a useful exercise for all concerned. This type of summative and formative evaluation can inform project management and future project planning. Many organisations structure their youth work in a continuous programme of short-term projects, which provide flexibility and fresh ideas to retain the interests of ongoing participants and/or reach new target groups.

Reflection and evaluation can assist participants to recognise and implement their learning. A range of criteria can be used to review the information collection and the analysis of findings. Involving young people in identifying and applying the evaluation criteria can be a powerful method of enabling participation and learning. Young people can often identify the reasons for any difficulties or unexpected outcomes from a different perspective. The experience will also assist participants to anticipate consequences in future projects or related actions.

Once the data on a project has been collected, various formats for dissemination could be considered in relation to their relevance for the target audience, the purpose of dissemination and available resources. A celebration at the end of a project could include dramatic, visual and participative activities to raise awareness of the issues addressed or the achievements of the participants with other young people and relevant agencies. The launch of a report at a meeting or conference enables everyone involved to celebrate the end of an often demanding project. Face-to-face discussions of the issues raised with an element of training can be useful. A presentation to agencies that may have additional resources to allocate to future projects could incorporate an action plan and budgetary implications for follow-on work, following the proposal outline in Box 10.11 in the previous chapter. Deciding on an appropriate method of dissemination requires an understanding of the audience, what information they need or would be interested in and some interesting ways in which it could be passed on to them.

Different versions of a report may be appropriate for different audiences: a full report for funders, summaries for young people or the public, and alternative media used for specific groups. Checking out the appropriateness of language and information for an audience can be important; the level of detail and terminology may vary greatly. A report for a manager might be a brief outline of work carried out with recommendations for future projects; a presentation to a community might involve a newsletter article, web page or display; a funding bid might include a feasibility study. A report may require several drafts to be circulated to participants to allow corrections or amendments to be made.

Different methods of distribution can be used to widen dissemination of the success of a project. Flyers, which summarise the activities and include a form for ordering a copy of the report, can be distributed at community events or door to door. Copies of reports can be made available to those who request them and put on the web, which could also link with other useful sources and limit paper wastage. Information can be distributed to mailing lists, conferences and members. A multi-method approach can assist dissemination to individuals whose access to computers, literacy or networks is limited.

A dissemination plan can be used to target the specific stakeholders who need to be informed about the project. Some projects have a policy of looking at the 'equality of dissemination' of information so that those directly affected by a project and those with the power and resources to effect any recommendations receive equal attention. In the example provided in Box 11.10, the resources made available for dissemination are equally divided between the residents in the area and non-residents, and between older and younger residents. The targeting of resources for dissemination means that proper attention is paid to the needs and interests of those affected by an issue as well as to ensuring that those in power have the information necessary to effect changes. Too often, the focus on project reporting is directed towards funders; paying attention to those directly affected can improve future project take-up and participation.

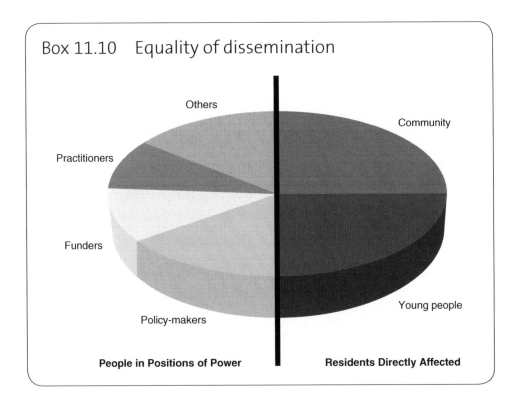

ESSENTIAL SKILLS FOR MANAGING A PROJECT

- Applying principles to project management
- Balancing interests
- Managing self
- Managing finance

- Applying for funding
- Managing budget controls
- Managing people
- Designing a job or task description
- Recruitment and selection
- Providing support and direction
- Handling disciplinary matters
- Managing project evaluation

FURTHER READING

Readers' interests in management could be addressed through reading about management and organisational theory in a range of organisational settings, such as Handy's (1999) introduction to managing organisations with various frameworks for analysis based on research. Also highly recommended is Adirondack and Simpson's (2006) guidance on managing voluntary organisations from policy making to day-to-day decisions while Tchami (2007) introduces cooperative structures for project development. Texts relating more specifically to youth work organisations could include Ingham and Harris' (2001: 56–8) relevant guidance for management of self and others, and Ord's (2012) presentation of various discussions about issues relevant to the current UK setting that may well apply elsewhere. Reading about Senge's (1990) understanding of a 'learning organisation' is relevant to management of a project that attempts to benefit all participants as well as the organisation through change and development.

12

ORGANISING STUDENT PLACEMENTS

This chapter focuses on how to make the most of the learning opportunities provided by work placements, which are usually a key element of programmes for students learning to be youth workers. The issues could also be relevant for work-based learning organised for new-to-the-field youth workers, apprenticeships or induction and orientation for new workers and volunteers. Arrangements to support the experience are explored from preparation to assessment – as well as how the learner can make the most of the experience. During induction to the profession, individuals can develop the essential skills required for practice that will sustain them throughout their professional careers. Ideally, effective planning, supervision and management of these experiences will enhance the learning and outcomes for all stakeholders. As well as the learner, the young people, staff, organisation and communities would also benefit.

APPRECIATING EXPERIENCES

Acquiring the essential skills for practice and learning to be a youth worker can involve a range of formal, informal and non-formal learning experiences. Professional development can take place through a natural progression of life choices and experiences, as well as through more structured formal learning programmes. Relevant knowledge and understanding, skills, interests, attitudes and habits that can be used in youth work may develop from an individual's background, upbringing or chance opportunities. Recognition of a pre-disposition or aptitude for youth work could arise through being a trainee youth worker or youth leader. Other life-changing experiences, whether potentially traumatic, such as rape, bereavement or homelessness, or positively transformative, such as encountering an inspirational role model or successfully completing a white water rafting course, may provide the motivation and foundation for becoming a youth worker. Many professionally competent youth workers have not gone through specific educational programmes in youth work; some may have pursued alternative study routes that nevertheless result in useful areas of understanding. A youth worker with knowledge of economics, history or sports science could have a range of frameworks and information to underpin discussions with young people. A politics, sociology or health background could be useful when developing issue-based materials. Skills in IT, arts or music could be passed on to young people. Box 12.1 provides some examples of informal 'acquisition learning' from life, intentional non-formal learning from reflective practice and formal education through training courses.

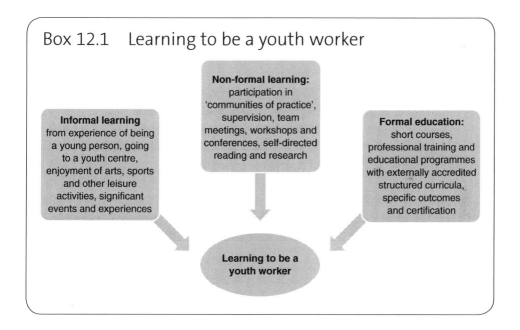

Box 12.1   Learning to be a youth worker

Informal learning from experience of being a young person, going to a youth centre, enjoyment of arts, sports and other leisure activities, significant events and experiences

Non-formal learning: participation in 'communities of practice', supervision, team meetings, workshops and conferences, self-directed reading and research

Formal education: short courses, professional training and educational programmes with externally accredited structured curricula, specific outcomes and certification

Learning to be a youth worker

Work-based placements bridge these definitions of learning as they are usually periods of immersion in the work environment through non-formal learning arrangements with supervision from an experienced practitioner which are organised as part of a formal learning programme. In addition, students will draw upon their informal learning from previous experiences throughout the placement. The work involved in a placement generally applies learning gained from other experiences and from formal educational settings to 'real-life settings'. A 'community of practice' provides support for making sense of the learning. Other youth workers and managers pass on skills as well as develop learners' understanding of a range of less tangible areas of professional practice, such as appropriate demeanour, managing varied responsibilities and scheduling. Learners observe and carry out interactions with staff, young people and members of communities, as well as professionals from other organisations and services, to learn about 'common sense' issues as well as the role of youth workers. Eraut (2000) describes this learning as the 'tacit understanding' and 'tacit knowledge in action' required for professional practice.

The 'real world' setting of work placements can also provide opportunities for learners to gain specific skills and a holistic understanding of issues and consequences of actions that may be difficult to develop elsewhere. Through experience and reflection on experience, the learner engages with punctuality and time management, teamwork, meetings and practice tools, such as conversation openers, games and procedures. 'Leadership and entrepreneurial skills, assuming responsibility and making decisions, and demonstrating high ethical standards' (Crebert et al., 2004: 162) can be practised and developed in a placement or project at the same time as addressing a genuine community need.

The chapter will refer to 'learners', who are usually students on a course; 'course providers' as the formal educational institutions and their staff who are responsible for issuing qualifications; and 'host organisations' that provide the setting and opportunities for work-based learning. 'Participants' refers to all of those involved: learners, tutors, managers and supervisors.

PREPARING FOR WORK-BASED LEARNING

The identification of appropriate work-based learning opportunities requires participants to clarify expectations with each other. The potential for a learner to benefit from the experience cannot be the only criteria for matching a learner with a host organisation; the young people's interests and the host organisation's priorities are also important considerations. A range of practical concerns as well as issues of compatibility of interests, values and working styles can affect the success of a learning experience. Criteria for the identification of appropriate work-based learning opportunities need to take into account the shared interests of participants as well as their specific concerns. For example, learners will be motivated by interests and accessibility; course providers will wish to secure sufficient placements that are safe and provide opportunities for relevant and supported learning experiences; and host organisations will need to ensure that ongoing work is enhanced rather than hindered by participation. Box 12.2 illustrates some of the criteria that may need to be used to select appropriate work-based learning opportunities.

Successful work-based learning arrangements can result from discussions and preparation as well as contracts or agreements so that participants understand their responsibilities at each stage. Host organisations may be identified by the learner or selected and assigned by the course provider who would also need to ensure the quality of the opportunity. If a learner chooses their own host organisation, the course provider may need to accommodate a wider variation

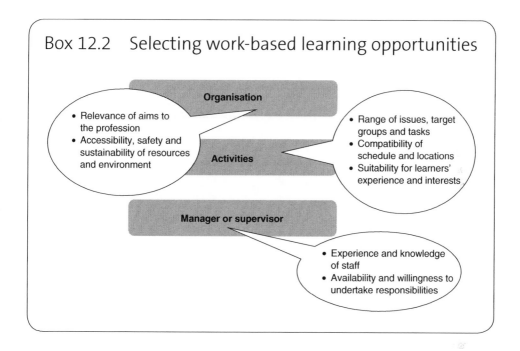

Box 12.2 Selecting work-based learning opportunities

Organisation

- Relevance of aims to the profession
- Accessibility, safety and sustainability of resources and environment

Activities

- Range of issues, target groups and tasks
- Compatibility of schedule and locations
- Suitability for learners' experience and interests

Manager or supervisor

- Experience and knowledge of staff
- Availability and willingness to undertake responsibilities

in learners' experiences, for example supervision or opportunities to undertake responsibility. Learners who continue to practise within their existing voluntary or employing organisation may not have any choice about who will manage or supervise their practice and professional development. Well-established patterns of expectations or work may be difficult to alter. If responsibilities for support, supervision and assessment of the learner are allocated to the host organisation staff, then training for work-based supervisors will need to ensure that criteria and requirements are clearly understood and agreed upon. Often, responsibilities are shared to enhance parity between different learners' experiences and monitor their quality, particularly if learners are marked differently according to their level of learning. Evaluation of all participants' experiences and the procedures can lead to continuous improvement. Box 12.3 outlines a checklist for course providers with procedures for arranging work-based learning opportunities.

Box 12.3 Learning provider procedure checklist

Procedures	Criteria, information and guidelines required
Registration of host organisations	• The course provider's requirements for host organisations, e.g. insurance, relevant policies and procedures, acceptable types of organisation and activities • What the learners require from the host organisation, e.g. dates, times, tasks, type of learners, management and supervision requirements • What information about the organisation is required by the course provider and the learners, e.g. staff contact details, types of opportunity available, requirements and expectations of learners [see also Box 12.4 for the learners' checklist] • How information about the organisation will be made available to learners and staff on the course • What the course provider will provide to the host, e.g. training, paperwork, fees, support
Matching	• Selection of host organisation: random allocation, based on preferences or learner choice • Ensuring that application, references, interview or training requirements from the organisation are addressed
Contract	• Agreements, contracts and set-up meetings to clarify the responsibilities and expectations of the host, course provider and learner • Learner induction and planned schedule • Learning outcomes expected to be addressed by the learner
Monitoring	• Contacts, three-way meetings: number and content, arrangements • Supervision requirements and records • Learner-maintained records: programmes of work, journal guidelines, health and safety audits • Supervisor/manager meetings
Assessment of learning	• Requirements for length, timescale, specific activities during the placement • Criteria and methods of assessment: observations, interviews, written reports • Guidelines for what to include in a portfolio of evidence • Weighting given to different elements of the assessment and manager/supervisor's input
Evaluation	• Feedback from learners about the host organisation and opportunities provided, and the supervisor • Feedback from host about contact with the course • Feedback from the course to the host about appropriacy and relevance of the experience for the learner

The identification and clear communication of a learner's expectations could assist in appropriate matching and selection arrangements. Specific hopes and fears may relate to work with a particular target group or issue, but may also be affected by concerns about travel time and costs. As well as consideration of practical issues, a learner could think about previous experience, levels of confidence, learning needs and interests, and the realistic availability of interesting and relevant opportunities. A learner may decide to build on knowledge developed in other settings or to develop a new area of work. Specific aspects may be more relevant to overall career plans, such as opportunities to work on certain issues, take initiative or manage a project. Others may feel that close supervision and guidance could address a lack of confidence in certain areas or their need for extra support. Although not all courses facilitate a high level of learner choice, the potential for maximising any available opportunities could depend on a learner's awareness of their preferences. Readiness to communicate and negotiate to plan a placement that addresses the learner's needs and interests could enhance the experience of all stakeholders. See Box 12.4 for a checklist to aid learners' preparation for the selection of an appropriate placement.

Box 12.4   Placement matching checklist

	Learner's 'location of self'	Questions for the host organisation
Support	❑ How far am I willing to or able to travel? ❑ What time/schedule do I have available? How many days/hours do I need to work? ❑ What support or challenge do I need? [e.g. am I confident or shy; outgoing or quiet; more comfortable or unsure in certain situations; needing close supervision or more independence; wanting opportunities to demonstrate taking initiative]	❑ What are the transport issues and requirements? [e.g. personal safety, travel time and cost, expenses] ❑ Is the organisation disability friendly and accessible? ❑ Will I be similar or different to others? [e.g. in relation to age or ethnicity, are there other students/learners there?] ❑ What personal qualities or experience do you expect or require? ❑ Do you have experience of supporting students who are...? [e.g. dyslexic, new to the field, unsure] ❑ What training or support is available?

(Continued)

(Continued)

	Learner's 'location of self'	Questions for the host organisation
Activities	❏ What experience of different activities do I have / do I want to develop? ❏ Do I need or want experience of activities that are similar or different to previous work?	❏ What activities are ongoing or developing? [e.g. one-to one work, group work, generic drop-ins, detached, research, advice, short-term projects, training, alternative education, outdoor education, mental health support, restorative justice, positive activities]
Types of groups or issues	❏ Do I need or want experience of work with individuals or groups who are similar or different to me or to previous work? ❏ Do I want an opportunity that is typical of the field or offering a unique or alternative experience?	❏ Who will I be working with? [e.g. young people who are urban or rural, single or mixed gender, volunteers, disabled, LGBT/questioning their sexuality, young parents, homeless, excluded, ex-offenders, 'at risk', carers]
Interests/skills	❏ What skills, knowledge and experiences do I have to offer?	❏ Would my enthusiasms, skills or experience be useful in this setting?

[e.g. sports, music, drama, cooking, dance, drugs, sexual health, gardening, the outdoors]

While host organisations need to check their readiness to offer opportunities for work-based learning, they may also identify some benefits. For example, a learner engaged in a formal programme of learning could provide young people in the host organisation with a perspective and approach to conversations and activities that is different to that of the usual staff. A student or trainee may be closer in age to the young people, which can provide a useful connection through shared interests and understanding, although some younger learners find the lack of a significant age gap to be difficult in relation to establishing professional relationships.

The availability of staff is paramount. Managing a placement and supervising a learner's professional development can be challenging, particularly for a small organisation that is already stretched in terms of staff time. Although a student might provide a useful 'extra pair of hands', the temporary nature of the arrangement and the management of inexperienced learners can be time-consuming. Not all learners are prepared for taking responsibility and may well require detailed instructions and close supervision. Host organisations need to consider whether staff are available to take on the challenge of providing adequate support for learning, as well as ensuring that young people's experiences and the ongoing work of the organisation are enhanced rather than jeopardised by the arrangements. Box 12.5 is a sample checklist for organisations checking their readiness for work-based learning. (See also Box 2.7 for an induction checklist.)

Box 12.5   Host organisation's readiness checklist

	Questions to consider
Does work-based learning fit with our values and culture?	• Do we look forward to the contribution of new ideas from different perspectives, e.g. the learner, the learning provider? • Do our managers and staff welcome the chance to pass on learning opportunities to others? • Would the young people and other members of communities we work with benefit from contact with a learner (or learners), e.g. as a positive role model?
Do we have sufficient staff to provide a positive experience for the learner?	Is someone available (and not on holiday): • To manage the placement and ensure that tasks are clear and carried out? • To supervise the learner to ensure that understanding and awareness of role and practice is developed? • To attend training and other information meetings required by the learning organisation? • To provide supervision and complete assessment reports? • To work alongside the learner? • To host visits to the workplace from the learning provider?
Can we provide appropriate tasks and duties for the learner?	• Do we have any useful work that someone new and/or inexperienced could carry out? • Are the tasks and duties sufficiently variable? • Would our programme of work enable the learner to meet the course provider's requirements? • Could we facilitate more than one learner at a time?
What other resources do we need to provide?	• Do we have sufficient working space for the learner? • Can we contribute to the learner's expenses? • Do we need payment for providing work-based learning?
What are our own requirements or procedures?	• Do we need the learner to complete our selection procedures, e.g. CV, application form, interview, approval by our Board? • What skills, knowledge or experience, e.g. reliability, clear motivation, willingness to learn, do we require? • What skills would we expect the learner to gain whilst on placement? • Do we require criminal record checks or pre-training prior to the learner starting with us, e.g. health and safety, diversity issues? • Do we have established induction and exit procedures? • Would the learner attend staff or other key meetings?

As relationships with young people and communities can take time to establish, learners in temporary arrangements for work-based learning may be asked to undertake a specific type of work, such as shadowing, co-working or short-term projects where exit arrangements may be easier. Fixed period agreements could range in length from three months for a typical student placement to several years for a working trainee studying part-time; the time differences would clearly affect the level and range of possible roles and responsibilities.

WORKING OUT A PROGRAMME

As professional practice values appropriate responses to individuals' needs and interests, host organisations are usually prepared to find a range of different opportunities to support learners' development. Planning an appropriate programme of work for a learner will depend on the availability of opportunities and resources within the host organisation and the skills, knowledge and experience that the learner possesses or develops through the placement. Learning providers may also stipulate certain tasks to complete to ensure that the learner is able to evidence specific learning outcomes from the experience. A learner may be required to complete a specific piece of work, such as a research project, which can provide a focus for independent activities and give space to a manager to get on with other work. A host may plan a set of tasks, role or project for a learner where help is needed. Understanding and matching various factors to find the perfect programme of work is not always possible. Difficulties can arise. A placement may be half completed before an opportunity for a project arises. A learner may turn out to be insufficiently prepared for the planned activities or may find them tedious. Early exchanges of information about expectations can alleviate some difficulties; however, building in some flexibility to address issues arising through regular communication and monitoring can assist the development of a suitable plan of action. Box 12.6 provides some examples of a variety of tasks that a learner may be able to undertake whilst on placement.

A programme of work should include a range of activities. Learners can 'try out' different tools, conversations and approaches to practice, and develop their understanding of complex relationships, such as the different ways in which staff interact and interpret their roles. Through engagement with different groups of young people, learners hear about a diversity of life stories and experiences, issues and circumstances. Outreach work in local communities means that learners get a view of different lifestyles and circumstances. Meetings with related organisations provide a deeper understanding of how youth work fits in to the wider picture of society and services. Incorporating elements of research, planning and facilitating face-to-face work and management tasks within a placement are desirable.

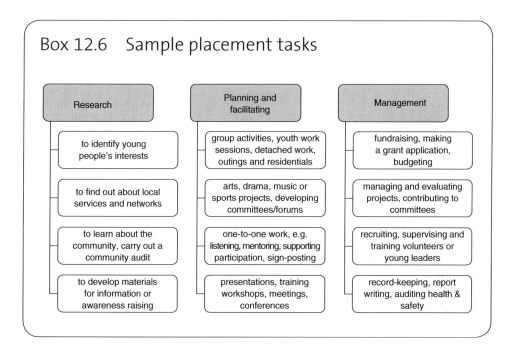

Box 12.6   Sample placement tasks

Research
- to identify young people's interests
- to find out about local services and networks
- to learn about the community, carry out a community audit
- to develop materials for information or awareness raising

Planning and facilitating
- group activities, youth work sessions, detached work, outings and residentials
- arts, drama, music or sports projects, developing committees/forums
- one-to-one work, e.g. listening, mentoring, supporting participation, sign-posting
- presentations, training workshops, meetings, conferences

Management
- fundraising, making a grant application, budgeting
- managing and evaluating projects, contributing to committees
- recruiting, supervising and training volunteers or young leaders
- record-keeping, report writing, auditing health & safety

Underestimating the time required to arrange and manage placements can lead to a number of problems, and a heavy administrative load is often a concern for all participants. Learners may take time to recognise the value of up-to-date and complete paperwork, which can lead to a backlog. Finding suitable times for three-way meetings may be difficult; efficient and current information records about placement opportunities can take time to maintain. Staff at the course provider as well as the host organisation may prioritise other work, particularly if students do not conform to usual schedules. A learner whose completion date is delayed may be left unsupported due to staff holidays. While learning about the impact of administrative demands on practice is a valuable lesson for new professionals, course providers may need to give thought to what might be feasible and to realistic expectations.

MEETING PROBLEMS

No matter how well planned, a range of difficulties can arise during placements and affect attendance, learner satisfaction or completion of the requirements. Anticipating what might go wrong can minimise errors as well as prepare those involved to deal with them. Discussions amongst all participants about expectations, constraints and preparation can also help to avoid serious issues. Conflicts may still arise between learner and manager due to personal or professional differences or inadequate communication. Some complications are due to circumstances out of anyone's control. A host organisation may experience staffing or funding cuts, restructuring or a burglary that means premises or equipment are not useable. Learning providers may need contingency planning in the form of alternative arrangements when completion of an agreement is impossible. However, many difficulties can become valuable learning experiences to be resolved through discussion and negotiation. Learning can be evidenced from an analysis of errors and poor practice through reflections and evaluation. Practice Example 12.1 outlines some examples of problems encountered by learners on placement.

PRACTICE EXAMPLE 12.1

Learners' placement problems

Inappropriate placement? They want me to wear a tie and proper shoes; I have to do the same thing every day, there's no variation; I don't feel fulfilled; My manager doesn't explain what I have to do; My supervisor keeps postponing the supervision sessions.

Poor practice? Staff: use inappropriate language; disrespect the young people; don't follow procedures or policies; waste resources.

Lack of opportunities: I don't have the chance: to work independently; to use my initiative; to complete the paperwork; for face-to-face work; to raise issues or questions.

Making mistakes: I keep: missing sessions; being late; saying the wrong thing; getting involved in criminal activity and being arrested; running out of money for transport or laundry. I can't keep up with the hours/paperwork; I don't know how to prioritise; I can't cope with the amount of work/hours.

External or unpredictable events: illness, family or close friend bereavement; car theft, personal attack or accident.

The cause of the difficulties is not always easy to ascertain. The learner's expectations, immaturity, perceptions and/or lack of preparedness may be key factors. Qualities such as confidence and emotional stability can assist individuals in minimising difficulties and dealing with issues arising (Judge and Bono, 2001). Doel's (2010) guide to social work placements emphasises how a student's mindset can affect their response to experiences. Those with a strong 'internal locus of control' are active learners in their learning experiences, whereas others who have passive expectations of learning being 'offered on a plate' sometimes struggle to resolve issues that come up. Assisting learners to develop awareness of their role and the need to take action to address any difficulties is vital when learning from experience. The placement may be an inappropriate match; the host organisation or personnel may be under stress; and/or the learner may be under-managed or poorly supervised. Finding out what is behind the statements is necessary before jumping to conclusions about causes and solutions. The following Practice Examples (12.2 and 12.3) demonstrate some of the difficulties that can arise in a placement, with some suggestions about ways the issues could be addressed through two-way discussions with learners about possible causes and ways forward.

A bored student?

My placement is nothing like what I expected: I'm doing the same thing every day and I've got hardly any face-to-face time with young people. I'm just filling in a database and making coffee. There don't seem to be any opportunities to develop anything new or get involved in interesting work.

Possible causes

- A temporary lull between projects? A lack of funding or wherewithal within the organisation to develop new work? A looming deadline for completion of the database work? The organisation's remit has changed or is different to what the learner expected?
- The learner's lack of attention span, assertiveness, flexibility or understanding of the organisation's work? Or the learner's exaggeration of the circumstances, unrealistic expectations or lack of access to the manager to discuss his concerns?
- The manager's lack of awareness of the learner's programme or discontent? Or the manager's perception of the learner as lacking in ideas or confidence in undertaking different types of work?
- The course provider's criteria for selecting placement hosts needs to be stricter or the course provider needs more up-to-date information about the host organisation's activities?

Possible ways forward:

- The course provider to review the learner's weekly records and discuss possible causes of boredom (as above) with the learner.
- The learner to ask questions in the organisation about other work going on, to be proactive about suggesting ideas for outreach, networking or project development, or to draw attention to the limited range of activities evident in the weekly record of work.
- The course provider to call a three-way meeting to review the learner's programme of work, bring up the lack of variation in activities and emphasise the need for face-to-face experience with young people as well as learning about office-based work. A plan is mutually agreed upon for the requirements of the placement to be addressed. If necessary, this may involve a secondment to a local youth group for part of the week.

PRACTICE EXAMPLE 12.2

Addressing a false start?

I just got off on the wrong foot with my manager. She right away thought I wasn't right for the job. I think she misinterpreted a few comments that I made and I was late a few times. Ever since, she's thought that I don't care about the work. It isn't true. I really want to learn. But her attitude towards me means that I'm not getting opportunities to take responsibility. I have tried to assert myself and to make suggestions about what I could do, but she is very dismissive and doesn't really listen. I would really like the chance to plan and facilitate a session, but she clearly doesn't think that I'm capable and doesn't have the time or inclination to make the arrangements for this to happen. I don't think that she respects me.

Possible causes?

- The learner has made a poor impression and the manager does have low expectations?
- The learner is being oversensitive and misinterpreted the manager's attitude?
- The manager has not listened to or heard the learner's suggestions? There may be other issues of more immediate or pressing concern or the learner may not have articulated her suggestions clearly?

Possible ways forward:

- The tutor discusses the possible causes with the learner and probes for further specific evidence and articulation of difficulties.
- The learner takes responsibility for raising the issue with the manager and articulates her interest in taking on more responsibility.
- The tutor calls a three-way meeting to discuss how the placement is progressing – encouraging articulation from the learner about her hopes for the placement and from the manager about her impressions of the learner. A plan is mutually agreed upon for the learner to take more responsibility and to improve punctuality.

REFLECTING ON PRACTICE

Planning, carrying out and evaluating practice during a placement provide relevant experience from which a learner is able to learn. Through observation, active participation and critical reflection, learners develop generic skills and 'work process knowledge', a term coined by Boreham (2002, cited in 2004) to identify the 'active' knowledge used to guide and support work developed through problem-solving in the workplace and 'synthesizing knowhow with theoretical understanding' (Boreham, 2004: 209). By trying out new pieces of work, discussing their experiences and writing about what they have learned, learners develop their self-awareness, confidence and skills and increase the range of tasks and level of responsibility they are ready to fulfil. The process involves an exploration of their response to situations, their values and beliefs with colleagues, as well as the manager and supervisor, usually from within the host organisation, and with tutorial support from the course provider.

A learner engaging in work-based learning will have access to various sources for support and direction of their practice and professional development. Identifying and using a range of support is likely to be significant in relation to making the most of the experience. Working with learners to create a 'map' of the individuals and services offering support (see Box 12.7) could be a method for course providers to communicate to learners what support is available. Learners can also identify the strengths in their support systems and any gaps. The individuals on the support map will be able to provide different perspectives on incidents that arise as well as inform the learner's exploration of good practice. (See also Chapter 13 for ways to enhance reflection.)

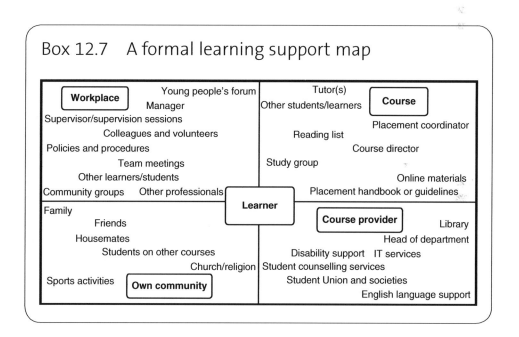

Box 12.7   A formal learning support map

Learners engaged in work-based learning are generally required to provide evidence of their experiences and critical reflection identifying their learning. In addition to fulfilling any of the host organisation's record-keeping requirements, learners will maintain more detailed and reflective records of practice such as session evaluations and journaling for submission to the course provider and assessment of learning. Through this reflection, learners identify good practice and relate their learning to other experiences, including reading and the course.

The difference between records and reflections can be seen in this description of the process:

> [M]ost students have used reflection to 'upgrade' from the 'making sense' stage of learning to that of 'making meaning'. This is essentially still a surface approach to learning; the module team, however, had hoped that reflection would lead to deeper learning where students worked with meaning, or where their learning was transformed in some way following the experience. Although for some students this was achieved, it was by no means universal. (Smith et al., 2007: 139)

While records of work may note what took place and monitor outcomes or achievements, reflective activities are intended to promote 'experiential learning', or the 'active transformation and integration of different forms of experience' (Weil and McGill, 1989: 246). Experiential learning depends not only on observation and participation in relevant activities and projects in a 'real life' work environment, but on different ways of making sense of experiences. In addition to the written records mentioned above, discussions, reading and evaluation are methods that can be used to stimulate critical reflection and experiential learning. In tutorials and supervision, learners are encouraged to apply their learning from the classroom, their reading and previous experiences to a new context, a skill that will continue to enhance their professional development throughout their career.

> We currently interpret experiential learning as the process whereby people, individually and in association with others, engage in direct encounter and then purposefully reflect upon, validate, transform, give personal and social meaning to and seek to integrate the outcomes of these processes into new ways of knowing, being, acting and interacting in relation to their world. Experiential learning therefore enables the discovery of possibilities that may not be evident from direct experience alone. (Weil and McGill, 1989: 248)

Records, supervision sessions and written pieces often use established models to structure a learner's reflections. Models for reflective practice have established key critical questions to enhance in-depth observation and analysis. Prompts that stimulate recall and thinking are key elements of Kolb and Fry's experiential learning cycle (1975) (Box 8.12 in Chapter 8), Gibbs' (1988) model of reflection (Box 12.8 below) and Johns' (1995) reflective tool based on 'ways of knowing' (1995) (see Box 13.7 in the next chapter). Common practice is to identify a situation or event that caused the learner to question the actions that took place and to analyse possible issues arising and the implications for professional practice and development. As Emslie describes in a case study of youth work education:

> Thought, feeling, knowledge and the influence of context become the subject of deliberation, judgment, discussion and appraisal. The way critical reflection is used

to improve students' decision making capacities and assist with the integration of theory and practice was observed. Moreover the exercise of human agency and responsible action is promoted, alerting students to their capacity for transformative action and professional youth work. (Emslie, 2009: 425)

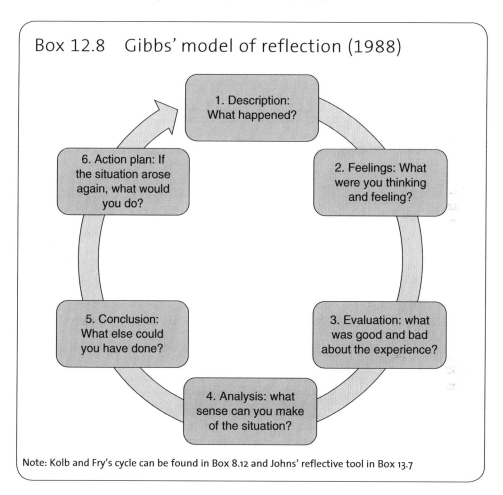

Box 12.8   Gibbs' model of reflection (1988)

1. Description: What happened?

2. Feelings: What were you thinking and feeling?

3. Evaluation: what was good and bad about the experience?

4. Analysis: what sense can you make of the situation?

5. Conclusion: What else could you have done?

6. Action plan: If the situation arose again, what would you do?

Note: Kolb and Fry's cycle can be found in Box 8.12 and Johns' reflective tool in Box 13.7

IDENTIFYING AND ASSESSING LEARNING

Ongoing and summative feedback in relation to learning outcomes and continuous development needs is good practice in any youth work project, but is particularly significant during a period of focused learning. Feedback to learners should mean that the learner is clear about what constitutes good or poor practice and understands the implications of different ways of working. Assessment and feedback on evidence presented about a learner's experiences and learning can assist the learner in developing an awareness of strengths as well as professional development needs. In more formal arrangements, criteria for passing and/or marking the evidence generally require standardised and specific types of learning. In England, the Youth Work National Occupational Standards (Learning and Skills Improvement Service, 2012), Community Development (LLUK, 2009) and Management and Leadership (MSC, 2008), which are established through consultations with various stakeholders including employers, provide some relevant definitions of professionalism and the underpinning knowledge and understanding required for practice. The standards can be useful in identifying learning objectives and outcomes from work-based learning.

A range of methods for gathering different types of evidence can assist in the process of identifying learning, achievements and development needs. Written records are generally used as a basis for formal assessment of how the learner has engaged with the opportunity, has reached certain learning goals and is ready to transfer these to future experiences. Additional methods may include evidence from other participants, such as interviews and reports, observation of practice and discussions with young people. Utilising a 360-degree approach, feedback could be elicited from various individuals encountered during the placement. In addition to self-evaluation, the perspectives of young people, colleagues, the manager/supervisor, members of communities, other professionals and the tutor could be collected. Allowing the learner to identify their own projected learning outcomes and evaluate their learning at the end of the experience could enhance their capacity for continuous professional development. Assessment of work-based learning may attempt to analyse evidence in a critical or appreciative approach, incorporate intuitive judgement and/or recognise the validity of different approaches and voices.

In a formal course of professional training, consideration needs to be given to the minimum requirements to pass the assessment. Guidance or ground rules may be provided by an educational, professional or government body about particular standards that need to be reached, however assessment is not always straightforward. Even quantitative assessment can require interpretation. For example, an attendance requirement may designate a specific number of hours in particular types of work. Questions can arise in relation to evidence and practicability. If the host organisation changes their programme or experiences a sudden funding crisis, alternative arrangements may not be possible within the time frame. Course providers will need to identify procedures for what to do when situations out of a learner's control impact on their work.

Involving young people in an appraisal of a youth worker's practice (see Box 12.9) could provide opportunities for relevant voices to be heard. How this is carried out can affect the content, quality or depth of this feedback, for example what young people are able or feel empowered to say may be determined by the ways in which they are asked for their opinions. Some methods may provide opportunities for a consensus, whilst others may be more effective in hearing individual voices, for example a group discussion may provide more possibilities for individuals to be supported in order to develop their understanding of the process and capacity for articulating their views. Whether the topics and criteria for an appraisal are set or any subject can be raised by the young people will also affect the nature and meaning of the findings.

The ethical questions that can arise when assessing learning or practice are similar to those involved in any qualitative research, such as validity, reliability and appropriacy or 'trustworthiness, rigor and quality' (Rolfe, 2006: 304). For example, the evidence

---

Box 12.9   Involving young people in appraisals

The young people

- interview the youth workers to assess their practice
- discuss the youth worker's practice and record their findings
- communicate their feedback to a blog, webpage or evaluation from
- email feedback to the youth workers or tutor
- are asked by the youth workers for feedback in a meeting, interview or evaluation exercise
- are interviewed by the manager or tutor about the youth workers' practice

---

of a manager in the assessment of a learner's development may be valid in relation to employability, but unless the manager has been working alongside the learner, the evidence may not be relevant in relation to the learner's ability to form relationships with young people. Interpreting the manager's evidence may also require an understanding of whether the manager has sufficient information about the course provider's expectations, whether developing a relationship with other staff is a key learning outcome and whether the manager is, in fact, someone difficult to please. A comparison of the feedback from one manager with that of another in a different setting raises further questions about the reliability of this common assessment requirement. Recognition of the strengths and weaknesses of specific approaches and methods can assist in identifying measures that can be taken to enhance the quality of evidence or judgements. 'Distance travelled' (Dewson et al., 2000) compares the learner's starting point with a final evaluation that may provide valid evidence of the effect of the placement on the learner.

Evidence-based assessment can include analysis and evaluation of records of work to meet certain requirements for hours of working and types of activities undertaken. Some arrangements may also include specific activities to be completed, such as a community audit; session planning, facilitation and evaluation; a funding application; practice tools or materials; or a project report. Similar difficulties may be encountered if assigning a measure to this evidence. Some supervisors are very particular in relation to learners' timesheets – noting gaps in punctuality or participation. Others may collude in learners' laxity, signing the sheet for a week without checking whether the learner was even physically present. While the factors relating to perceived good performance as a learner on placement may not relate directly to the qualities required of a youth worker, a high degree of correlation probably exists in key areas such as reliability, motivation and communication. Learners who regularly turn up on time, let managers know when issues get in the way of regular attendance, contribute their ideas to discussions and ask questions, and make their engagement with the experience apparent to others will probably be treated more favourably if difficulties then arise.

EVALUATING THE EXPERIENCE

Reviewing the arrangements and evaluating the work-based learning experience can lead to improvements for future agreements made between the course provider and the organisation. A course provider needs to know whether the procedures for matching, induction and supervision ran smoothly; whether documents and communication have been clear; whether any issues that arose indicate a need for new policies. While all participants should be encouraged to raise issues and take a proactive role in sorting them out during the placement, a final review can provide an opportunity to consider issues related to future developments or efficiency. Feedback from learners and others directly involved in a placement about the opportunity provided by a particular host organisation could address learner satisfaction and learning, as well as whether the requirements of the programme were difficult to meet. Reviewing the information provided and induction experiences may impact on the course provider's document reviews or supervisor training. The learner's evaluation of the opportunity in Box 12.10 suggests some questions that may be used to raise issues to feed back to the host organisation for reconsideration of managerial or organisational arrangements. A similar list could be used to check with the host organisation about their readiness for the experience and whether any lessons had been learned that could inform future practice.

Box 12.10　Learners' evaluation

Initial agreements

- Was the information provided about the opportunity prior to starting the agreement reasonably accurate?
- Was the induction sufficient?
- Were you given the opportunity to talk about what you wanted from the placement/project?

Programme of work

- Were travel arrangements feasible?
- Were the timings and schedule appropriate?
- Were there sufficient opportunities to work with young people?
- Did you feel sufficiently supported so you knew what to do?
- Was the work sufficiently varied?
- Was the work placement sufficiently challenging?

Ending the arrangement

- Were you given the opportunity to tie up any loose ends?
- Did you have a discussion with your manager at the end of the agreement to evaluate the arrangements?

> **Overview**
>
> - Were you able to meet the learning outcomes and other requirements that were originally agreed?
> - What would you describe as the most significant contribution to your learning from this experience?
> - What was the least satisfactory aspect of this experience?
> - If possible, would you like to return to work with this organisation?
> - Would you recommend this organisation to another student?
> - What changes would you recommend for future arrangements with this organisation?

ESSENTIAL SKILLS FOR ORGANISING PLACEMENTS

- Appreciating experiences
- Preparing for work-based learning
- Working out a programme
- Meeting problems
- Reflecting on practice
- Identifying and assessing learning
- Evaluating the experience

FURTHER READING

For useful suggestions on using a placement to improve employability in a general guide to managing a placement from the student's perspective, see Neugebauer and Evans-Brain (2009).

Parker (2010) explores the perceptions and experiences of stakeholders when social work students fail their placements, and raises a number of relevant issues for youth work placement coordinators in relation to the significance of open relationships based on an awareness of power.

Although 'recognised' standards quickly go out of date, the following lists may be accessed via the internet and may still provide some guidance for developing learning outcomes and criteria for assessment of learning:

The United Kingdom's Quality Assurance Agency for Higher Education Subject Benchmark Statement: Youth and community work (QAA, 2009)

LLUK (2009) National Occupational Standards for Community Development

Youth Work National Occupational Standards (Learning and Skills Improvement Service, 2012)

MSC (2008) National Occupational Standards for Leadership and Management

The Students Partnership Worldwide (2010) guide for youth participation in development also contains some relevant standards.

13

USING SUPERVISION

Supervision is a process of critical reflection in which youth workers discuss ongoing work and professional development issues with another practitioner, such as a manager, a practice tutor or a peer in order to identify clarity about roles, and the relationships between values, practice and development. This chapter identifies the essential skills required for effective provision and use of managerial, professional and/or educational supervision and goes through the stages of supervision, from understanding and agreeing the type of supervision being undertaken, to establishing the supervision relationship and examining practice through supervision sessions and then moving on through evaluation and exit.

Supervision, like youth work, can be a process of dialogue and problem-posing with both parties working together and learning from each other to deepen understanding. A developmental approach based on mutual respect can enable both supervisor and supervisees to learn from each others' perspectives in a relationship that is both supportive and challenging. Good supervision can provide a structure for professional youth work practice where supervisees reflect on recent work and plan future developments that are consistent with youth work principles. Challenging discussions about practical and ethical dilemmas are required to assist a youth worker to maintain focus for participative and anti-oppressive practice. Freire (1972) describes this as 'praxis', reflection and analysis of issues arising from practice to identify and plan transformative action. Without this 'liberating education' (see below), both youth workers and youth work can become forces for domestication rather than liberation.

Liberating education consists in acts of cognition, not transferrals of information ... Through dialogue, the teacher-of-the-students and the students-of-the-teacher cease to exist ... The teacher is no longer merely the-one-who-teaches, but one who is himself taught in dialogue with the students, who in turn whilst being taught also teaches. They become jointly responsible for a process in which all grow. In this process, arguments based on 'authority' are no longer valid; in order to function, authority must be on the side of freedom, not against it. Here, no one teaches another, nor is anyone self-taught. People teach each other. (Freire, 1972: 79–80)

Plans for good practice, professional development and organisational change can be positive outcomes of stimulating and challenging discussions. Monitoring changes and development in individuals and groups, as well as relationships and issues related to power, can lead to increased understanding and awareness of a situation and ways forward. A core focus of sessions can be to identify the levels of participation by young people to ensure that relevant interests and needs are addressed. A review of projects or activities may be used to question whether alternative strategies may be appropriate. Additionally, supervision often leads to a consideration of ways to implement any organisational change necessary to address barriers to participation caused by particular structures or practices within the workplace.

HAVING A PLANNED APPROACH TO SUPERVISION

A planned approach to supervision requires attention to the periods before, during and after the supervision relationship. Prior to starting supervision sessions, both supervisor and supervisee seek clarification and agreement about the type of supervision and what they bring to the relationship. The relationship and meetings are established with agreements about structure and any recording. Once the focus of the sessions is on practice, supervision includes reviews of ongoing work and discussion of relevant issues. Plans to address the issues through work and professional development are made and then reviewed in subsequent sessions. Exiting from a supervision arrangement can include a number of methods for ensuring that the supervisee continues to develop professionally. The stages in a planned approach are suggested in Box 13.1.

Box 13.1 A planned approach to supervision

Preparing for supervision	• Understanding the type of supervision required • Locating self in relation to identity, skills and experience, and boundaries
Establishing the supervision relationship	• Exchanging information about the above • Making practical arrangements to meet • Structuring the sessions • Record-keeping

(Continued)

(Continued)

Examining practice	• Listening and valuing experience
	• Providing critical feedback
	• Reviewing practice
	• Identifying issues
Moving on	• Action planning
	• Reviewing what has been achieved
	• Identifying learning outcomes
	• Allowing the relationship to end

UNDERSTANDING THE TYPE OF SUPERVISION REQUIRED

While the primary function of youth work supervision is to focus on the core values of youth work in order to maintain, support and develop professional practice, some supervision arrangements may provide more focus on the related managerial and developmental functions, which can affect the process, content and outcomes of supervision. (See Box 13.2 for a diagram about the functions of supervision.) Supervision provided by a line manager, for example, would tend to address professional values and practice within the context of the organisational aims and resources. The supervisee's job description and workload would be taken into consideration and a priority put on the successful completion of duties and responsibilities. A manager's responsibilities for quality assurance, resources, services and personnel may assist supervision to address key concerns in practical ways. However, free discussion of issues arising may be more impractical, particularly if supervision records might be used to monitor performance or to carry out disciplinary procedures. Similarly, supervision undertaken as part of an educational curriculum tends to emphasise the professional development function with the specific learning objectives, standards and requirements defined by the training provider. The sessions may include instruction on how to approach certain tasks, recommendations for reading and research and evaluation of learning. The supervisor's role in assessment of the supervisee's learning outcomes could significantly obstruct reflection on practice or the questioning of whether young people's needs were addressed. As an individual youth worker could receive managerial supervision from a line manager; non-managerial supervision for a specific project; external supervision from a colleague in another organisation; and, if undertaking training, student supervision from the educational agency, clarification from the outset of an arrangement, particularly with regards to whether the supervision is managerial or non-managerial, reported or confidential, can help both parties to utilise the sessions appropriately.

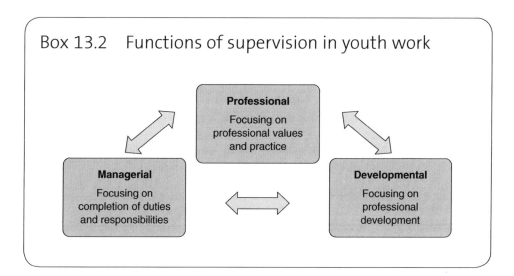

Box 13.2   Functions of supervision in youth work

Professional
Focusing on professional values and practice

Managerial
Focusing on completion of duties and responsibilities

Developmental
Focusing on professional development

Youth workers may need to seek out supervision in situations where there are gaps or unevenness in the provision or functions of supervision. Without adequate managerial supervision, individuals can be unsupported or unclear about how to prioritise or carry out their work. Some supervision may focus on control and containment to minimise resource use or change and miss out on facilitating the development of professional practice or professionalism. Alternative or additional arrangements for peer supervision, co-supervision and consultancies from within or external to the organisation may be sought out to address any gaps in available supervision. Co-supervision arrangements can provide an equal relationship without hierarchy, which may be particularly attractive to an individual feeling that their existing supervision is constrained by over-powerful managerial or assessment functions. Supervision from within the organisation can bring familiarity with the context, the available resources and organisational aims, culture and procedures. External supervision, arranged with someone who is unconnected with the supervisee's organisation, can provide a new perspective unconstrained by organisational culture. A colleague or youth worker met at a conference or networking event could provide useful peer supervision with feedback and support based on experience of similar responsibilities and challenges. Alternatively, an organisation without experience of youth work may seek out external supervision for their youth work employees to ensure that appropriate managerial and professional decisions are made. Consultancies, or short- and fixed term external supervisory arrangements, can provide access to particular knowledge or experience, particularly when lacking within an organisation.

LOCATING SELF

Preparation for supervision could also include participants taking time to identify their hopes and fears with regards to supervision, as well as any strengths or limitations that may affect the supervisory relationship or agenda. 'Location of self' or reflection on previous personal, political and work experiences to analyse and evaluate any acquired skills, knowledge, attitudes and values that may be relevant to the supervision, is a useful starting point. This reflection can enable supervisors to be clear and open about what they are able to offer as well as any gaps. Similar reflection and preparation by supervisees can enable them to articulate their needs and interests and to take a more active role in setting an agenda for supervision that will address them. (See Practice Example 13.1 which illustrates 'location of self' and Box 4.3 in Chapter 4 contains some additional examples): The process can be developed into ongoing 'self supervision', which Hawkins and Shohet (2006:42) say requires individuals to monitor and confront their ways of working.

PRACTICE EXAMPLE 13.1

A supervisor's 'location of self'

An experienced practitioner was asked to supervise a recently qualified youth worker who was starting a group aiming to raise young women's educational and career aspirations. Before meeting the supervisee, the supervisor reflected on her own experience in order to 'locate' her perspective and identify relevant strengths as well as gaps. The supervisor had not worked with a young women's group before, but had a good understanding of starting and developing mixed gender projects, and of some of the issues faced by young women. For example, she was aware that homeless young women in the area were exchanging sex for a place to stay and personal experience of sexism enabled her to make links between societal attitudes and the young women's perceived and genuine options.

To address the identified gaps, the supervisor visited a couple of young women's projects proactively involved in specific anti-sexist activities and staff training, carried out some reading about challenging sexism and discussed methods of promoting positive images of women and girls with colleagues. She focused on her own current practice and involved young women in developing some peer education materials and activities on sex working to build their confidence, assertiveness and enquiry skills. These various forms of professional development enhanced the direction and feedback she could provide for the new youth worker and enabled her to suggest up-to-date reading material and contacts.

The identification of boundaries in relation to practical arrangements for supervision is also a significant part of preparation and location of self. Box 13.3 lists some relevant topics for consideration, such as preferences for scheduling and venues as well as style and/or approaches to supervision. While some supervisory situations have less flexibility, arrangements to suit the individuals concerned can often be accommodated. Communication and establishing a common understanding about practicalities, expectations and ways of working can assist the supervisory relationship to flourish. Discussion of these key points could provide an opportunity for participants to get to know each other, clarify arrangements and reach agreement on the function and nature of the relationship.

Box 13.3 Identifying boundaries for supervision

Arrangements	
Contacts, timing and dates	When and where do I wish to be contacted or can messages be left? What time do I have available for supervision sessions? Can I allocate an interruption-free time slot on a specific day and time? How long do I think the meetings should be and how frequent? Would it be better to arrange (and diary) several meetings in advance? How long can I commit myself for? When do I think I would like to review the arrangements? Would I prefer an open-ended or fixed term agreement?
Venue	Can I travel to meetings or do I need them to be held at my workplace? Where can we meet undisturbed? Is the venue appropriate in relation to privacy, safety, atmosphere and comfort?
Approach to supervision	Do I prefer or need formally recorded and structured meetings or more free-flowing discussion? Do I have flexible approaches to practice or a preference for clear ground rules and boundaries?
Records	What records will be kept and who will have access to them? Do I need my own records of the sessions? What records does the organisation require and what is their purpose? Who is responsible for the records? Do I have any control over them?
Ethical boundaries	What issues would raise ethical questions for me? What issues would I report to a manager, a training agency, the social services or the police? What personal, political or professional information do I consider to be relevant or irrelevant for these sessions?
Cancellations and punctuality agreements	How much notice do I need for cancellations? How have I responded to previous cancellations? How would I prefer cancellations to be handled? How strongly do I feel about punctuality? How have I responded to late arrivals in the past? What arrangements would I like to establish in relation to time-keeping?
Own development needs	What do I expect from the other participant in relation to experience, issues or areas of work? What support, information or learning do I need to make this arrangement useful or work well?
Other issues to consider	What problems have I encountered previously in relation to supervision? What issues have been raised in feedback? How have I reacted to challenges or advice?

KEEPING APPROPRIATE RECORDS

Records of sessions reflecting the supervisees' language and ideas can show that a supervisor values the supervisee's experience and perspective. A record can remind both parties of the issues discussed to provide continuity between sessions, monitor development, identify patterns in issues arising and, in student supervision, assist in the completion of assessment forms. Going through a record of a session together to check accuracy can establish mutual understanding of key issues and any action for subsequent sessions. Sometimes minimal records are sufficient. Summarising the points at the end of a session can preclude the need for taking extensive and intrusive notes during the sessions.

Reaching agreement on the purpose and content of the records is essential. Clarity about any monitoring or reporting requirements and whether these could be used as evidence in appraisal or promotion, disciplinary matters or assessment must be established prior to recording. A manager may be required to follow established procedures for quality assurance. Student supervision may have particular forms for assessment purposes. Shared understanding about what happens to records could help to reduce problems arising from unexpected demands made at a later date. (See Practice Example 13.2 which illustrates the importance of having clarity about supervisory roles and records.)

PRACTICE EXAMPLE 13.2

Conflicting roles and records

A youth worker, who was also a part-time student, asked her manager for suggestions about how to extend her experience of supervision. The manager arranged for her to provide *internal non-managerial supervision* for an individual from another team. A series of sessions was negotiated for the purpose of mutual learning. The supervisee used the sessions to raise and discuss some difficulties he was experiencing with his manager.

After a while, the supervisees' manager contacted the student to make enquiries about her opinion of the supervisee's practice and what information she had about why the supervisee had missed a particular work session. As the student and supervisee had agreed previously that the records would only be used to provide a reminder of issues raised, the student said that the information was confidential. The manager stated that it was the organisation's usual practice to use supervision recordings as evidence in disciplinary matters.

The student had not been provided with the policies, procedures or authority within the organisation to carry through issues raised within supervision and had not understood that she would be taking on a formal supervisory role. She had initiated and negotiated a more supportive type of peer supervision, which she felt was being compromised by demands for records for formal disciplinary procedures. She had learned a useful lesson about the importance of clarity about roles and records.

STRUCTURING THE SESSIONS

Supervision can take place within a series of regular and structured two-way meetings to ensure that professional values are maintained through continuous critical reflection; other arrangements may be much more ad hoc.

Supervision carried out at regular intervals and within a format that is suitably structured to ensure that sufficient time is allocated for key issues and planning can be particularly effective. While a formal agenda is not essential, the establishment of a pattern for the supervision sessions can encourage focused and useful discussion. Agreements about the structure of the sessions and other protocols can clarify the power relationship and responsibility for the issues raised, and their prioritisation can be shared. Supervisees can become involved in planning the session and actively addressing their own learning needs by raising any topics of concern. The agenda in Box 13.4, for example, encourages the supervisor to take responsibility for moving the session on and the supervisee to be responsible for identifying relevant issues. The supervisee can be asked to prioritise points within the time constraints of a particular session. This dialogical approach encourages the development of plans that are realistic and practical.

Box 13.4   A supervision agenda

Agenda items	Supervisor's prompts	Supervisee's actions
1 Share news	• Tell me what's going on... • Any good or positive developments at work since we last met?	Reflects on recent practice prior to the session to identify positive as well as negative practice issues for discussion
2 Set the agenda	• What do we need to talk about during this session? • Is there anything left over from the last session? • Can we make a list?	Brings along any records of work, such as a diary or notes from the last session. Reviews these prior to the session and identifies any matters arising.
3 Review ongoing work	• Let's look at how your work is going with the 'xyz' project. • How have your work plans with 'abc' been progressing?	Raises any issues that have caused concern or second thoughts. Passes on sufficient information for the supervisor to understand the context.

(Continued)

Agenda items	Supervisor's prompts	Supervisee's actions
(Continued)		
4 Focus on issues	• Let's focus on the issues/ items on the list in more detail.	Attempts to recall accurate details of the circumstances surrounding events, such as exact words used, emotions felt and expressed and relevant contributory factors.
5 Plan	• What plans can we make to address the issues arising? • What new plans do you have for the 'abc' and 'xyz' projects?	Makes sure to raise any issues that would make plans unrealistic.
6 Confirm next meeting	• When should we meet again?	Confirms satisfactory arrangements. Raises any concerns.
7 Agree record	• Can we agree that these notes are an accurate record of the important points raised?	Checks for accuracy.

Both parties are responsible for ensuring that the sessions address relevant youth work issues and practice – although a supervisor who is supervising a student takes ultimate responsibility for this. The purpose of supervision is to challenge and develop practice rather than resolve personal issues. While some individuals need time to settle into a session through greetings and chat about family, health or holidays, both need to make sure that this does not take up much time in the session. If someone appears to need extra time to discuss domestic arrangements or emotional responses to situations or if an individual appears overly distressed or depressed, the supervision session should be brought to an end. Communicating continued interest in providing support for a supervisee's professional development through supervision can be separated from signposting the individual to useful alternative means of support for their emotional health.

LISTENING

Supervisors strive to provide an appropriate balance between stimulating reflection, listening and feedback. Attentive listening can enable a full exploration of issues and feedback should assist progression towards understanding of how they can be addressed. Initially, supervisees are encouraged to outline their recent work experiences and a supervisor listens attentively to hear the supervisees' perspective on what has taken place. As supervisees recall and articulate their experience, they begin to explore their roles and responsibilities, the consequences of their actions and other influences on situations. Paying attention to the detail in what supervisees are saying, both verbally and non-verbally, about particular circumstances and feelings generated can assist a supervisor to gain a full picture and understanding of a supervisee's experiences. Careful listening also allows a supervisor to recall information later in the session or in subsequent sessions, and to focus on the supervisee's account and agenda. According to Egan, good attending in counselling enables the:

> 'helper to listen carefully to what clients are saying, both verbally and nonverbally. Total or complete listening involves three things: (1) observing and reading the client's nonverbal behaviour – posture, facial expression, movement, tone of voice and the like; (2) listening to and understanding the client's verbal messages; and (3) listening in an integrated way to the person in the context of both the helping process and everyday life.' (1986: 79)

Supervisors, as well as counsellors, have identified that responses conveying a listener's interest and demonstrating that information has been heard can encourage further exploration of an issue. Active listening techniques (Rogers, 1969 and Egan, 1986), such as 'paraphrasing the feelings and content' can convey interest and 'clarifying and summarising', can convey understanding. However, attempting empathy or 'thinking in someone else's terms', such as in the active listening approach used by counsellors and described by Rogers and Farson below are likely to be beyond the remit of youth work supervision.

> Active listening carries a strong element of personal risk. If we manage to accomplish what we are describing here – to sense deeply the feeling of another person, to understand the meaning his experiences have for him, to see the world as he sees it – we risk being changed ourselves. For example, if we permit ourselves to listen our way into the psychological life of a labor leader or agitator – to get the meaning which life has for him – we risk coming to see the world as he sees it. It is threatening to give up, even momentarily, what we believe and start thinking in someone else's terms. It takes a great deal of inner security and courage to be able to risk one's self in understanding another. (1987: 327)

A supervisor may use other counselling skills, such as avoiding interpretative statements and asking relevant open questions rather than probing, to allow the supervisee to explore issues and incidents on their own terms, provide their own emphasis and identify meaning that is significant to them.

PROVIDING FEEDBACK

A supervisor responds to what supervisees say about their practice with positive and critical feedback, as well as suggestions for further thought.

Highlighting a supervisee's description of good practice can affirm and confirm positive developments, as well as identify and value the particular skills and knowledge underpinning their actions. Positive feedback will ensure that supervisees are aware of how to continue this approach. Building on good practice and making further plans to extend young people's involvement or participation can further enhance supervisees' professional development.

Supervisors are also required to provide an alternative perspective and more challenging or critical feedback in relation to professional values and practice. A supervisor should not ignore or collude with poor practice. If a supervisee describes inappropriate, dangerous or oppressive practice, a clear professional perspective is required. Critical feedback may be necessary when supervisees use inappropriate language, express oppressive attitudes or tell the supervisor about situations where mistakes have been made without any apparent intention of addressing the consequences. A supervisor is responsible for ensuring that supervisees recognise bad practice, learn from their mistakes and develop ways to address them.

In order to stimulate supervisees to look at their practice in new ways, feedback can provide new frames of reference to alter a supervisee's way of looking at a situation (see Box 13.5 for some 'framing' techniques). Using metaphors or a contrasting situation, for example, can assist in a change of perspective. Supervisors need to monitor their responses to make sure that a relevant tool provides insight rather than gets in the way of communication. If a framing technique is over-used, the method can lose meaning or if misused or misapplied, the frame is only confusing. For example, a supervisor may identify a tradition or pattern of behaviour within an organisation that in her mind illuminates the organisational culture. Partial evidence could lead to an inaccurate analysis, and continuous reference to 'organisational culture' as a catch-all explanation for issues arising could become unhelpful.

Box 13.5   'Framing' techniques

Metaphor: using a parallel example or symbol to highlight themes that may be similar to the current topic.

Jargon and catchphrases: using familiar language or slogans that relate to a subject.

Contrast: providing a definition of a situation in terms of what it is not.

Spin: talking about various aspects of a subject, such as the positive or negative implications.

Stories: using as an anecdote, myth or legend, to engage attention and emotion.

(Adapted from Fairhurst and Sarr, 1996: 101)

The provision of appropriate feedback requires a supervisor to be able to assess and understand supervisees' responsibilities and roles. A supervisor needs clarity about the level of control or power that a supervisee can exert in the context of the work setting. An awareness of available resources, potential for change and a clear view of the type of work that a supervisee should be carrying out also enhances appropriate feedback or direction. Effective supervisors are able to provide positive, constructive and informative reactions and suggestions. When thinking is stimulated and debates are carried out on a level that is understood, supervisees can be encouraged to continue to develop their awareness and practice. This 'conversational learning', as described by Baker et al. (see below), can enable learners to construct meaning and transform experiences into new knowledge. The reference to 'ontological resource' highlights the value of dialogue in developing a deep understanding of self and others, which supervision can provide.

> Taking the time to hear other perspectives through the telling of each other's stories can often provide a path for returning to the questions or decisions at hand in ways that are easier to hear. In storytelling and in recursive conversations, new ways of framing can be grasped – apprehended – and the ontological recourse informs the learning. (Baker et al., 2005: 420)

REVIEWING THE SUPERVISEE'S PRACTICE

Reviewing practice and applying principles to practice are the essential ingredients in professional supervision. A supervisor assists youth workers to focus on different aspects of practice. A review could include looking at the overall programme of work, a particular work responsibility or session, any developments since the last supervision session, recent events or issues arising. The process can involve reviews of work records and other relevant documents for problem-solving, planning and/or evaluation. Recording forms, diaries and evaluation sheets can be useful bases for discussion. The review can then relate to whether the practice meets the requirements of the post or placement, addresses professional values and principles, makes practical sense in relation to the time and resources available, and involves sufficient variation, change and development for both the young people involved and the youth worker.

Supervision can assist youth workers in making sense of organisational or managerial targets. The process of an overall review of a programme of work can start with an analysis of how supervisees actually spend their time in comparison with the needs of the young people and their communities, the job description, project brief or student placement requirements. The needs of the young people may be contradictory. An organisation's expectations may not be feasible or fall within professional boundaries. Supervision can assist supervisees in identifying and negotiating feasible ways of moving forward. Supervisees can explore methods of asserting themselves, raising issues or challenging rules or requirements. Alternatively, supervisees may need to find a way to work within constraints that is compatible with the profession and resources.

A useful tool to structure reflection on practice could be Johns (1995) series of questions based on Carper's four 'ways of knowing' (cited in Johns). The questions are designed to facilitate learning from experience in a process of defining and understanding practice that liberates an individual from previous ways and empowers action to effect changes. Box 13.6 outlines Johns' questions.

Box 13.6   Johns' (1995) reflective tool

Aesthetics	What was I trying to achieve? Why did I respond as I did? What were the consequences of that for the young person/colleague/ member of the community directly concerned? Others? Myself? How was this person (or these people) feeling? How did I know this?
Personal	How did I feel in this situation? What internal factors were influencing me?
Ethics	How did my actions match with my beliefs? What factors made me act in an incongruent way?
Empirics	What knowledge did or should have informed me?
Reflexivity	How does this connect with previous experiences? Could I handle this better in a future similar situation? What would be the consequences of alternative actions for: The young person/colleague/member of the community directly concerned? Others? Myself? How do I now feel about this experience? Can I support myself and others better as a consequence? What have I learned from this experience? (Have I changed my ways of knowing?)

EVALUATING YOUTH WORK PRACTICE

A review of a specific piece of work can evaluate practice in relation to youth work aims and values. A supervisor can provide questions that supervisees apply to a project, event or provision to identify whether good youth work practice has been carried out. Box 13.7 provides some examples of how to stimulate a professional analysis of participation. Through analysis, supervisees begin to identify issues and problems.

Box 13.7   Evaluating supervisees' practice

A supervisor could invite supervisees to review a piece of work through asking:

- How do members participate in decisions made about the design, management and evaluation of this provision?

- Who would feel unwelcome or excluded from this group?
- How was this piece of work inclusive?
- How would the current members react to new members?
- How would (a specific group, such as wheelchair users, younger members, non-readers) participate in this activity?
- What are the reasons for targeting this specific group? Does this relate to issues of exclusion or oppression from other activities?
- How does this work fit into organisational priorities, your job description, anti-oppressive practice?

A supervisor encourages a supervisee to examine issues from the perspective of groups and individuals in the community, the agency and the profession. Planning and prioritising will need to balance various considerations or needs, such as young people's needs, organisational priorities and youth work values. Organisational priorities will often impact on planning. Whether the priorities have been formally set, evolved through habit or discussed with managers, the process of identifying problem areas and making plans may challenge existing ways of working. Supervisees need to think about the impact of changes they plan and how to involve others in that change.

Role clarity is an important outcome of supervision. Evaluation is based on an understanding of youth work roles and practice. A supervisor assists supervisees to come to an understanding of how the aims of the profession relate to their work practice. Supervisees examine underlying principles as well as the overall aims of their job, project or placement. The evaluation identifies practice that conforms to the aims, as well as practice that conflicts. Practice Example 13.3 illustrates instances of a supervisor using supervision to address a supervisee's poor practice.

Tackling poor practice through supervision

Supervisee doesn't address own power

Supervisee: I can't believe the attitude of workers in this organisation. They have such low expectations of the young people and they speak to them really disrespectfully. No one plans anything and there is no structure to the sessions.

Supervisor asks questions: *What is your response when the issues arise (in the immediate or short term)? Where could you raise these issues? How could you influence positive change?*

Supervisee finds a worker incapable

Supervisee (a manager): I've told the youth worker that she needs to distance herself more from the young people. When we discuss different options with the young people, she intervenes with her opinions. The idea is to offer them the opportunity to make

(Continued)

PRACTICE EXAMPLE 13.3

(Continued)

their own decisions, not to influence their choices. Despite several review sessions where I have pointed out that she needs to be a worker offering options, not a member of the group stating opinions, she seems unable to grasp her role.

Supervisor raises possible underlying causes: Before we dismiss her capability to understand the need for distance, we could consider other possible explanations. (If necessary, the supervisor could also prompt: She could need further clarification or more specific instruction. Perhaps she is not listening to you. She may disagree with you or have a different perception of their needs.)

Supervisee has 'tried everything'

Supervisee: I have an unreliable member of staff who is continually late, makes excuses for missing meetings and leaves early without explanation. I've tried talking with her, recording disciplinary warnings, changing the schedule, trying to find out what's going on... I've no idea what to do.

Supervisor presents an alternative perspective: So your understanding is that the individual is unreliable. Perhaps she sees herself as being put upon, excluded or denied responsibility? She could feel unneeded or under-utilised. What are some of the possible causes of lack of motivation? Addressing the professional development and practice needs arising

---

Whether issues are identified by supervisees or the supervisor, reflection on practice can assist supervisees to find ways forward. Developing methods to avoid or address difficult situations in the future forms part of learning. A supervisor may use suggestions or invite further analysis to assist supervisees in working on issues. Supervisees can be asked to reflect on discrepancies within their accounts or behaviour. A supervisor may provide factual information, positive suggestions or 'handy hints' from experience or an area of expertise. Supervisors may confront supervisees with an alternative frame of reference or ask the supervisee to look at a situation from another point of view. A supervisee might be engaged in a discussion of the moral or professional questions arising from a situation, or be provided with a parallel scenario for analysis and discussion. Assisting supervisees to 'unpack' or analyse issues and situations is often a useful method of developing practice. Provision of a framework for analysing the circumstances or contributory factors in the situation could assist in the development of requisite skills or strategies to develop a more professional approach.

Supervision can be used to plan specific steps to address barriers and progress work towards long-term goals. Practice Example 13.4 provides an illustration of how supervision can be used to identify an issue and naturally lead on to relevant planning. Supervisees can be encouraged to identify the strengths of a situation to build a solution based on reality, what can be achieved within a specific period with indicators of achievement, and what resources can be used. Establishing clearly communicable aims can assist the supervisee to see how others might be involved in taking the plans forward. A supervisor expresses interest in supervisees' opinions and takes care not to provide all the answers. Supervisees are encouraged to come up with their own solutions to problems and analyses of situations.

> One of our greatest difficulties in any dispute is to recognize or, even more difficult, to accept that the certitude we feel about our own rightness and goodness is equaled by the certitude of the opposing individual or group about their rightness and goodness. If tension is to be reduced, it is this pattern that must somehow be dissolved.' (Rogers, 1978: 123).

This affirmative approach allows supervisees to acknowledge mistakes, present their practice honestly and make practicable plans to address their errors.

Using supervision to address development needs

PRACTICE EXAMPLE 13.4

A Deaf youth worker brought up complaints about her workplace during *external supervision*. She felt unsupported; her hearing manager was prejudiced; she had insufficient assistance to produce reports to schedule. She was on the point of taking out grievance procedures due to what she saw as bullying and oppressive behaviour.

The supervisor listened carefully and then encouraged the supervisee to consider the situation from the manager's perspective. As her written reports were sufficiently coherent for the organisation's requirements and she presented herself confidently and articulately, how was the manager to know that she was having difficulty? The supervisee began to recognise that perhaps she had not sufficiently communicated her needs or her career and professional development aspirations to her manager.

The supervisor was able to assist the supervisee to put together a sensible and costed-out development plan, which would enable her to access available resources for English language support and further career development. The shared perspective of the external supervisor in relation to the importance of enabling Deaf people's participation, along with some ideas about related practice, provided an understanding of the barriers as well as some suggestions for ways forward.

(Note: Deaf is capitalised in recognition of the linguistic and cultural identity of Deaf communities.)

IDENTIFYING LEARNING

Encouraging supervisees to recognise their learning in relation to specific pieces of work or recognising what they have achieved is part of the ongoing process of supervision. A supervisor may create opportunities for reflection on specific areas of practice or draw out learning from issues arising. A formal or thorough review at certain key points can assist recognition of the journey taken and help to identify learning from the process. Acknowledgement of what has been achieved could include going back to the original agreement, contract or ground rules and reviewing progress. Carrying out regular evaluation of professional development assists in the identification of learning and progression.

Student supervision has a clear educative and assessment function. Learning outcomes are generally specified and set by the training and/or professional agency. Part of each supervision session could focus on these outcomes and both supervisees and the supervisor can identify areas of development which are relevant to youth work practice. The evaluation process at the end of a time-specified placement could also focus on what a student has learned and how certain competencies or learning outcomes have been addressed. Additional and related learning outside of specified outcomes can highlight current issues based on actual practice and enhance ongoing reflective practice.

REVIEWING ARRANGEMENTS

A supervisor should encourage supervisees to provide feedback about supervisory practice and address the relevant issues: reviewing whether a supervisory arrangement has been useful and whether the sessions should continue, change or end (see Box 13.8 for some suggested topics for evaluation). Regularly scheduled communication about the arrangements can include formative evaluation to ensure that supervision continues to meet supervisees' needs. Such reviews can also highlight whether issues of power are negatively affecting the supervision. Summative evaluation at the end of an arrangement could include more formal evaluation forms or appraisals of progress if necessary.

Box 13.8   Evaluating supervision

A supervisor could:

- ask how the supervisee is feeling about the supervision at the end of each session
- check whether the suggestions, information and advice discussed during supervision have been followed up
- notice whether the work plans have been implemented
- designate a time for review of the sessions and the supervision records, such as the middle and/or end of a work placement or after the completion of a specific piece of work or project
- invite the supervisee to comment on whether the supervision has covered relevant issues of concern
- use open questions to find out whether the sessions are meeting the supervisee's needs

- review the arrangements for suitability to both parties at regular intervals
- provide opportunities for supervisees to indicate their level of satisfaction with the approach to supervision being used
- review the agenda points that supervisees bring to the session to assess whether they have been fully addressed.

A supervisee could reflect on whether:

- the timing and venue for sessions were convenient
- sessions were uninterrupted
- copies of supervision records were provided, accurate or useful
- enough information was provided
- confidentiality was discussed
- issues could be raised and discussed
- sufficient support was felt
- sufficient challenge or stretch was felt
- plans made in supervision were implemented and practicable
- feedback about the sessions was invited and received well.

ALLOWING THE RELATIONSHIP TO END

Either party may wish to end a supervisory relationship. A decision to end a supervisory arrangement may arise due to external changes or readiness for a change expressed during a discussion and review of the relationship. A supervisee may require a supervisor with a different perspective or understanding of issues, or who is accessible at different times or venues. The type of supervision, the level of agreement or understanding between the supervisor and supervisee, and any of the issues arising may affect whether such changes are possible. Negotiating a change within a large organisation might be agreed, and ending an arrangement with an external supervisor is usually straightforward.

A supervisor may end a supervisory relationship because the supervision is not proving to be effective or feasible. As a supervisor is responsible for supervisees' professional approach to practice, continuing supervision may not be possible with a supervisee who refuses to address concerns raised. If a range of approaches have been attempted and a supervisee remains unresponsive, a supervisor may need to end the arrangement. In internal, particularly managerial supervision arrangements, additional procedures may be required, such as disciplinary procedures. Supervisors of students usually need to alert the training agency about such issues.

The ending of a supervisory relationship generally includes an exit strategy, particularly when the ending is expected, agreed and/or otherwise accepted. Highlighting the positive aspects of the supervision, the learning that has been achieved on both sides and options for future supervision is an important aspect of an exit strategy. Supervisees should be clear about ways to move forward and be provided with contacts and methods to promote their continued professional development.

ESSENTIAL SKILLS FOR USING SUPERVISION

- Having a planned approach to supervision
- Understanding the type of supervision required
- Locating self
- Keeping appropriate records
- Structuring the sessions
- Listening
- Providing feedback
- Reviewing the supervisee's practice
- Evaluating youth work practice
- Identifying learning
- Reviewing arrangements
- Allowing the relationship to end

 FURTHER READING

Many books about supervision aimed at nurses, counsellors or social workers can provide relevant frameworks, discussions of issues and methods. A few are suggested here: Brown and Bourne (1996); Carroll and Holloway (1999); Carroll and Tholstrop (2001); Kadushin (1992); Pritchard (1995). Hawkins and Shohet's (2006) book presents a useful outline of supervision from different perspectives, including a 'seven-eyed' supervision model that can be easily transferred to a youth work setting. Tash's (1967) exploration of developing supervisory relationships illustrates the value of regular and continuous supervision.

APPENDIX: YOUTH WORK DEFINITIONS

The definitions of terms in this section relate to their application in youth work practice and include some suggestions for further reading. Cross references within the list appear in italics.

Ableism: A belief in the superiority of individuals who conform to an assumed physical or mental norm and discrimination against individuals with different learning, mental or physical abilities, appearance, impairment or illness sometimes known as 'disabilism'. Includes personal or individual *prejudice* as well as *societal, institutional* and internalised *oppression*. (See Oliver, 1996, and *a social model of disability*.)

Accountability: Communicating to *stakeholders* about on-going work, financial records or plans so that relevant parties can provide feedback or informed decisions.

Activist: An unpaid individual whose own perspective or beliefs provide the motivation for practice. An activist is usually unconstrained or governed by external standards.

Advocate: Acting or speaking on behalf of an individual or group; or, supporting a cause that does not directly affect oneself.

Ageism: Generalised and negative assumptions about individuals who appear to be of a specific age group that can lead to the denial of equality of opportunity or treatment. Often directed at younger or older people with derogatory language or references to lack of abilities to understand or make their own decisions. (See Snape and Redman, 2003.)

Aims: The purpose, direction or goals of an organisation, group or project that can be used to identify changes that need be made, consider whether plans actually address them and evaluate *outcomes*.

Animator or animateur: An individual whose goal is to transform individuals and groups through their participation in social, educational and creative activities and projects that enhance self-expression.

Anti-oppressive practice: Addressing or countering the effects of *oppression* through proactive work that raises awareness of *prejudice*, illuminates different experiences and challenges discriminatory practice or attitudes.

Appreciative Inquiry: A strengths-based approach to youth and community work, research and organisational management that explores possibilities for change by establishing what the individuals, organisations or communities concerned identify as strengths, 'dreams' and ways to work towards these and make the changes sustainable (Cooperrider and Whitney, 2005).

Area youth worker: Works with young people within a designated geographic area, which may be defined by political, natural or built boundaries and may be larger than a particular neighbourhood.

Audit: A check or review to make sure that standards are being met and that system controls are in place, such as financial records, health and safety systems, organisational policies. A social audit checks and reports on an organisation's impact on society and ethical behaviour; a community audit (or community profile) examines a community's strengths and any gaps in services. (See Hawtin and Percy-Smith, 2007 and Holdsworth, 2002.)

Autonomy: Self-government, independence and the capacity to make and act on decisions. Young people develop their capacity to make decisions through their involvement in self-governing organisations.

Black perspective: Recognition of the collective capacity of black people to define, develop and advance their own political, economic, social, cultural and educational interests (Best, as cited in Sapin, 2005). Youth work practice with a black perspective promotes an understanding of black peoples' cultures and histories as well as challenging the social constructs of '*race*' and *racism*.

Budget: A plan outlining how resources will be obtained (the income) and used (the expenditure) during a period, usually including headings for staffing, equipment and *running costs*.

Capital: Cash and resources, including the assets of an organisation, such as a building, computers, furniture, equipment, vehicles. Capital expenditure is usually a separate budget heading from *running costs* or staffing.

Caste: A hereditary system that dictates social position and status. See also *class*.

Catchment area: An organisation's geographical target area, which may define boundaries for practice and/or address eligibility for membership or participation in a project.

Centre-based youth work: Carried out within a venue or facility that may be purpose-built for young people's activities or owned and used by other groups and purposes, such as a church, sports centre or school.

Challenge: Raising awareness of or addressing unfair, discriminatory or unprofessional *practice*, attitudes or information, including questions to stimulate thinking; pointing out contradictory facts; bringing attention to motivation or procedures; requesting or demanding an explanation, justification or proof. (See Mullaly, 2002.)

Class and classism: A social construct that distinguishes economic and social status and is often used as an indicator of an individual's position, status or power in society. Classism is based on prejudiced assumptions about individuals and groups from specific classes that can lead to discrimination and denial of equality of opportunity and access to resources. *Caste*, inheritance and heritage through family trees or ancestry are related prejudices.

Codes of practice: The requirements and expectations of workers and members outlined in relation to organisational standards and how they can be achieved. Issues such as equality, ethics, conflicts of interest, duty of care, respect for young people, *accountability* and *confidentiality*, are addressed and detailed in *policies* and *procedures*, such as those related to fees, contracts, quality assurance or evaluation.

Community work: Work with individuals and groups in a community to bring them together for collective activities and action in relation to issues that affect them.

Community development work: Work as a *facilitator* and *enabler* to improve the capacity of a community to address their physical, economic, political, educational and social needs.

Confidentiality: An agreement to protect and limit the use of information, particularly when related to individuals' personal details, history or circumstances.

Conflict resolution: Although 'conflict' usually refers to irresolvable differences between individuals or groups, such as opposing values or fundamental needs, positive work related to conflicts could include peacemaking based on understanding of these differences or mediation to identify ways of defusing anger and aggression. (See Thompson, 2006, and MacBeth & Fine, 1995).

Consensus: A widely held understanding of a concept or general agreement within a group or community that could be based on an accurate analysis or a false premise. A full consensus can be reached when participants negotiate and agree a decision. Genuine consensus depends on access to and understanding of accurate evidence, a wide exploration of views and unanimous and voluntary compliance. (See Brunson, et al., 2002, for ways to use arts to develop consensus.)

Cultural competence: The confidence to interact with the individuals and organisations from another culture or identity that may be enhanced by relevant knowledge, understanding and practice.

Deficit model: The perception of a community, group or individual as inadequate, lacking something or failing to meet an often ill-defined goal, which assigns blame and responsibility to them rather than examining the circumstances or the 'service' they receive.

Depreciation: A figure or percentage of purchase price used in budgets to indicate the level at which an item decreases in value over time. Enables financial resources to be allocated for replacement of a larger piece of equipment or vehicle when necessary.

Detached young people: Are not connected to or supported by family, school, employment or other social institutions and services. (See also *exclusion*.)

Detached youth work: Going out into a community to make contact and build relationships for informal education, signposting and enjoyable activities with young people in their own 'space'. See also *street-based youth work*, Arnold et al. (1981), Crimmens et al. (2004) and Tiffany (2007).

Discrimination: Different and unequal treatment of individuals, bodies or groups because of perceived differences.

Dissemination: Distribution and publicity about research *findings* or information.

Diversity: Recognition of the range of different individuals, ethnic groups, groups of interest and identities that supports their rights to *equal opportunities*. (See Faulkner et al., 1994, for discussion of diversity in relation to practice.)

Emancipator: Works with individuals to set them free from oppression, slavery, restricted aspirations or limited opportunities.

Empower: To promote opportunities for other to develop their skills and confidence or self-esteem, which enables them to exercise their power to make decisions or take actions.

Enabler: Provides the resources and opportunities to make something possible or feasible. The term is applied positively to the role of a community or youth worker or negatively to someone assisting an abuser.

Equal opportunities: Access to basic social justice, employment and services, such as health, education, housing, without negatively discrimination.

Evaluation: Reviewing records to determine the value, success, quality, importance, extent or condition of a group or project, particularly in relation to the original aims, objectives and targets. Can be external or internal, ongoing (formative) or at the end (summative).

Evidence-based practice: Using methods or procedures that have been monitored through research and/or *evaluation* and been found to be successful or effective.

Exclusion: Not being permitted or being able to participate fully so that access to social or economic opportunities that are available to others, such as education, housing, employment, family life, the arts or sports, is denied. Some young people may 'self exclude'. Poverty, prejudice or lack of information, welcome or confidence may prevent participation. Schools may deny young people the opportunity to attend school on a temporary or permanent period for disciplinary reasons. Sometimes referred to as social exclusion. See also *financial exclusion*.

Exit strategy: A planned withdrawal from a commitment that keeps those concerned informed about any resulting changes. For example, when a worker is unable to continue with a particular group of young people or to provide supervision for a colleague, those concerned are informed about any alternative arrangements.

Face-to-face work: Working directly with young people or other members of the community; usually distinguished from responsibilities for management in job descriptions.

Facilitator: Assists a group to find their own ways of addressing tasks or finding solutions to problems by sharing observations and questioning to develop the processes of participation, communication and decision-making. (See Hunter, et al., 1995.)

Feminist: An advocate of political, economic and social equality for women and girls. (See an articulation of feminist of youth and community work with girls and young women in Batsleer, 1996, and of detached work in Benetello, 1996.)

Financial exclusion: A lack of access to or ownership of certain financial mechanisms or products, such as pensions, life assurance and savings accounts, which can disadvantage individuals and/or present barriers to full participation in society.

Formal education: Generally refers to learning undertaken in an educational institution, with "a prescribed learning framework, an organised learning event or package', the presence of a designated teacher or trainer, the award of a qualification or credit, (and) the external specification of outcomes" (Eraut, 2000: 114). See also *informal learning* and *nonformal learning*.

Funder: Agencies and individuals that provide resources, particularly financial support, such as national or local governments, charities, community associations or any combination of these.

Goals: The planned changes that an organisation or group wants to make or address, which can be identified clearly as solutions to problems or specific positive developments. (See also *targets*).

Grievance procedures: The steps undertaken by an employee making a complaint against unfair or unreasonable treatment.

Grounded knowledge: Knowledge that is gained from firsthand experience of living or working in an area that, if clearly defined and acknowledged, can provide a valuable context and perspective for practice. See also *location of self*.

Heterosexism: Discrimination, prejudice against or oppression of lesbian, gay, bi-sexual and transgendered people based on assumptions that heterosexuality is the norm and other identities are inferior, an attitude also referred to as heteronormativity. (See also Hill, 2007.)

Idealism: A belief in and pursuit of perfection, particularly in relation to standards and principles (see *pragmatism* as a contrast).

Impact: Long-term and sustainable changes resulting from activities whether positive or negative (see also *outcomes*).

Inclusion: Work to involve diverse individuals and groups in activities and services, particularly those who are usually excluded or not involved.

Induction: Procedures that introduce a new member, volunteer or employee into the resources, policies, procedures and practice of a group or organisation to enable full and safe participation.

Informal educator: Passes on information and skills so that others develop and learn to make positive and informed choices in a responsive rather than curriculum-based approach.

Informal learning: unintentional learning from life's experiences.

Informed consent: Steps taken to ensure that participants have sufficient information to make a decision about whether they wish to be involved, particularly when participants are young or potentially vulnerable and when issues of confidentiality are at stake, for example, through publicity or research reports.

Institutional oppression: Discrimination and oppression within specific institutions or organisations that '*can thrive in a tightly knit community, so that there can be a collective failure to detect and to outlaw …*' (Macpherson, 1999: 6.17)

Internal locus of control: An individual's belief in her/his ability or power to control various factors in her/his life, which leads to taking an active and assertive role in approaching experiences as positive learning opportunities (Judge & Bono, 2001).

Internship: A structured and supported short-term arrangement for work experience carried out usually with no or minimal pay for the purposes of developing an individual's understanding of an organisation's role and way of working.

Intervention: A proactive activity, piece of work or plan of action.

Issue-based practice: When the focus of an activity or project is on political or social issues such as *sexism, racism, hetero-sexism, ableism, ageism, class* and poverty (see also *anti-oppressive practice*) or particular areas of concern such as crime, drugs, gangs, sexual health, educational achievement, social relationships, homelessness, the environment.

Location of self: Identification, analysis and evaluation of one's skills, knowledge, attitudes and values as well as their origins, particularly in relation to experience and identity. Location of self requires a reflection and audit on the effects of identity on one's *paradigm*, as well as others' perceptions and power. Other relevant topics include the effects of privilege and various forms of capital (See *social capital* and Bourdieu, 1983) on perspective.

Lone-working: Undertaking youth work alone is often considered risky as workers or volunteers can be accused of undesirable behaviour without witnesses or become victims without back up. Many organisations have a 'lone working policy' which requires staff to work in tandem with colleagues, particularly during outreach or detached work.

Marginalised: A group or individual excluded from or ignored by mainstream services. Occurs through *oppression* and *discrimination*.

Misconduct: Inappropriate actions by an employee or volunteer that may warrant a verbal or written warning with a clear explanation of what improvement is needed. Gross misconduct is more serious and can lead to dismissal.

Mission statement: Overall aim(s) condensed into a sentence or paragraph about what an organisation plans to achieve and why. More concrete, 'action-oriented' and clearly related to outcomes than a *vision* statement.

Mobile youth work: use of a vehicle or mobile unit, such as a purpose built van or converted bus, temporarily parked in a public setting, such as an urban street, park, festival or rural area, as an attractive contact point or centre for activities or information.

Monitoring: Recording and checking change and development using particular indicators at regular intervals to measure progress, particularly in relation to the group's established *aims*, *objectives* and *targets*.

Neighbourhood work: *Community work* with residents within a small locality to bring them together to address relevant issues and develop community relationships and *social capital*.

Networking: Developing and establishing links and relationships with individuals and organisations generally through informal exchanges of information. Networks can become forums or partnerships for regular information exchange or sharing of resources.

Nonformal learning: learning from intentional, often work-based experiences, outside of a formal learning environment, such as supervision or non-accredited in-service training. Although 'nonformal' is useful to distinguish these experiences from *informal learning* from life experiences, the term is not universally utilised. Non-formal learning is often referred to as *informal education*, e.g. Smith, 1998.

Non-profit and not-for-profit: Generally used interchangeably to refer to organisations whose main aims are not to make a profit. Non-profits reinvest all profits into the organisation; some not-for-profit may generate a surplus.

Objectives: Demonstrate how the *aims* are going to be reached through outlining a programme or set of activities that are required.

Oppression: Cruel and/or unfair treatment backed up by societal or cultural forces; denial of life, human rights and/or equal opportunities. Examples include *racism, sexism, heterosexism, ageism, class or caste systems, ableism*. Oppression can also be internalised to affect an individual's self-perception and self-esteem. See also *institutional* and *societal oppression*.

Organisational culture: *Policies* and ways of working established through individual and organisational *practice*, such as *institutional oppression* in relation to access, flexibility and discrimination; generally incorporating well-established habits that may include unwritten *procedures* that are difficult to *challenge* or change.

Outcomes: Planned or unexpected changes, benefits and results arising from a group or project. Hard outcomes are measurable and quantifiable, such as specific outputs or targets easily identified through counting. Soft outcomes are qualitative benefits that may be difficult to measure or count. Unplanned outcomes not anticipated in the original plan possibly occur because of unusual circumstances or individuals. (See The Young Foundation, 2012, framework for young people's services.)

Outreach work: Publicity and recruitment or other activities that encourage young people to come to mainstream provision centres or facilities, such as 'taster sessions'. Sometimes refers to external, satellite or extension programmes.

Overheads: The ongoing expenditure required to maintain an organisation such as core staff, rent/mortgage.

Paradigm: a belief system or perspective that influences understanding and perceptions based on experiences and developed knowingly and unwittingly.

Participation: Taking an active part, for example, in issues and decisions that affect one's life. Young people take an active part in developing youth work activities and organisations.

Participative: Describes activities and approaches that involve others in determining content and/or agenda rather than passively observing. (See Sapin & Watters, 1990, for discussion and examples of participative learning.)

Partnership: A formal or informal arrangement and agreement between organisations, groups or individuals to share responsibility for specific work, activities or resources.

Placement: Voluntary work-based learning experience arranged by a learning organisation as part of a course. In some situations, the placement requirements may be met through an apprenticeship, traineeship, internship, part-time job or self-created experience.

Policy: Definitions of boundaries, roles, relationships and responsibilities that are guided by an organisation's *principles* and *values* and provide a basis for consistent decision-making and resource allocation. Generally, policies are contained within written documents, but may be understood or part of *organisational culture* (see also *procedures* and *Codes of practice*).

Power: The opportunity and ability to control one's own and others' lives.

Practice: Work that is carried out based on the values and principles of a profession. What a worker or organisation actually does as opposed to their policies or theoretical approach.

Pragmatism: A way of thinking or dealing with decisions or issues, which generally means prioritising the results of an action. *Outcomes* and outputs may be seen as more important than *principles*, *values* or process.

Praxis: Action based on reflection: an examination and analysis of reality in order to understand what is going on and to identify practical ways forward that can transform that reality (Freire, 1972). See also Smith, 1994.

Prejudice: A fixed like or dislike based on ignorance or without any reason that can limit expectations, aspirations and attainment of self-determination, employment, responsibilities, understanding and learning of self and others. See also *oppression*.

Principles: The *values* and fundamental and often generalised truths or assumptions on which a profession or organisation is based, which may be written down or simply understood. Youth work principles include having respect for young people, establishing voluntary participation, being accountable, maintaining confidentiality and involvement in continuous professional development.

Probationary period: An initial, limited period of monitoring of a newly appointed worker for suitability in the post, generally for three to six months.

Procedures: Agreed or imposed steps to be followed in particular circumstances that are meant to ensure efficiency, safety, equity or other quality assurance concerns and that implement or maintain organisational policy. Often designed to protect an organisation from litigation through systematic responses and prescribed time-scales for actions (see also *Codes of practice*).

Quality assurance: Providing evidence of good practice and effective *procedures* for maintaining good quality of service or organisation, usually through documentation regarding the systems in place, such as *policies* and *codes of practice*.

'Race': Grouping people according to arbitrary visual physical characteristics or cultural differences, despite the 'human race' referring to the whole of humanity. Often associated with assigning values, such as inferiority or superiority, and prejudices towards particular 'race' categories. See *racism*.

Racism: *Discrimination* on the basis of *'race'* or skin colour, which generally benefits people perceived as 'white'. Racism includes personal or individual *prejudice* as well as institutional and societal *oppression*. 'Unwitting racism' (Scarman, 1981) is based on *prejudice*, ignorance, thoughtlessness and racist *stereotyping*.

Revenue: Income generated by activities, such as fees, sales, sponsorship. See also *capital*.

Risk assessment: identifying potential dangers involved in an activity or setting to determine ways to minimise. (See also *safeguarding* and NCVYS, 2007.)

Risky behaviour: Activities that may cause or are perceived to cause harm to health, self or others, such as drinking, smoking, fighting, carrying out sexual or criminal activity, driving too fast, climbing too high or riding on top of trains. Sometimes also minor infractions of the law, such as graffiti.

Running costs: Expenditure on items that will be used rather than kept, such as insurance, postage, stationery, rent, heat and electricity. Usually a separate budget heading from *capital* expenditure or staffing.

Safeguarding: the 'duty of care' responsibilities of individuals and organisations working with children and young people to promote their welfare, minimise risks and act on any concerns about their suffering or risk of suffering significant harm. (See Banks, 2006 & 2010, for discussion of the ethics of duty of care.)

Sessional work: Part-time employment for specific weekly time schedules, usually to carry out face-to-face sessions with young people.

Sexism: Discrimination on the basis of gender, which generally, although not exclusively, benefits men. Sexism includes personal or individual prejudice as well as *societal*, *institutional* and *internalised oppression*.

Sign-posting: Providing contact information about alternative individuals, services or organisations that may be able to address specific needs or interests, such as names, postal/e-mail addresses and/or telephone numbers.

Social capital: The benefits of social interactions and informal organisations that develop a sense of trust and community (see Putnam, 1995 or Bourdieu, 1983).

Social enterprise: an organisation engaging in business for social or environmental benefit that generates at least partial income for reinvestment in the 'mission'.

Social model of disability: A definition of *ableism* that recognises that fear, ignorance and prejudice, barriers and discriminatory practices disable people rather than impairments; and that equality for disabled people lies in restructuring society rather than the disabled person.

Socialisation: Training individuals to function within society and to fit in with what is considered to be normal social behaviour (social norms).

Societal oppression: *Discrimination* and *oppression* sanctioned and upheld by society through attitudes and practices within, for example, the media, the education system, religions. See also *institutional oppression*.

Stakeholder: An individual or group directly affected by an issue or with a personal or professional interest in a service or organisation.

Statutory organisation or service: Legally required by a government, for example, a legal statute requiring certain services to be provided for a population.

Stereotype: A commonly held, limited and standard idea or image of a group, or of individuals who are perceived to be a group.

Strategy: A longer-term plan to reach an *aim* that includes more detail than a *vision* or *mission* statement, more specific *objectives* and a time-scale.

Street-based youth work: The development of youth work activities out-of-doors rather than indoors, which is often literally on the streets or pavements/sidewalks but may also take place in or around mobile units. See also *detached youth work* and *mobile youth work*.

Supervision: Critical reflection on practice with an experienced practitioner to identify and address professional practice dilemmas and development needs, which may be combined with responsibilities for management or assessment. (See Sapin, 1998, for different perspectives on supervision.)

Targets: Specific *goals* of an organisation identified and used in planning, monitoring and evaluation, such as the number of outputs or *outcomes*.

Third sector: The range of non-governmental organisations, including groups of young people and youth forums, which are generally *non-profit*, such as community organisations, charities, faith groups, but may also include social enterprises and cooperatives. Third sector organisations may receive partial funding from public (first) and private profit-making (second) sectors.

Traineeship: where an individual is employed to undertake a relevant programme of learning either alongside or as part of their job as an apprentice (with a short-term contract) or as a trainee or worker-in-training (whose contract may continue after completion of the programme).

Transgendered: Individuals who have undergone surgery and hormone treatment in order to acquire the physical characteristics of the opposite gender or (sometimes) individuals whose identity does not conform to conventional notions or definitions of male and female gender, but combines or moves between these identities or traits (see also *transsexual*).

Transsexual: Individuals who have changed or who want to change gender due to emotional and psychological self-identification with a different gender than the one whose physical characteristics are possessed (see also *transgendered* as the terms are often used interchangeably).

Values: The fundamental beliefs that underpin a perspective or profession, such as the belief that an anti-oppressive, positive (warm, fun and welcoming), participative approach to work with young people is of benefit.

Vision: A group or organisation's verbal description of a future ideal often articulated in a brief statement that conveys their beliefs and *principles* in a clear and concise form.

Xenophobia: A prejudiced and intolerant view of other people, customs or cultures perceived as being from a different nation or nationality, which often leads to leading to fear or dislike associated with *racism*.

Young person-centred: Aims and practice that focus on young people's perspectives, interests and decisions.

Youth and community work: Work with different groups in communities to develop relevant activities and enable them to have a say in issues that affect them. See also *community work* and *youth work*.

Youth support worker: A *youth work* position for an individual with basic training and no managerial responsibilities for other staff.

Youth warden: An individual who works with young people in parks or recreational areas using the environment as a setting for activities – often interacting with the environment through specific 'green' or gardening projects.

Youth work: Working with young people to develop enjoyable activities that address their expressed needs and interests in a voluntary relationship based on mutual respect.

REFERENCES

Adirondack, S. M. and Simpson, S. (2006) *Just About Managing? Effective Management for Voluntary Organisations and Community Groups* (4th edn). London: London Voluntary Service Council.

Alderson, P. (2008) *Young Children's Rights: Exploring beliefs, principles and practice* (2nd edn). London: Save the Children and Jessica Kingsley.

Arnold, J., Askins, D., Davies, R., Evans, S., Rogers, A. and Taylor, T. (1981) *The Management of Detached Work: How and why*. Leicester: National Association of Youth Clubs.

Arnstein, S. R. (1969) 'A ladder of citizen participation', *Journal of the American Institute of Planners*, 35(4): 216–24.

Baker, A. C., Jensen, P. J. and Kolb, D. A. (2005) 'Conversation as experiential learning', *Management Learning*, 36(4): 411–27.

Banks, S. (2006) *Ethics and Values in Social Work* (3rd edn). Basingstoke: Palgrave Macmillan.

Banks, S. (ed.) (2010) *Ethical Issues in Youth Work* (2nd edn). Oxon: Routledge.

Batsleer, J. (1996) *Working with Girls and Young Women in Community Settings*. Aldershot: Arena.

Belenky, M., Clinchy, B., Goldberger, N. and Tarule, J. (1986) *Women's Ways of Knowing: The development of self, voice and mind*. New York: Basic Books.

Bell, J. (1999) *Doing Your Research Project: A guide for first-time researchers in education and social science* (3rd edn). Maidenhead: Open University Press.

Belton, B. (2010) *Radical Youth Work: Developing critical perspectives and professional judgement*. Lyme Regis: Russell House.

Benetello, D. (1996) *Invisible Women: Detached youth work with girls and young women*. Leicester: Youth Work Press.

Benson, J. (2010) *Working More Creatively With Groups* (3rd edn). Oxon: Routledge.

Best, J. (2000) 'To Whom is Accreditation Acceptable as a Qualification in Community Work?' Unpublished PhD dissertation, Youth and Community Studies, Manchester Metropolitan University.

Boal, A. (2002) *Games for Actors and Non-Actors* (2nd edn). London: Routledge.

Boal, A. (1998) *Legislative Theatre: Using Performance to Make Politics*. London: Routledge.

Boreham, N. C. (1988) 'Models of diagnosis and their implications for adult professional education', *Studies in the Higher Education of Adults*, 20(2): 95–108.

Boreham, N. (2004) 'Orienting the work-based curriculum towards work process knowledge: a rationale and a German case study', *Studies in Continuing Education*, 26(2): 209–27.

Bourdieu, P. (1983). 'Forms of capital' in J. C. Richards (ed.) *Handbook of Theory and Research for the Sociology of Education*. New York: Greenwood Press.

Brown, J.M. (ed.) (2008) *Mahatma Gandhi: The essential writings*. Oxford: Oxford University Press.

Brown, A. and Bourne, A. (1996) *The Social Work Supervisor*. Buckingham/Milton Keynes: Oxford University Press.

Brunson, R., Conte, Z. and Masar, S. (2002) *The Art in Peacemaking: A guide to integrating conflict resolution education into youth arts programs*. Washington, DC: National Center for Conflict Resolution Education.

Burton, P. (1993) *Community Profiling: A guide to identifying local needs*. Bristol: SAUS Publications.

Carper, B. A. (1978) 'Fundamental patterns of knowing in nursing'. *Advances in Nursing Science* 1(1) 13–24.

Carroll, M. and Holloway, E. (eds) (1999) *Counselling Supervision in Context*. London: SAGE.

Carroll, M. and Tholstrop, M. (2001) *Integrative Approaches to Supervision*. London: Jessica Kingsley.

Carson, C. (ed.) (1988) *The Autobiography of Martin Luther King Jnr*. New York: Warner Books.

Charity Commission (2009) *Safeguarding Children: Protecting children in your organisation* (March): www.charitycommission.gov.uk/charity_requirements_guidance/charity_governance/managing_risk/protection.aspx (accessed 12 April 2012).

Chambers, R. (2002) *Participatory Workshops: A sourcebook of 21 sets of ideas and activities*. London: Earthscan.

Christiano, G. J. (2002) 1950's *Street Games, Street Talk: The Bronx, NY*. My Recollection: www.myrecollection.com/christianog/games.htm/ (accessed 4 November 2012).

Cleary, T. (1994) *Dhammapada: The sayings of buddha*. New York: Bantam Books.

Cleaver, E. (1969) *Eldridge Cleaver: Post prison writings and speeches*. New York: Random House/Ramparts.

Cleaver, H., Cawson, P., Gorin, S. and Walker, S. (eds) (2009) *Safeguarding Children: A shared responsibility*. Chichester: Wiley-Blackwell.

Cohen, M. B. and Mullender, A. (eds) (2003) *Gender and Group Work*. London: Routledge.

Collins, M. (2010) *Examining Sports Development*. Abingdon: Routledge.

Conger, J. A. and Riggio, R. E. (2007) *The Practice of Leadership: Developing the next generation of leaders*. San Francisco, CA: Jossey-Bass.

Cooperrider, D. L. and Whitney, D. (2005) *Appreciative Inquiry: A positive revolution in change*. San Francisco, CA: Berrett-Koehler.

Crebert, G., Bates, M., Bell, B., Patrick, C. and Cragnolini, V. (2004) 'Developing generic skills at university, during work placement and in employment: graduates' perceptions', *Higher Education Research & Development*. 23(2):147–65.

Crimmens, D., Factor, F., Jeffs, T., Pitts, J., Pugh, C. and Spence, J. (2004) 'The role of street-based youth work in linking socially excluded young people into education, training and work', Joseph Rowntree Foundation, ref. 654, June, National Youth Agency.

Davies, B. (2005) 'Youth work: a manifesto for our times', *Youth and Policy: A special feature*, No. 88. Leicester: National Youth Agency.

Davies, T. and Cranston, P. (2008) *Youth Work and Social Networking Final Research Report, September 2008: How can youth work best support young people to navigate the risks and make the most of the opportunities of online social networking?* Leicester: National Youth Agency.

Devi, M. (2010) *The Queen of Jhansi*. London: Seagull Books.

Dewson, S., Eccles, J., Tackey, N. D. and Jackson, A. (2000) *Guide to Measuring Soft Outcomes and Distance Travelled, August 2000*. DfEE RR219. London: Department for Education and Employment.

Doel, M. (2010) *Social Work Placements: A traveller's guide*. London: Routledge.

Driskell, D. (2002) *Creating Better Cities with Children and Youth: A manual for participation*. London: Earthscan.

Eastwood, M. and Norton, M. (2010) *Writing Better Fundraising Applications: A practical guide* (4th edn). London: Directory of Social Change.

Egan, G. (1986) *A Systematic Approach to Effective Helping* (3rd edn). Belmont, CA: Brooks/Cole, Wadsworth.

Emslie, M. (2009) 'Researching reflective practice: a case study of youth work education', *Reflective Practice: International and Multidisciplinary Perspectives*, 10(4): 417–27.

Eraut, M. (2000) 'Nonformal learning and tacit knowledge in professional work', *British Journal of Educational Psychology*, 70(1): 113–36.

Fairhurst, G. T. and Sarr, R. A. (1996) *The Art of Framing: Managing the language of leadership*. San Francisco, CA: Jossey-Bass.

Faulkner, A., Roberts-DeGennaro, M. and Weil, M. (eds) (1994) *Diversity and Development in Community Practice*. New York: Haworth Press.

Feinstein, J. and Kuumba, N. I. (2006) *Working with Gangs and Young People: A toolkit for resolving group conflict*. London: Jessica Kingsley.

Fletcher, A. (2008) *Youth Voice Glossary: The Freechild Project*: www.freechild.org/glossary.htm (accessed 4 November 2012).

Freire, P. (1972) *Pedagogy of the Oppressed* (translated from the Portuguese by M. Bergman Ramos). New York: Herder and Herder.

Flores, K. S. (2008) *Youth Participatory Evaluation: Strategies for engaging young people*. San Francisco, CA: John Wiley & Sons.

Gandhi, M. (1931) 'Young India, Bombay, India', in R.K. Prabhu and U.R. Rao (eds), *The Mind of Mahatma Gandhi: Encyclopedia of Gandhi's thoughts*. Ahmedabad, India: Navjeevan Trust, www.mkgandhi.org/ebks/mindofmahatmagandhi.pdf (accessed 4 November 2012).

Garvey, M. and Blaisdell (ed.) (2005) *Selected Writings and Speeches by Marcus Garvey*. USA: Dover Publications.

Gibbs, G. (1988) *Learning by Doing: A guide to teaching and learning methods*. Oxford: Further Education Unit, Oxford Polytechnic.

Goldstein, J. H. (ed.) (1994) *Toys, Play, and Child Development*. Cambridge: Cambridge University Press.

Hammond, S. A. (1998) *The Thin Book of Appreciative Inquiry* (2nd edn). Bond, OR: Thin Book Publishing Co.

Handy, C. (1999) *Understanding Organisations* (4th edn). London: Penguin.

Hart, R. (1992) *Children's Participation: The theory and practice of involving young citizens in community development and environmental care*. London: Earthscan.

Hawkins, P. and Shohet, R. (2006) *Supervision in the Helping Professions* (3rd edn). Buckingham: Open University Press.

Hawtin, M. and Percy-Smith, J. (2007) *Community Profiling: A practical guide – Auditing social needs* (2nd edn). Maidenhead: Open University Press.

Henderson, P. and Thomas, D. N. (2002) *Skills in Neighbourhood Work* (3rd edn). New York: Routledge.

Hill, R. J. (2007) 'Challenging homophobia and heterosexism: lesbian, gay, bisexual, transgender and queer issues', *New Directions for Adult and Continuing Education*, 112.

Holdsworth, P. (2002) *DIY Community Street Audit Pack*. London: Living Streets.

hooks, b. (1996) *Killing Rage, Ending Racism*. London: Penguin.

Hope, A. and Timmel, S. (1984)*Training for Transformation: Handbook for community workers*. Gweru, Zimbabwe: Mambo Press.

Hudson, M. (2009) *Managing Without Profit: Leadership, management and governance of third sector organisations* (3rd edn). Directory of Social Change.

Hunter, D., Bailey, A. and Taylor, B. Jr. (1995) *How to Create Group Synergy: The art of facilitation.* Cambridge, MA: Da Capo Books.

Ingham, G. and Harris, J. (2001) *Delivering Good Youth Work: A working guide to surviving and thriving.* Lyme Regis: Russell House Publishing.

Johns, C. (1995) 'Framing learning through reflection within Carper's fundamental ways of knowing in nursing', *Journal of Advanced Nursing*, 22: 226–34.

Joseph, J., Akpokavi, A. B., Chauhan, V. and Cummins, V. (2002) *Towards Global Democracy: An exploration of black perspectives in global youth work.* London: Development Education Association.

Judge, T. A. and Bono, J. E. (2001) 'Relationship of core self-evaluations traits – self-esteem, generalized self-efficacy, locus of control, and emotional stability – with job satisfaction and job performance: a meta-analysis', *Journal of Applied Psychology*, 86(1): 80–92.

Kadushin, A. (1992) *Supervision in Social Work.* New York: Columbia University Press.

Kindon, S., Pain, R. and Kesby, M. (2007) *Participatory Action Research Approaches and Methods: Connecting people, participation and place.* Abingdon: Routledge.

Kolb, D. A. and Fry, R. (1975) 'Toward an applied theory of experiential learning', in C.L. Cooper (ed.) *Theories of Group Process.* London: Wiley, pp. 27–56.

Learning and Skills Improvement Service (2012) *Youth Work National Occupational Standards.* http://repository.excellencegateway.org.uk/fedora/objects/eg:4931/datastreams/DOC/content (accessed 4 November 2012).

Ledwith, M. and Springett, J. (2010) *Participatory Practice: Community-based action for transformative change.* Bristol: Policy Press.

Lee, H. D. P. (2003) *Plato: The republic* (revised edn). London: Penguin.

Le Fevre, D. N. (2007) *The Spirit of Play: Cooperative games for all ages, sizes and abilities.* Findhorn, Scotland: Findhorn Press.

Lewin, K. (1946) 'Action research and minority problems' *Journal of Social Issues*, 2: 34–46.

LLUK (2009) *National Occupational Standards for Community Development.* London: Lifelong Learning UK, www.fcdl.org/nos/208-cdnos-full-version (accessed 4 November 2012).

LLUK (2010) *National Occupational Standards for Youth Work.* London: Lifelong Learning UK, www.lluklegacy.org/cms/uploads/National-Occupational-Standards-for-Youth-Work.pdf

Lounsberry, A. (1900) *A Guide to the Trees.* Toronto: W. Briggs.

Luft, J. (1982) 'The Johari Window: A Graphic Model of Awareness in Interpersonal Relations', NTL Reading Book for Human Relations Training, NTL Institute.

Luxmore, N. (2000) *Listening to Young People in School, Youth Work and Counselling.* London: Jessica Kingsley.

MacBeth, N. and Fine, N. (1995) *Playing with Fire: Creative conflict resolution for young adults.* Gabriola Island, BC, Canada: New Society Publishers.

Macpherson of Cluny, Sir W. (1999) *The Stephen Lawrence Inquiry: Report of an inquiry.* London: HMSO.

MSC (2008) *National Occupational Standards for Management and Leadership.* London Management Standards Centre, www.management-standards.org/standards/full-list-2008-national-occupational-standards (accessed 4 November 2012).

Maslow, A. H. (1943) 'A theory of human motivation', *Psychological Review*, 50: 370–96.

Max-Neef, M. A. (1991) *Human Scale Development: Conception, application and further reflections.* New York: Apex Press.

McLeod, J. and McLeod, J. (2011) *Counselling Skills: A practical guide for counsellors and helping professionals* (2nd edn). Maidenhead: Open University Press.

McGregor, D. (1960) *The Human Side of Enterprise.* London: McGraw Hill.

Merton, B. et al; in the Youth Affairs Unit, De Montfort University (2004) *An Evaluation of the Impact of Youth Work in England*. Research Report RR606. Nottingham: Department for Education and Skills.

Mullaly, R. P. (2002) *Challenging Oppression: A critical social work approach*. Ontario: Oxford University Press.

Mullender, A. and Ward, D. (1991) *Self-directed Group Work: Users take action for empowerment*. London: Whiting & Birch.

Munro, E. (2008) *Effective Child Protection* (2nd edn). London: SAGE.

National Youth Agency (2004) *Ethical Conduct in Youth Work: A statement of values and principles from the National Youth Agency*. Leicester: National Youth Agency.

NCVYS (2007) *Keeping it Safe: A young person-centred approach to safety and child protection* (2nd edn). London: National Council for Voluntary Youth Services.

Niebuhr, R. (1987) *The Essential Reinhold Niebuhr: Selected essays and addresses*. New Haven, CT: Yale University Press.

Neugebauer, J. and Evans-Brain, J. (2009) *Making the Most of Your Placement*. London: SAGE.

Nkrumah, K. (1964) *Consciencism: Philosophy and ideology for decolonization and development with particular reference to the African Revolution*. London: Heinemann.

NSPCC (2011) *Safe Network*. National Society for the Prevention of Cruelty to Children: www.safenetwork.org.uk/ (accessed 4 November 2012).

Oliver, M. (1996) *Understanding Disability: From theory to practice*. Basingstoke: Macmillan.

Ord, J. (ed.) (2012) *Critical Issues in Youth Work Management*. Oxon: Routlegde.

Pakroo, P. (2011) *Starting and Building a Non-profit: A practical guide* (4th edn). Berkeley, CA: Nolo.

Parker, J. (2010) 'When things go wrong! Placement disruption and termination: power and student perspectives', *British Journal of Social Work*, 40(3): 983–99.

Pershing, J. (ed.) (2006) *Handbook of Human Performance Technology: Principles, practices, and potential* (3rd edn). San Francisco, CA: Pfeiffer.

Planck, M. (1949) *Scientific Autobiography and Other Papers*. New York: Philosophical Library.

Poole, M. S. (1981) 'Decision development in small groups: a comparison of two models', *Communication Monographs*, 48: 1–24.

Pringle, M. K. (1986) *The Needs of Children* (3rd edn). London: Hutchinson.

Pritchard, J. (ed.) (1995) *Good Practice in Supervision*. London: Jessica Kingsley.

Pruitt, B. and Thomas, P. (2007) *Democratic Dialogue: A handbook for practitioners*. International IDEA, United Nations Development Programme, Organization of American States and Canadian International Development Agency.

Putnam, R. D. (1995) 'Bowling alone: America's declining social capital', *Journal of Democracy*, 6(1): 65–78.

QAA (2009) *Subject Benchmark Statements: Youth and community work*. QA 283 02/09. Gloucester: Quality Assurance Agency for Higher Education, www.qaa.ac.uk/Publications/InformationAndGuidance/Documents/YouthandCommunity09.pdf (accessed 4 November 2012).

Rogers, A. (1981) *Starting out in Detached Work*. Leicester: National Association of Youth Clubs, www.infed.org/archives/nayc/rogers_starting_out_in_detached_work.htm (accessed 4 November 2012).

Rogers, C. R. (1957) 'The necessary and sufficient conditions of therapeutic personality change', *The Journal of Consulting Psychology*, 21: 95–103.

Rogers, C. R. (1967) *On Becoming a Person: A therapist's view of psychotherapy*. London: Constable and Robinson.

Rogers, C. R. (1969) *Freedom to Learn*. Columbus, OH: Charles E. Merrill Publishing Co.

Rogers, C. R. (1978) *Carl Rogers on Personal Power: Inner strength and its revolutionary impact*. London: Constable and Co.

Rogers, C. R. and Farson, R. E. (1987) 'Active listening', in S.D. Ferguson and S. Ferguson (eds), *Organizational Communication* (2nd edn). New Brunswick, NJ: Transaction Publishers.

Rogers, V. (2011a) *101 Things to Do on the Street: Games and resources for detached, outreach and street-based youth work* (2nd edn). London: Jessica Kingsley.

Rogers, V. (2011b) *Let's Talk Relationships: Activities for exploring love, sex, friendship and family with young people*. London: Jessica Kingsley.

Rolfe, G. (2006) 'Validity, trustworthiness and rigour: quality and the idea of qualitative research'. *Journal of Advanced Nursing*. 53(3): 304–10.

Roseland, M. (2005) *Toward Sustainable Communities: Resources for Citizens and their Governments* (revised edn). Gabriola Island, BC, Canada: New Society Publishers.

Sapin, K. (ed.) (1998) 'Supervision of Practice and Professional Development – Keeping Track of Community and Youth Work – 1', Community Work Unit, University of Manchester.

Sapin, K. (ed.) (2005) 'A Black Perspective in Community and Youth Work 2005', a Community Work Unit conference report, University of Manchester.

Sapin, K. and Watters, G. (1990) *Learning from Each Other: A handbook for participative learning and community work learning programmes*. Manchester: The William Temple Foundation.

Scarman, L. G., Baron (1981) *The Brixton Disorders 10–12 April 1981: Report of an inquiry by the Rt Hon. the Lord Scarman; presented to Parliament by the Secretary of State for the Home Department*. London: HMSO.

Seacole, M. (1857) *Wonderful Adventures Of Mrs Seacole in Many Lands*. London: James Blackwood.

Senge, P. M. (1990) *The Fifth Discipline: The Art and practice of the learning organization*. London: Doubleday.

Shier, H. (2001) 'Pathways to participation: openings, opportunities and obligations, in line with article 12.1 of the United Nations Convention on the Rights of the Child', *Children & Society*, 15(2): 107–17.

Smith, K., Clegg, S., Lawrence, E. and Todd, M. J. (2007) 'The challenges of reflection: students learning from work placements', *Innovations in Education and Teaching International*, 44(2): 131–41.

Smith, M. (1988) *Developing Youth Work: Informal education, mutual aid and popular practice*. Milton Keynes: Open University Press (also available as e-text).

Smith, M. K. (1994) *Local Education: Community, conversation, praxis*. Buckingham: Open University Press.

Snape, E. and Redman, T. (2003) 'Too old or too young? The impact of perceived age discrimination', *Human Resource Management Journal*, 13 (1): 78–89.

Students Partnership Worldwide (2010) *Youth Participation in Development: A guide for development agencies and policy makers*. London: SPW/DFID-CSO Youth Working Group, March, www.restlessdevelopment.org/file/youth-participation-in-development-pdf (accessed 4 November 2012).

Tash, M. J. (1967) *Supervision in Youth Work: The report of a two-year training project in which selected youth workers acquire skill in supervising*. London: National Council of Social Service.

Tchami, G. (2007) *A Handbook for Cooperatives for use by Workers' Organizations*. London: International Labour Organisation, www.ilo.org/empent/units/cooperatives/WCMS_160205/lang–en/index.htm (accessed 4 November 2012).

The Young Foundation (2012) *Framework of Outcomes for Young People*. London: Catalyst, Department for Education, www.youngfoundation.org/publications/framework-of-outcomes-for-young-people/ (accessed 4 November 2012).

Thompson, J. L. (1997) *Strategic Management: Awareness and change*. London: International Thomson Business Press.

Thompson, N. (1993) *Anti-discriminatory Practice*. Practical Social Work Series. Basingstoke: Palgrave Macmillan.

Thompson, N. (2006) *People Problems*. Basingstoke: Palgrave Macmillan.

Thompson, N. (2011) *Promoting Equality: Working with diversity and difference*. Basingstoke: Palgrave MacMillan.

Thorpe, M., Edwards, R. and Hanson, A. (1993) *Culture and Processes of Adult Learning*. London: Routledge/Open University Press.

Tiffany, G. A. (2007) *Reconnecting Detached Youth Work: Standards and guidelines for excellence*. Leicester: Federation for Detached Youth Work.

Tuckman, B. W. (1965) 'Developmental sequence in small groups', *Psychological Bulletin*, 63: 384–99.

United Nations (1989) *Convention on the Rights of the Child*. Geneva: Office of the UN High Commissioner for Human Rights.

Unks, G. (ed.) (1995) *The Gay Teen: Educational practice and theory for lesbian, gay and bisexual adolescents*. New York: Routledge.

Waterman, R. H. Jr., Peters, T. J. and Phillips, J. R. (1980) 'Structure is not organization', *Business Horizons*, 23(3): 14–26.

Wates, N. (2000) *The Community Planning Handbook: How people can shape their cities, towns and villages in any part of the world*. London: Earthscan.

Weil, M. and McGill, I. (1989) in M. Weil and I. McGill (eds) (2005) *Making Sense of Experiential Learning: Diversity in theory and practice* Buckingham: Open University Press.

Whaley, S. (2007) *Fundraising for a Community Project: How to research grants and secure financing for local groups and projects in the UK*. Oxford: How to Books.

Williams, S. and Edelston, J. (eds) (2010) *Connect, Challenge and Change: A practical guide to global youth work*. London: Development Education Association.

Wood, J. and Hine, J. (eds) (2009) *Work with Young People*. London: Sage.

Wylie, T. (2004) *Costing Street-based Youth Work*. NewYork: Joseph Rowntree Foundation.

INDEX

Entries are arranged in word-by-word alphabetical order which takes account of spaces, hyphens, dashes and diagonal slashes between words. Locators followed by a 'g' suffix indicate a definition, a 't' suffix indicates a table, diagram or practice example.